Digital Community
Engagement

Digital Community Engagement

Partnering Communities with the Academy

Rebecca S. Wingo
Jason A. Heppler
Paul Schadewald

University of
CINCINNATI | PRESS

About the University of Cincinnati Press

The University of Cincinnati Press is committed to publishing rigorous, peer-reviewed, leading scholarship accessibly to stimulate dialog among the academy, public intellectuals and lay practitioners. The Press endeavors to erase disciplinary boundaries in order to cast fresh light on common problems in our global community. Building on the university's long-standing tradition of social responsibility to the citizens of Cincinnati, state of Ohio, and the world, the Press publishes books on topics that expose and resolve disparities at every level of society and have local, national and global impact.

University of Cincinnati Press, Cincinnati 45221

ucincinnatipress.uc.edu

Published in 2020

ISBN 978-1-947602-51-9 (hardback)
ISBN 978-1-947602-21-2 (e-book, PDF)
ISBN 978-1-947602-24-3 (e-book, EPUB)
DOI: 10.34314/wingodigital.00001

An enhanced open-access edition of this book is available at:
https://ucincinnatipress.manifoldapp.org/projects/digital-community-engagement

Wingo, Rebecca S., editor. | Heppler, Jason A., editor. | Schadewald, Paul, editor.
Digital community engagement : partnering communities with the
    academy / Rebecca S. Wingo, Jason A. Heppler, Paul Schadewald.
1st Edition. | Cincinnati : University of Cincinnati Press,
    2020. | Includes bibliographical references and index.
LCCN 2019045934 (print) | LCCN 2019045935 (ebook) | ISBN 9781947602519 (hardback) |
    ISBN 9781947602212 (pdf) | ISBN 9781947602243 (epub)
LCSH: Information technology--Social aspects. | Community development. |
    Digital media--Social aspects. | Digital communications--Social aspects. | Social change. |
LCC HM851 .D5165 2020 (print) | LCC HM851 (ebook) | DDC 303.48/33--dc23
LC record available at https://lccn.loc.gov/2019045934
LC ebook record available at https://lccn.loc.gov/2019045935

Designed and produced for UC Press by Jennifer Flint
Typeset in Baskerville URW

Printed in the United States of America
First Printing

Contents

Acknowledgments

We would first like to thank our community-based partners and acknowledge those who contributed their work to this volume. This book is for you, and this book is because of you.

We also want to acknowledge the dedication of the faculty, staff, and students who made the projects possible and whose reflection, insights, and knowledge will inspire future projects. Successful digital community engagement (DiCE) initiatives often demand work across silos and depend upon the behind-the-scenes efforts of civic engagement professionals, librarians and archivists, and technology personnel. Integrating DiCE into scholarship, teaching, and service can also entail risk for faculty members, especially if their institution's tenure, promotion, and reappointment policy does not reward community-engaged work. We hope that the case studies included in this volume will strengthen and encourage faculty who are doing this work, and make a small contribution to the movement to value engagement in higher education.

The catalyst for this volume was a DiCE symposium hosted by Macalester College's Jan Serie Center for Scholarship and Teaching, where Rebecca Wingo served as a postdoc in Digital Liberal Arts. The postdoc position and subsequent symposium were funded through a generous grant from the Andrew W. Mellon Foundation designed to bring together faculty and staff from Macalester and the University of Minnesota around issues in digital research and pedagogy. In addition to Wingo and Paul Schadewald, the planning team included Alexis Logsdon, Brooke Schmolke, and Chris Wells from Macalester, as well as Jennie Burroughs, Rebecca Moss, and Ben Wiggins from the University of Minnesota. We are grateful to the faculty and staff at the Serie Center, including Britt Abel, Adrienne Christiansen, Jacqueline Huppert, Theresa Klauer, Marga Miller, and Chris Wells. For Chris's unwavering support for the harebrained ideas of a wide-eyed postdoc, we will always be indebted. Terri Fischel's strategic support in time, space, and food from the library also helped launch the symposium. We would also like to specifically thank the contributors that helped us shape our vision at that symposium: Ariel Beaujot, Julia Brock, Karlyn Forner, Allison Schuette, Amy Sullivan, Megan Telligman, and Liz Wuerffel. Many of the ideas that we batted about at the conference room table are in our introduction.

There are a number of additional people to whom we owe thanks for their support and time. We want to acknowledge Macalester's Civic Engagement Center within the Kofi Annan Institute for Global Citizenship for their generous support of Schadewald's contribution to this project. Early in the process, Teresa Mangum provided advice and encouragement, as did Chad Gaffield. Liz Scarpelli, Sarah Muncy, and Sean Crowe at the University of Cincinnati Press have been masterful at shepherding this project, especially in thinking through the open access platform. Our open access mission would have been far too costly without the support of Associate Provost Keisha Love and her office's Toward an Open Monograph Ecosystem (TOME) grant. We are also grateful for the press's careful choice of our peer reviewers, who saw the value of our work and provided valuable feedback.

The students in our classes inspired our projects and were key conversation partners. We especially want to thank students in Wingo's graduate public history seminar who helped frame some of our advice for community engagement: Robbie Due, Alysha Federkeil, Phuong Le, Jack Raslich, Kevin Rigsbee, Tony Russomanno, Aidan Shackleford, Jason Sorn, and Corey Swearingen.

Finally, this volume would not have been possible without our contributors who were—without fail—timely, flexible, and responsive to edits. Their belief in the project sustained us even as we all navigated the rather murky waters of what it means to publish open access. The projects in this volume are inspirational. They show us a future pathway for community engagement and higher education by helping to form and inform a cohesive practice of digital community engagement.

Digital Community Engagement

A Letter to Future Community Partners

Hello and welcome!

We're glad you found this book. We wanted to make sure this volume provided more than just stellar examples of partnerships with academic institutions. We also wanted to make sure it was useful to you. Unlike the rest of this book, this is the only time we're going to speak directly to you as a potential community partner. These are the nuts and bolts of how to approach a partnership with academics and how to navigate this book.

We identified a few key questions that you might like answered before diving in:

What is this book?

This book is a collection of nine case studies about successful partnerships between community partners and academic institutions—but with a twist. Each of the partnerships also includes significant digital components both inside and outside of university and college classrooms. We think that together the examples demonstrate a cohesive practice of digital community engagement, or what we fondly refer to as DiCE.

We didn't just ask scholars to write about their projects; we asked them to include the voices and perspectives of their community partners. As a result, the majority of our chapters are co-authored, and in a variety of different ways. We hope that part is particularly useful.

While we think the examples and advice from each of the contributors transcend all aspects of community engagement, the advice for the digital components is particularly strong. We asked our authors to "lift the hood" to make the projects as easy to understand as possible. We live in a digital age but it's not always clear what choices go into tool or platform selection, nor is it always clear how those choices will impact the community partners. The clarity with which our contributors write about their technology choices should better prepare you for when you enter into your own partnerships.

How do partnerships form?

Community partnerships typically form in three ways:
1. the community approaches the scholars,
2. the scholars approach the community, or
3. the partnership grows out of a prior involvement.

In all cases, however, the community should be a co-creator in shaping and defining the project. Here are some examples (in order):

1. *SNCC Digital Gateway*: Veterans of the Student Nonviolent Coordinating Committee (SNCC), frustrated at the inaccurate representation of SNCC in academic texts, approached Duke University to create a digital project that centered veteran voices.
2. *People's Archive of Police Violence in Cleveland*: After police shot and killed Tamir Rice, a group of archivists from the national conference (which was meeting in Cleveland) approached local community groups to see if their skills could be used for social change.
3. *Remembering Rondo*: Scholars at Macalester College reconstituted an old partnership with a local community organization, Rondo Avenue, Inc., to tell the history of African Americans and highway construction in St. Paul, Minnesota.

What are the steps in forming a partnership with academic institutions?

It might seem daunting to approach a college or university and ask for help with your project. But at our core, most of us have come to this with a passion for local history and a desire to make a difference. We recommend starting by researching the institution as a whole and then narrowing down with whom you want to work through the following steps:

Step 1: Research the college or university online. Look at the institution's mission statement to see if they have a focus on community or civic engagement. If they do, use that to your advantage by stating how your organization or project idea fits with the institution's mission. Even if they do not have an explicit statement, the chances are high that there are still plenty of faculty and staff willing to work with you.

Step 2: Search online to see if the institution has a center for civic or community engagement, or a dedicated staff member who responds to requests and ideas like yours. Not all institutions do, but they are great places to start because they're trained in connecting you with the right people or partners and have a responsibility for supporting equitable, long-term, and mutually beneficial partnerships.

Step 3: You can also reach out directly to an academic department or office, based on your initial ideas, topic themes, or desired outcomes. Do you need a map? Email or call the Geography Department. Would you like to create an archive? Email or call an archivist in the library. Even if the people you contact cannot help you, they likely know who can.

What general advice do you have about working with academics?

We have four main pieces of advice. The first is about trust. We understand that you're risking a lot bringing your project to an academic institution, particularly if you are from a group historically marginalized by or within the academy. Academics are trying to feel out the partnership as much as you are.

Have a conversation about what a mutually beneficial relationship might look like; this is a key component of building trust. Start small and build on the relationship from that first (we hope successful) project knowing that you can withdraw from the partnership at any time. Starting small also means that you won't lose too much time or investment in case the partnership doesn't work out.

Second, establish a clear understanding of roles and responsibilities and a schedule of communication with your academic partner(s) early on. The conversations between community members and the scholar(s) are full of creativity and generativity, and they will make your project better. More than that, a communication schedule keeps you accountable to each other as you work together to establish and meet deadlines.

Third, have a conversation about digital sustainability before you start building the project. Ask questions such as: is this a small, finite project, or part of a larger vision? For the latter, you may need to choose different technologies. Ask about control over the data and the project once the partnership is complete. What is your maintenance agreement? This section of our introduction (see * on page 22) is particularly helpful for thinking through these and other questions.

Last, higher education runs on different schedules from the real world. We generally define time by semesters or quarters and if your partner is a professor, they might not be available in the summer. Some community engagement projects are tailor-made for the classroom, but some of our teaching schedules are determined up to two years in advance. Ask us up front about our timelines so we can think through how to best integrate your project and you can determine what works best for you.

How do I use this book?

Let the projects in this book inspire you! Partnerships in this book have formed in classrooms, stemmed from research agendas, and developed in response to institutional missions. There are some great ideas in this book, but they certainly aren't the only options.

We recommend skipping the first half of the introduction and getting straight to the good stuff: the summaries of all the projects in this collection (see * on page 17). Then you can pick and choose which ones seem most interesting to you.

Since this volume is committed to the voice of our community partners, we encourage you to add yours as well. If you're reading this online, you can join the conversation in the book by selecting sentences and passages, providing commentary, or asking questions. If you're reading this in print and really like a particular chapter, we suggest you go to the online version and read the conversations happening there too.

We hope this book helps shape your future partnerships. Please let us know if you have any questions or concerns!

Rebecca S. Wingo

Jason A. Heppler

Paul Schadewald

Introduction

Rebecca S. Wingo, Jason A. Heppler, and Paul Schadewald

We assembled this book because, when we needed this book, it did not exist. And yet, scholars across a variety of disciplines were already involved in community-engaged digital projects. How were they navigating the fragile relationships between communities and the academy? What aspects of community engagement change with the addition of digital components? How do communities change the technologies scholars choose? If we grouped these projects together, would there be something cohesive that might be called digital community engagement?

We fondly refer to our volume as DiCE, our attempt at an acronym for digital community engagement that accidentally stuck. This volume is a series of nine curated case studies focusing on projects that emerged through the creative engagement of community partners with academic faculty, staff, and students. These partnerships formed in classrooms, through institutional initiatives, and as components of individual research agendas. We collected essays from scholars who co-authored with their community partners (wherever possible) to describe their projects, the digital components, and what made them successful and meaningful. The projects all take various shapes, form partnerships along different lines, include and define "community" in distinct ways, and utilize a host of digital tools. We believe that, when viewed as a whole, these exemplary projects form a cohesive practice.

What is DiCE?

DiCE blends established digital humanities, public humanities, and community engagement practices. We recognize the importance of digital and public humanities broadly construed, grounded in many of the discussions, whether theoretical, practical, or pedagogical. We three editors, however, are trained as historians. We play to our strengths in this volume by drawing from the larger field of digital and public humanities while situating ourselves more firmly in digital and public history. Our academic contributors are also primarily historians, but not exclusively so. Although we looked outside of our discipline, the projects we found most compelling were typically history-related or otherwise examined change over time. This focus created greater cohesion for the projects described in this volume and helped us draw upon the vibrant conversations in history and related fields.

Scholars in these fields are increasingly thinking about community engagement in the digital age. During the National Council on Public History's annual meeting in 2017, a working group called "Meeting in the Middle: Community Engagement in a Digital World" assembled to discuss common issues in using digital methodologies when partnering with communities and using digital platforms to reach a wider public.[1] The American Historical Association held its first workshop on digital community engagement during the 2018 Getting Started in Digital History workshops. Imagining America, an organization that brings together scholars, students, and community partners, released a special issue of *Public* about digital civic engagement in 2018. Serge Noiret and Mark Tebeau are currently editing the *Oxford Handbook of Digital Public History* that includes a couple of chapters on community engagement and shared authority.

Ours is the first volume fully devoted to DiCE, but its exploratory (rather than definitive) nature will perhaps raise more questions than it will answer. Even the three fields we draw upon—digital history, public history, and community engagement—have contested meanings and definitions. The number of definitions on "What is Digital Humanities?" alone is staggering (and occasionally quite poignant and funny). Rather than offering yet another definition for either digital humanities or digital history, we instead want to highlight and embrace digital humanities' potential for social change. In what we hope isn't misguided optimism, we believe that digital humanities has the capacity to positively shape the study of the arts, culture, and social sciences. We believe it can do so while promoting inclusion, justice, and recovery with beneficial impact for communities.

This element of the humanities, however, needs constant invigoration lest the field become complacent, or worse, hidebound and irrelevant. Kathleen Woodward, citing Herbert Blau's 1969 essay that "bursts with blooded thought [. . .] about participatory democracy in the wake of the student revolution," argues that we need to "reclaim that sense of intellectual urgency."[2] Gerald Early further explores this disciplinary tension in his article on the historical links between the humanities and social change: "At any given moment, [humanists] see themselves either as cultural gatecrashers and agents of radical social change or cultural gatekeepers and champions of tradition."[3] Digital humanists have built upon this analog work as they interrogate the power structures that undergird everything from individual technological choices to the field writ large.[4] These same choices in technology have implications for the communities involved, including ownership, sustainability, and reach. It is this civically engaged current that shaped our selection of the included projects, as you'll read in the chapters ahead.

Public humanists increasingly sought the inclusion and participation of diverse voices in humanistic inquiry since the social and cultural turn of the 1960s.[5] More specifically, public historians have actively invited the public to participate in history-making. Nina Simon's *The Participatory Museum* is an inspired exploration of how museums across the globe are staying relevant in the twenty-first century by developing scalable participatory experiences. Of particular note is Simon's chapter on co-creating history with the public that describes the museum as a place for dialogue and community engagement, centered on the needs of the community itself.[6] In a similar vein, the edited volume *Letting Go?: Sharing Historical Authority in a User-Generated World* probes what it means for museums and museum practitioners to share authority with the public in an increasingly complicated world.[7] The popularity of the term "a shared authority" can be traced back to Michael Frisch's book *A Shared Authority: Essays on the Craft and Meaning of Oral and Public History*. In this sweeping collection of essays, Frisch delves into the potential of treating the public as equal partners in history-making.[8]

Given the works outlined above, it should come as no surprise that public and digital history have intertwining trajectories. This is not because publishing academic scholarship online calls upon some cosmic forces that merge the web and the ability to reach a wider public, and thus digital public history is born. Stommel succinctly states, "Doing public work is different from making academic work public. Available is not always accessible."[9] Writing for the web requires a similar ability to communicate beyond the academy. Sheila Brennan also argues that "understanding audiences is not a skill most humanities scholars are taught in graduate school, but it is a key element for successful digital projects."[10]

Good communication skills aren't the primary reason digital and public history can be a powerful pairing. Digital tools and platforms open opportunities for public humanists who have, more often than not, been in the vanguard of the "digital turn." Public digital humanities practitioners (especially archivists and librarians) have always been one step (or more) ahead of traditional humanists in integrating digital tools and critically examining structures of information on the web.[11] Public historians specifically, as Simon and the contributors to *Letting Go?* demonstrate, have the drive to experiment as they work to make good, relevant history. It was the insatiable curiosity of historians who experimented with the digital medium that forced a field to grow around them.[12] Incidentally, this is also what makes digital and public history so much fun.

A few preeminent scholars have specifically examined how the digital affects public history. As Sharon Leon argues, "to use fully the affordances of digital technologies, public historians have begun to shift the ways in which they work, organize and structure historical content, and engage with public audiences."[13] Leon reserves a section of her argument to specifically address the web as a portal through which the public can engage with history as active participants, rather than just as passive consumers. This follows a shift in the very infrastructure of the web itself, from "read" to "read-write."[14] The web generates exciting opportunities for public engagement outside of and in addition to traditional venues.

In 2017, Stephen Robertson and Lincoln Mullen assembled twenty-five prominent digital historians, including Leon and one of our editors (Jason Heppler), to provide historians with the rationale and language to discuss digital scholarship in productive ways. The working group argues that one of the key differences between digital public history and print narratives is that digital projects often "[incorporate] the sources themselves as a central element, which can allow for more analysis and engagement. They also often take advantage of the digital medium to incorporate non-textual sources as well as visual argumentation including graphs and maps."[15] Also included in Robertson and Mullen's working group were Edward Ayers and William G. Thomas III, two authors of one of the first web-based digital history projects. *The Valley of the Shadow Project* chronicled daily life in two counties, one north and one south of the Mason-Dixon line, in the Civil War. The project sought materials and other ephemera from local community members (as well as archives, libraries, and museums) to contribute to the digital archive.

That's right. Digital projects involved community from its earliest days.

And it is with the intersection of digital and public humanities and history in mind that we turn our attention to the "community engagement" portion of DiCE. Communities commonly define themselves through three facets: shared demography, experiences/interests, and geography. Community exhibits itself, as Benedict Anderson once wrote, as a "deep, horizontal comradeship" that binds groups of people together.[16] In the pages ahead, our communities find themselves in shifting Venn diagrams of these facets. For example, the predominantly African American community of Rondo in St. Paul, Minnesota, defines itself through demography and geography, but also a shared fracture of that community by a concrete freeway bifurcating its neighborhood. The people of La Crosse, Wisconsin, share a statue with a controversial history even as its collective historical memory remains contested. This three-pronged definition of community, as these examples indicate, is fairly common throughout our volume.

We also observed an exciting trend in our collection: some projects used digital tools to bring together a community that did not previously recognize themselves as such. One of Amy Sullivan's projects brought together harm reduction workers in Minneapolis active in the 1980s via social media. Sullivan's event included people who organized the country's first women-focused needle exchange programs, among others. In so doing, the participants realized that they formed a broader community of harm reduction specialists; they comprised an important local and national history of which they didn't even know they were a part. Similarly, James Connolly and Patrick Collier maintain an online collection of daily diaries from residents of Muncie, Indiana. The diarists submit and interact with each others' entries anonymously. They form a virtual community and have never met in person—that they know of, anyway.[17] We don't have a crystal ball, but we suspect that many more academic projects will explore this type of community formation in the future.

When we use the term "community engagement," we refer to reciprocal (rather than extractive) academic collaborations with communities where each side is accountable to a project. This is akin to the fine distinction Frisch makes between "shared authority" and "*a* shared authority"; the former implies that historians have authority that they may deign to share, while the latter is built upon equal meaning-making by its very definition.[18] Simon likewise distinguishes between co-creation and collaboration: "Co-creative projects originate in partnership with participants rather than based solely on institutional goals." She continues, "While co-creative and collaborative processes are often quite similar, co-creative projects start with community as well as institutional needs."[19] Our decision to include or exclude a project from this volume typically fell along this line: are the projects built *with* communities, or *for* communities?[20] We sought projects for this volume that did not just provide venues through which community voices are heard, but that actively sought their equal co-creation.

Community-engaged practice is closely aligned with the goals and methods of civic engagement and civic tech, or the creation of tools "to improve public life."[21] Supporting our belief that the powers of digital humanities can be wielded for good, a major goal of civic engagement projects is to effect positive social change in a variety of ways, such as by influencing public policy or contributing expertise or labor to a community organization. Effecting broader social change is not a necessary outcome for DiCE projects, though, as our projects demonstrate, it may indeed be *an* outcome.

Similarly, DiCE projects often draw upon the approaches and values developed in the field of academic civic engagement, which encompasses community-based research, place-based engagement, public scholarship, and service learning or community-based learning. Over the past three decades, higher education networks and consortia such as the Association of American Colleges and Universities, Bringing Theory to Practice, Campus Compact, the Corella and Bertram F. Bonner Foundation, Imagining America, and Project Pericles have advanced the institutionalization of civic engagement on individual campuses and advocated for the importance of the civic mission in higher education. By drawing together practitioners, these networks have supported pedagogies focused on student development and learning through mutually beneficial campus-community partnerships and the valuing of engagement as components of faculty scholarship and work.[22] Scholars and leaders in the field have increasingly raised questions of equity in engaged practices and advocated for projects that are co-created with community stakeholders.[23]

While higher education's civic engagement mission provides broader frameworks for considering student development, campus-community collaborations, and faculty work, it rarely takes into account digital methodologies. Though student involvement is not mandatory in DiCE projects (and only half of the projects highlighted in this book have it), we believe that DiCE is, at least in part, an extension of the academic civic engagement movement.

It figures that digital and public history scholars have something to say about community engagement. "The public digital humanities starts with humans, not technologies or tools," Stommel notes. "[Its] terrain must be continuously co-constructed. There is no place within the public digital humanities for exclusion or anti-intellectualism. No place for hierarchies. . ."[24] The Arguing with Digital History working group also focused on the ethical considerations of community-engaged practice. Emphasizing community authority, they argue that "historians working with communities have an obligation to engage with those communities on their own terms."[25] In *Debates in the Digital Humanities*, Wendy Hsu addresses the potential power of community knowledge by asserting that when scholars practice listening, they can "learn from the public," and that when we do, we can yield a "more efficacious and engaged public humanities work." She ends the chapter with a plea: "Humanists, I urge you to leverage your knowledge of the digital as a tool of community building. Working, listening, and making in proximity with communities will bring us closer to the co-imagination of a socially just world."[26]

As the tone in all these works indicates, digital and public history scholarship about community-engaged practice has primarily been geared toward practitioners in the field. In large part, these works have focused on driving questions and practical information for public historians as they pursue community-engaged work. These publications are certainly important; however, we need to shift the conversation of DiCE back to the community.

Where our collection seeks to intervene is by exploring the impact of technology on community engagement from the perspective of academics and the communities we serve. Our volume tries to reverse the typical practice of talking *about* communities by talking *with* communities. We examine the ways that technology has empowered communities, promoted collaboration, constructed or collapsed barriers, and sparked new dialogue. We believe the case studies in this volume raise important questions for the broader civic engagement movement and public digital humanities fields: Who benefits from the digital projects and the knowledge they produce, and how? Who owns them? How does DiCE impact the benefits and risks to communities when they partner with the academy? What are the pedagogical implications? How can physical and digital projects compliment each other?

About this Volume

Before we introduce each chapter, we want to call attention to a few overarching themes of this volume. First, we argue that digital engagement may help reinvigorate humanities fields such as history, but it must do so in ways that contribute to the community and minimize risk. From the position of a historian, William G. Thomas III astutely remarked over ten years ago, "The Web 2.0 movement might allow historians and the public to make history together rather than separately. The professional barriers are significant, but our professional relevance is also at stake in the digital age."[27] Given the sharp decline in humanities majors over the past decade, we think Thomas was correct in his assessment that humanists need to actively assert their relevance.[28] Community engagement is certainly one way to do that, but communities aren't here to save our disciplines. As Wingo asserts in a later chapter, "communities aren't an endless supply of generosity that scholars can mine at will with no reciprocity or compensation."[29] Communities typically have more of a stake in the projects than their academic partners. Fruitful partnerships between communities and the academy help pave the way for digital projects that provide access to community sources while also enabling communities to act as archivists, curators, and experts themselves.[30]

Towards that end, our academic contributors made every effort to include their community partners as co-creators in their chapters as well as in the projects they describe. This looks different in each chapter, taking the form of full-fledged co-authorship, interviews, devoted written sections or vignettes, and solicited feedback. Although we privilege *digital* community engagement, we would not want to promote the idea that such projects are *entirely* digital. The labor involved includes countless hours of face-to-face time that are often unbound from the quarter, semester, or academic year. The amount of time spent in church basements, at powwows, at community centers, in neighborhoods, and in living rooms is an essential ingredient of co-creation and trust-building. In other words, our contributors keep their focus on people, not technology.

Second, our volume is not all-encompassing. We are missing important voices among Indigenous peoples, disability studies, and Queer studies, among others. We also recognize that our chapters are American-focused and that there is a growing interest in facilitating international public history conversations.[31] These voices are not absent for lack of trying. The academy often

overburdens those engaged with undervalued public scholarship and communities. Some of the people we asked could not participate for any variety
of reasons, knowing that they had to balance contributions to this book with
other commitments.

We also recognize that these and other communities with whom we
partner could become targets of harassment in a digital environment where
doxxing, cyberbullying, surveillance, threats of, or actual, violence, racism,
sexism, and bigotry are sadly prevalent. We hope that does not dissuade potential partners and institutions from working together to carve out safe spaces
to co-produce compelling projects. The choice of digital tools and approaches
to partnerships should always reflect mindfulness concerning privacy and
harassment. Some of these issues are addressed in the pages ahead.

Third, academic-community partnerships often navigate complicated
imbalances of power, particularly if the academic collaborators are white and
the communities with whom they partner are marginalized or underrepresented. Since there is no universal code of collaborative conduct, we asked
the contributors to address how they adapted their partnerships to reflect a
more egalitarian practice. Each negotiation of power happens on an individual basis and is often contingent on the people involved. We hope that the
examples to come will at least provide some insight into successful practices.

Furthermore, public scholarship in general is undervalued in the
academy. For non-tenure-track faculty, librarians, practitioners, and staff, this
type of labor is often conducted outside of their assigned duties. Some places
have institutionalized community engagement as part of their mission; others
have not. The academy rarely affords these scholars the security and remu-
neration needed to advance their projects and careers. Speaking to tenure
and promotion specifically, a joint white paper by the American Historical
Association, Organization of American Historians, and National Council
on Public History has noted that community engagement—"a vital component of public history"—is largely "relegated to the undervalued category of
service." The effect is that public historians take on a larger workload. To
remain engaged in the field they must remain publicly engaged scholars, yet
their promotion is largely judged on the basis of traditional publications.[32]

Women often bear the brunt of this undervaluation. They have taken on key leadership roles in digital public history and community engagement projects (indeed, most of our contributors are women), yet that labor is still undervalued by professional structures. While we know that women are under-cited across academic fields, the same structures in academic labor also slow the advancement of women and fail to recognize contributions, leadership, and innovation.[33] These structures, labor, and prestige will require continual work and revision.

The nine DiCE projects that follow reflect a diversity of topics and forms of academic-community collaborations. They share common struggles with central issues such as how to establish generative relationships, support shared authority, and find ways to sustain projects through uncertain economic and political moments. DiCE projects emerge in academic courses, as the product of individual professors' activism or research projects, or in alliances formed by entities such as libraries and archives both attached to and detached from the academy. The DiCE projects featured in this book all reconstitute or amplify voices otherwise marginalized or silenced in history and the present. We believe that academics and communities can learn from each others' methodologies, and have assembled a collection of inspiring chapters that share a common commitment to co-creative collaborations.

We open with what is perhaps the most seamless co-authorship represented in the book: the *SNCC Digital Gateway*. The Student Nonviolent Coordinating Committee (SNCC), formed in the 1960s as a multiracial grassroots activist movement, focused on Black voter registration in the American South. SNCC veterans were frustrated by the academy's Great Man focus for a movement that rejected the top-down approach to leadership and actively invited women to participate. In 2013, they did something brave: they approached Duke University Libraries and the Center for Documentary Studies and asked them to help tell a different story. The result was the *SNCC Digital Gateway*, a web portal with SNCC artifacts, interviews with veterans, and modern resources for other activist organizers. Part of their funding stipulated that one of the deliverables be a document about the collaboration. Karlyn Forner, the project manager, introduces the collaborative document in Chapter 1, and the remainder is a guide to the successful partnership, co-authored by sixteen community and campus partners.

Chapter 2 features the *People's Archive of Police Violence in Cleveland* (*PAPVC*). In November 2014, Cleveland police officer Timothy Loehmann shot and killed Tamir Rice, a twelve-year-old Black youth. The following August, the Society of American Archivists convened in Cleveland for their annual conference, among them Melissa Hubbard, who, along with others, approached community groups seeking justice and the prevention of future violence to document police violence in the northern Ohio city. Unlike the *SNCC Digital Gateway* and many of the other projects in this volume, the *PAPVC* is freestanding, unattached to any academic institution. It is an anomaly in our collection. Hubbard explores the ethics of creating the archive, issues of ownership, and positionality. The Cleveland community partners involved in the *PAPVC* are the exact audience the *SNCC Digital Gateway* hopes to serve.

The three chapters that follow all center around a shared methodology: the History Harvest. The History Harvest is a pedagogically driven community digitization event in which community participants bring their items of significance for contribution to a digital archive. Chapter 3 examines the partnership between Rebecca Wingo, her students at Macalester College, and the Rondo community. In the late 1960s, the twin cities of Minneapolis and St. Paul weaponized interstate construction by building a highway through the central business district of a predominantly Black community called Rondo. Marvin R. Anderson, the co-founder of Rondo Avenue, Inc., spent the better part of fifty years fighting for recognition for what happened to his community. The partnership between Wingo and Anderson resulted in a three-year collaboration producing the *Remembering Rondo History Harvest*, the co-creation of panels for the Rondo Commemorative Plaza, and an internship on the RCR project that seeks to build a land bridge over the highway. The depth of the partnership (and ultimately friendship) between Anderson and Wingo demonstrates the value of longevity in community engagement—when scholars and communities focus on broader goals rather than singular points of engagement, the sky's the limit on the types of projects that can follow.

The flexibility of the History Harvest is one of its strengths. Chapter 4 discusses the same methodology, reimagined and reshaped to fit the historically Black Antioch A.M.E. Church northeast of Atlanta. In this chapter, co-authors Julia Brock, Elayne Washington Hunter, Robin Morris, and Shaneé Murrain discuss their variation on the History Harvest with the Antioch A.M.E. Church. As with Rondo, the production of the archive produced generative conversations and served as a mechanism by which the archive actually became secondary to developing a long-standing partnership between the congregation and the collaborators at the University of West Georgia and Agnes Scott College. The partners involved are still negotiating and navigating community needs.

Chapter 5 explores the History Harvest as an instrument for meaning-making. Amy Sullivan, a collaborator on the first Rondo History Harvest, turned the model toward her own research. She and her students hosted what can only be described as two overdue reunions, one between harm reduction specialists active in Minneapolis in the 1980s, and the other between Oklahoma Girl Scouts cut off from one another and their camp after the murder and sexual assault of three campers in 1977. Both groups experienced extreme trauma and silencing. What's genuinely compelling about Sullivan's application of the History Harvest, however, is that she reconstituted these powerful groups via digital means. As previously mentioned, the harm reduction activists and advocates in Minneapolis did not even recognize their role in the history of harm reduction until Sullivan assembled them for the Harvest. Likewise, the Girl Scouts knew they were part of a significant story but were never afforded an opportunity to share and document their experiences. They suffered their PTSD alone, until Sullivan used a Facebook group to bring former campers together in Oklahoma. Campers flew in from all over the country to attend the reunion. The furthest was from Oregon.

The project featured in Chapter 6, *Everyday Life in Middletown* (*EDLM*), also used digital means to form their communities. In *EDLM*, Patrick Collier and James Connolly at Ball State University follow up on Middletown Studies, founded in Muncie, Indiana, in 1929. Based on the British theory of Mass Observation, the project seeks (and historically sought) to record the minutiae of the daily life of ordinary American citizens by soliciting diaries. *EDLM*'s diarists are anonymous and their work is screened for any information that may reveal their identities. Diaries interact with each other anonymously as well, sparking conversations across race, gender, and socioeconomic status that may not otherwise occur. The project site is a searchable digital archive of day diaries that includes visualization tools developed by the project team to produce accessible textual analysis. While *EDLM* is place-based in Muncie, Collier and Connolly hope to export the model to other communities.

Chapter 7 counters another form of invisibility—the *Invisible Project* is a placed-based collection of digital stories designed to raise awareness about homelessness in Porter County, Indiana. The project is the result of a partnership between two Valparaiso University professors, Allison Schuette and Elizabeth Wuerffel (Departments of English and Art, respectively), and Megan Telligman, the then-coordinator of the Porter County Museum (now at Indiana Humanities). Together with Valparaiso students, the team created a hybrid project that combined the searchable online archive of digital stories, art, and infographics with a travelling exhibition that toured the county, and audio spotlights on public radio. The authors address the ethics of telling the stories of homelessness when it carries so much stigma. They navigate this in a variety of ways, including giving final say concerning publishing the edited stories to the individuals interviewed. Local advocates later used the project to influence the mayor's decision to build new affordable housing.

The next project, *Hear, Here*, also significantly influenced public policy in La Crosse, Wisconsin, when it contributed to the retirement of a large, caricaturish statue of a Native American located on sacred Ho-Chunk lands. *Hear, Here* is a pedagogical oral history project produced by Ariel Beaujot, a history professor at the University of Wisconsin–La Crosse. The project's main interface is a series of signs posted around downtown La Crosse inviting passersby to call a phone number and listen to a place-based oral history; the caller is then invited to contribute their own story. Beaujot and her students actively partnered with local community organizations to amplify the voices of marginalized communities in La Crosse, once a "sundown town." There is a web portal with archived stories, a contribution hub, and a sample curriculum for expansion of the project into other classrooms and cities. As the project collected stories, Beaujot noticed a confluence around a downtown statue called "Hiawatha." She then sought out story contributors and local activist groups to see how her project, students, and skills as a historian might be useful. The statue is slated for relocation to private property away from La Crosse's historic downtown.

Wrapping up the volume, Aubrey Thompson, a staff member at the University of California, Davis, and Ildi Carlisle-Cummins of the California Institute for Rural Studies reflect on the lessons they learned while collaborating to research and produce the podcast episode "There's Nothing More Californian than Ketchup," which explores the controversial history of the mechanical tomato harvester. The fruits of their collaboration became the first podcast of the California Institute for Rural Studies' *Cal Ag Roots* project, which "puts historical roots under current California food and farming change movements by telling the story of California agricultural development in innovative, useful and relevant ways." Their chapter includes text and audio conversations between the two collaborators about how their research attempted to bridge the campus-community divide while drawing on academic and community knowledge to provide historical background on contemporary agricultural issues. The authors grapple with their own positions as scholars and advocates and the institutional responsibility of UC Davis in the creation of the tomato harvester, which made California's Central Valley the center of U.S. tomato production but also concentrated farm production and put farmer laborers out of work.

In addition to the campus-community collaborations highlighted in these chapters, DiCE projects often require campus collaboration among faculty, archivists, librarians, technology specialists, and civic engagement professionals to create ethical, effective, and sustainable projects. These campus collaborations must overcome institutional silos, different reporting structures, and systems that may not sufficiently recognize the often-invisible labor that academic staff contribute behind the scenes. For example, civic engagement staff can facilitate projects that build on existing partnerships, train class-based projects in ethical engagement, and nurture community relationships after individual class projects have ended. Archivists and librarians too consider ways to maintain projects and make them accessible for stakeholders beyond the boundaries of a course. Successful campus collaborations draw upon the assets of higher education for community benefit and help higher education institutions fulfill their civic missions.

*   As we noted previously, DiCE is a blending of digital public humanities and community engagement practices. But what exactly does the digital change about community engagement? Primarily, it asks new questions about our technological choices, the ownership of digital material, the sustainability of the technology chosen for a project, and access to funding. While books have a well-defined path for preservation, digital products do not. One only needs to look as far as Myspace and its accidental deletion of twelve years of music produced by its community to see the fragility of digital material.[34] There are both up-front and long-term decisions to be made about infrastructure, tools, platforms, and frameworks, as well as ease of use, for different technology options. Choices about infrastructure, like any aspect of a DiCE project, require input from the community. Such projects need to meet community members where they are—whether that engages ease of use, capabilities that can take into account things like language or culture, or accessibility. Such choices also mean determining who becomes responsible for a project's long-term access and preservation, among academic staff and community members, as well as funding sources. Despite the internet's seeming ubiquity and easy access, the "cloud" has monetary and labor costs that are borne by institutions, projects, and people. Similar to any digital humanities project, such choices must be thought through; what changes is that those decisions are coordinated with the community.

It is equally significant that there are some aspects of community engagement that do not change with the addition of the digital. Digital technologies do not change the need to decenter the academy by placing the community's own knowledge and questions at the fore, which opens the opportunity for genuine co-creation.[35] Poorly conceived, however, a digital project may offer a substandard substitute for real engagement—a form of distancing rather than creating relationships across difference. Digital technologies also do not change the need to take deliberate steps to earn community trust, built at the speed of the community. This is an organic process of face-to-face contact, transparency, and open communication, as well as a healthy mixture of structured and informal engagement (regular check-ins and attendance at community functions). In the best-case scenario, stakeholders legitimately enjoy one another, and these small encounters can build up to larger successes.

It's past time for a volume of this nature, and we hope the examples to follow inspire new projects that advance the conversations about community engagement in the digital age. Community members have the most at stake in the success of the project. Their inclusion in this volume is essential—their voices, their willingness to trust academic institutions, their comfort with sharing stories, and their eagerness to co-create form the backbone of any DiCE project. We've tried to reciprocate their time, trust, and efforts by publishing this volume as an open access book, which we hope, in some small way, reduces potential barriers between our work and those we seek to serve. Like other forms of academic-community partnerships, digital community engagement can be either empowering or disempowering. We do this for our partners and those partners to come.

Notes

1. Several of the contributors to this volume participated in this working group including Ariel Beaujot, Julia Brock, and Karlyn Forner.
2. Kathleen Woodward, "The Future of the Humanities in the Present and in Public," *Daedalus* 138, no. 1 (2009): 117. See also Herbert Blau, "Relevance: The Shadow of a Magnitude," *Daedalus* 98, no. 3 (1969): 654-676.
3. Gerald Early, "The Humanities and Social Change," *Daedalus* 138, no. 1 (2009): 52. For an examination of the societal role of social scientists, see Steve Fuller, "Humanity: The Always Already—or Never to Be—Object of the Social Sciences?" in *The Social Sciences and Democracy*, ed. J. W. Bouwel (London: Palgrave Macmillan, 2010), 262.
4. The most comprehensive work in this vein was assembled in Dorothy Kim and Jesse Stommel, *Disrupting the Digital Humanities* (New York: Punctum Books, 2018). We also recommend Moya Z. Bailey, "All the Digital Humanities are White, All the Nerds are Men, but Some of us are Brave," *Journal of Digital Humanities* 1 (2011); Alan Liu, "The Meaning of the Digital Humanities," *PMLA* 128 (2013): 409-423; and Elizabeth Losh and Jacqueline Wernimont, eds., *Bodies of*

Information: Intersectional Feminism and Digital Humanities (Minneapolis: University of Minnesota Press, 2018), especially the chapter by Sharon Leon.

5. An overview of public history would be an entirely different book that might trace the discipline from the early museum musings of George Brown Goode in the late 1800s, to Carl Becker's address to the AHA in 1931, to G. Wesley Johnson's opening preface for the first volume of *The Public Historian* in 1978. Our field is constantly moving and shifting to meet the demands of an ever-changing public. In addition to mining the footnotes in this introduction, we recommend: Sheila A. Brennan, "Public, First," in *Debates in the Digital Humanities*, eds. Matthew K. Gold and Lauren F. Klein (Minneapolis: University of Minnesota Press, 2016); Paula Hamilton and James B. Gardner, eds., *The Oxford Handbook of Public History* (New York: Oxford University Press, 2017); Cherstin M. Lyon, Elizabeth M. Nix, and Rebecca K. Shrum, eds., *Introduction to Public History: Interpreting the Past, Engaging Audiences* (Lanham: Rowman & Littlefield Publishers, 2017); Roy Rosenzweig and David Thelen, *The Presence of the Past: Popular Uses of History in American Life* (New York: Columbia University Press, 2000); and Faye Sayer, *Public History: A Practical Guide* (London: Bloomsbury Publishing, 2015).

6. Nina Simon, *The Participatory Museum*, (Santa Cruz: Museum 2.0). See Chapter 8: Co-Creating with Visitors.

7. Bill Adair, Benjamin Filene, and Laura Koloski, eds., *Letting Go?: Sharing Historical Authority in a User-Generated World* (Philadelphia: Pew Center for Arts & Heritage, 2011).

8. Michael Frisch, *A Shared Authority: Essays on the Craft and Meaning of Oral and Public History* (Albany: SUNY Press, 1990).

9. Jesse Stommel, "Public Digital Humanities," in *Disrupting the Digital Humanities*, eds. Dorothy Kim and Jesse Stommel (New York: Punctum Books, 2018), 85.

10. Brennan, "Public, First."

11. Orville Vernon Burton, "American Digital History," *Social Science Computer Review* 23, no. 2 (2005): 206-220; Roy Rosenzweig, "The Road to Xanadu: Public and Private Pathways on the History Web," *Journal of American History* 88, no. 2 (2001): 548-579; and William G. Thomas III, "Computing and the Historical Imagination," in *Companion to Digital Humanities*, eds. Susan Schreibman, Ray Siemens, and John Unsworth (Hoboken: Blackwell Publishing, 2004).

12. Douglas Seefeldt and William G. Thomas III, "What is Digital History?," *Perspectives* (2009).

13. Sharon Leon, "Complexity and Collaboration: Doing Public History in Digital Environments," in *The Oxford Handbook of Public History*, ed. Paula Hamilton and James B. Gardner (New York: Oxford University Press, 2017), 46.

14. Leon, "Complexity and Collaboration," 58-63.

15. Arguing with Digital History working group, "Digital History and Argument," white paper, Roy Rosenzweig Center for History and New Media (November 13, 2017), 19.

16. Benedict Anderson, *Imagined Communities: Reflections on the Origin and Spread of Nationalism* (New York: Verso, 2016), 7.

17. This phenomenon is not unique to our volume. The *Georgetown Slavery Archive*, for example, located the descendants of the 272 enslaved women, men, and children they sold to keep their university afloat in 1838. These citizens did not know they were a community until researchers actively traced their lineage back to the GU272.

18. Michael Frisch, "From A Shared Authority to the Digital Kitchen, and Back," in *Letting Go?: Sharing Historical Authority in a User-Generated World*, eds. Bill Adair, Benjamin Filene, and Laura Koloski (Philadelphia: The Pew Center for Arts and Heritage, 2011): 126-137.

19. Simon, *The Participatory Museum*, 263.

20. Our question here borrows language from Laurenellen McCann, "Building Technology With, Not For, Communities: An Engagement Guide for Civic Tech," *Medium* (blog). March 30, 2015.

21. For more on civic tech, see Laurenellen McCann, *Experimental Modes of Civic Engagement in Civic Tech: Meeting People Where They Are* (Chicago: Smart Chicago Collaborative, 2015). For a more comprehensive literature review on campus-community partnerships, see Amy Driscoll and Kevin Kesckes, "Community-Higher Education Partnerships," Portland State University, Center for Academic Excellence (2009).

22. For examples of influential work from consortia, see Ben Berger and Jan R. Liss, "The Periclean Diamond: Linking College Classrooms, Campuses, Communities, and Colleagues via Social and Civic High Engagement Learning," (September 2012); Julie Ellison and Timothy K. Eatman, "Scholarship in Public: Knowledge Creation and Tenure Policy in the Engaged University," (2008); Donald Harward, ed., *Well-Being and Higher Education: A Strategy for Change and the Realization of Higher Education's Greater Purpose* (Washington, D.C.: AAC&U, 2016); and Ariane Hoy and Matthew Johnson, eds., *Deepening Community Engagement in Higher Education: Forging New Pathways* (London: Palgrave Macmillan, 2013).

23. For works focused on equity, co-creation, and new models of student learning, see Maria Avila, *Transforming Civic Engagement through Community Organizing* (Sterling: Stylus Publishing, 2018); Mary Beckman and Joyce F. Long, eds., *Community-Based Research: Teaching for Community Impact* (Sterling: Stylus Publishing, 2016); Donald W. Harward, ed., *Transforming Undergraduate Education: Theory That Compels and Practices That Succeed* (Landham: Rowman & Littlefield, 2011); Susan Sturm, Tim Eatman, John Saltmarsh, and Adam Bush, "Full Participation: Building the Architecture of Engagement and Diversity in Higher Education," (September 2011); John Saltmarsh and Matthew Hartley, eds., *"To Serve a Larger Purpose": Engagement for Democracy and the Transformation of Higher Education* (Philadelphia: Temple University Press, 2012); and Randy Stoecker, *Liberating*

Service-Learning and the Rest of Higher Education (Philadelphia: Temple University Press, 2016).

24. Stommel, "Public Digital Humanities," 81.

25. Arguing with Digital History working group, "Digital History and Argument," white paper, Roy Rosenzweig Center for History and New Media (November 13, 2017), 10.

26. Wendy F. Hsu, "Lessons on Public Humanities from the Civic Sphere," in *Debates in the Digital Humanities,* eds. Matthew K. Gold and Lauren F. Klein (Minneapolis: University of Minnesota Press, 2016).

27. William G. Thomas III, "Interchange: The Promise of Digital History," *Journal of American History* 95, no. 2 (2008): 472.

28. Benjamin M. Schmidt, "The History BA since the Great Recession: The 2018 AHA Majors Report," *Perspectives* (November 26, 2018).

29. Wingo, Chapter 3.

30. Bill Adair, Benjamin Filene, and Laura Koloski, "Introduction," in *Letting Go?: Shared Historical Authority in a User-Generated World* (Philadelphia: Pew Center for Arts & Heritage, 2011), 10-15.

31. See especially the work of Thomas Cauvin, President of the International Federation for Public History.

32. Kristin Ahlberg, et al., "Tenure, Promotion, and the Publicly Engaged Academic Historian: A White Paper by the Working Group on Evaluating Public History Scholarship," 6-7. See also KerryAnn O'Meara, Timothy Eatman, and Saul Petersen, "Advancing Engaged Scholarship in Promotion and Tenure: A Roadmap and Call for Reform," *Liberal Education* (Summer 2015), and KerryAnn O'Meara and R. Eugene Rice, eds., *Faculty Priorities Reconsidered: Rewarding Multiple Forms of Scholarship* (San Francisco: Jossey-Bass, 2005).

33. Leon, "Beyond the Principal Investigator," and Bailey, "All the Digital Humanities Are White, All the Nerds Are Men, But Some of Us Are Brave."

34. Daniel Cohen and Roy Rosenzweig, *Digital History: A Guide to Gathering, Preserving, and Presenting History on the Web* (University of Pennsylvania Press, 2005), 233-246; Daniel V. Pitti, "Designing Sustainable Projects and Publications," in *Companion to Digital Humanities*, 471-487; "Myspace deleted 12 years' worth of music in a botched server migration," *The Verge*, March 18, 2019 (accessed June 24, 2019).

35. Brennan, "Public, First."

Works Cited

Adair, Bill, Benjamin Filene, and Laura Koloski. "Introduction." In *Letting Go?: Sharing Historical Authority in a User-Generated World*. Edited by Bill Adair, Benjamin Filene, and Laura Koloski, 10–15. Philadelphia: Pew Center for Arts & Heritage, 2011.

Adair, Bill, Benjamin Filene, and Laura Koloski, eds. *Letting Go?: Sharing Historical Authority in a User-Generated World.* Philadelphia: Pew Center for Arts & Heritage, 2011.

Ahlberg, Kristin, et al. "Tenure, Promotion, and the Publicly Engaged Academic Historian: A White Paper by the Working Group on Evaluating Public History Scholarship."

Anderson, Benedict. *Imagined Communities: Reflections on the Origin and Spread of Nationalism.* New York: Verso, 2016.

Arguing with Digital History working group. "Digital History and Argument." White Paper. Roy Rosenzweig Center for History and New Media. November 13, 2017.

Avila, Maria. *Transforming Civic Engagement through Community Organizing.* Sterling: Stylus Publishing, 2018.

Bailey, Moya Z. "All the Digital Humanities Are White, All the Nerds Are Men, but Some of Us Are Brave." *Journal of Digital Humanities* 1 (2011).

Becker, Carl. "Everyman His Own Historian." *American Historical Review* 37, no. 2 (January 1932): 221–236.

Beckman, Mary and Joyce F. Long, eds. *Community-Based Research: Teaching for Community Impact.* Sterling: Stylus Publishing, 2016.

Berger, Ben and Jan R. Liss. "The Periclean Diamond: Linking College Classrooms, Campuses, Communities, and Colleagues via Social and Civic High Engagement Learning." September 2012.

Blau, Herbert. "Relevance: The Shadow of a Magnitude." *Daedalus* 98, no. 3 (1969): 654–676.

Brennan, Sheila A. "Public, First." In *Debates in the Digital Humanities.* Edited by Matthew K. Gold and Lauren F. Klein. Minneapolis: University of Minnesota Press, 2016.

Burton, Orville Vernon. "American Digital History." *Social Science Computer Review* 23, no. 2 (2005): 206–220.

Cohen, Daniel and Roy Rosenzweig. *Digital History: A Guide to Gathering, Preserving, and Presenting History on the Web.* Philadelphia: University of Pennsylvania Press, 2005.

Driscoll, Amy and Kevin Kesckes. "Community-Higher Education Partnerships." Portland State University. Center for Academic Excellence, 2009.

Early, Gerald. "The Humanities and Social Change." *Daedalus* 138, no. 1 (2009): 52–57.

Ellison, Julie and Timothy K. Eatman. "Scholarship in Public: Knowledge Creation and Tenure Policy in the Engaged University." *Imagining America.* 2008.

Frisch, Michael. *A Shared Authority: Essays on the Craft and Meaning of Oral and Public History*. Albany: SUNY Press, 1990.

Frisch, Michael. "From A Shared Authority to the Digital Kitchen, and Back." In *Letting Go?: Sharing Historical Authority in a User-Generated World*, 126–137. Edited by Bill Adair, Benjamin Filene, and Laura Koloski. Philadelphia: Pew Center for Arts and Heritage, 2011.

Fuller, Steve. "Humanity: The Always Already—or Never to Be—Object of the Social Sciences?" In *The Social Sciences and Democracy*, 240–264. Edited by J. W. Bouwel. London: Palgrave Macmillan, 2010.

Goode, George Brown. "The Museums of the Future." In *A Memorial of George Brown Goode Together with a Selection of His Papers*. Washington, D.C.: Government Printing Office, 1901.

Hamilton, Paula and James B. Gardner, eds. *The Oxford Handbook of Public History*. New York: Oxford University Press, 2017.

Harward, Donald W. ed. *Transforming Undergraduate Education: Theory That Compels and Practices That Succeed*. Landham: Rowman & Littlefield, 2011.

Harward, Donald W., ed. *Well-Being and Higher Education: A Strategy for Change and the Realization of Higher Education's Greater Purpose*. Washington, D.C.: AAC&U, 2016.

Hoy, Ariane and Matthew Johnson, eds. *Deepening Community Engagement in Higher Education: Forging New Pathways*. London: Palgrave Macmillan, 2013.

Hsu, Wendy F. "Lessons on Public Humanities from the Civic Sphere." In *Debates in the Digital Humanities*. Edited by Matthew K. Gold and Lauren F. Klein. Minneapolis: University of Minnesota Press, 2016.

Johnson, G. Wesley. "Editor's Preface." *Public Historian* 1, no. 1 (1978): 4–10.

Kim, Dorothy and Jesse Stommel. *Disrupting the Digital Humanities*. New York: Punctum Books, 2018.

Leon, Sharon. "Beyond the Principal Investigator: Complicating 'Great Man' Narrative of Digital History." In *Bodies of Information: Intersectional Feminism and Digital Humanities*. Edited by Elizabeth Losh and Jacqueline Wernimont. Minneapolis: University of Minnesota Press, 2018.

Leon, Sharon. "Complexity and Collaboration: Doing Public History in Digital Environments." In *The Oxford Handbook of Public History*. Edited by Paula Hamilton and James B. Gardner. New York: Oxford University Press, 2017.

Liu, Alan. "The Meaning of the Digital Humanities." *PMLA* 128 (2013): 409–423.

Losh, Elizabeth and Jacqueline Wernimont, eds. *Bodies of Information: Intersectional Feminism and Digital Humanities*. Minneapolis: University of Minnesota Press, 2018.

Lyon, Cherstin M., Elizabeth M. Nix, and Rebecca K. Shrum, eds. *Introduction to Public History: Interpreting the Past, Engaging Audiences*. Lanham: Rowman & Littlefield Publishers, 2017.

McCann, Laurenellen. "Building Technology With, Not For, Communities: An Engagement Guide for Civic Tech." *Medium* (blog). March 30, 2015.

McCann, Laurenellen. *Experimental Modes of Civic Engagement in Civic Tech: Meeting People Where They Are*. Chicago: Smart Chicago Collaborative, 2015.

O'Meara, KerryAnn and R. Eugene Rice, eds., *Faculty Priorities Reconsidered: Rewarding Multiple Forms of Scholarship*. San Francisco: Jossey-Bass, 2005.

O'Meara, KerryAnn, Timothy Eatman, and Saul Petersen, "Advancing Engaged Scholarship in Promotion and Tenure: A Roadmap and Call for Reform," *Liberal Education* (Summer 2015).

Pitti, Daniel V. "Designing Sustainable Projects and Publications." In *A Companion to Digital Humanities*, 471–487. Edited by Ray Siemens, John Unsworth, and Susan Schriebman. Oxford: Blackwell, 2004.

Porter, Jon. "Myspace deleted 12 years' worth of music in a botched server migration." *The Verge*. March 18, 2019. https://www.theverge.com/2019/3/18/18271023/myspace-music-videos-deleted-2003–2015-server-migration.

Rosenzweig, Roy. "The Road to Xanadu: Public and Private Pathways on the History Web." *Journal of American History* 88, no. 2 (2001): 548–579.

Rosenzweig, Roy and David Thelen. *The Presence of the Past: Popular Uses of History in American Life*. New York: Columbia University Press, 2000.

Saltmarsh, John and Matthew Hartley, eds. *"To Serve a Larger Purpose": Engagement for Democracy and the Transformation of Higher Education*. Philadelphia: Temple University Press, 2012.

Sayer, Faye. *Public History: A Practical Guide*. London: Bloomsbury Publishing, 2015.

Schmidt, Benjamin M. "The History BA since the Great Recession: The 2018 AHA Majors Report." *Perspectives* (November 26, 2018).

Seefeldt, Douglas and William G. Thomas III. "What is Digital History?," *Perspectives* (2009).

Simon, Nina. *The Participatory Museum*. Santa Cruz: Museum 2.0, 2010.

Smithies, James. "Digital Humanities, Postfoundationalism, Postindustrial Culture." *Digital Humanities Quarterly* 8, no. 1 (2014).

Stoecker, Randy. *Liberating Service-Learning and the Rest of Higher Education*. Philadelphia: Temple University Press, 2016.

Stommel, Jesse. "Public Digital Humanities." In *Disrupting the Digital Humanities*, 79–90. Edited by Dorothy Kim and Jesse Stommel. New York: Punctum Books, 2018.

Sturm, Susan, Tim Eatman, John Saltmarsh, and Adam Bush. "Full Participation: Building the Architecture of Engagement and Diversity in Higher
Education." *Imagining America*. September 2011.

Thomas, William G., III. "Computing and the Historical Imagination." In *Companion to Digital Humanities*. Edited by Susan Schreibman, Ray Siemens, and
John Unsworth. Hoboken: Blackwell Publishing, 2004.

Thomas, William G., III. "Interchange: The Promise of Digital History." *Journal
of American History* 95, no. 2 (2008): 452–491.

Woodward, Kathleen. "The Future of the Humanities in the Present and in
Public." *Daedalus* 138, no. 1 (2009): 110–123.

1

Learn from the Past, Organize for the Future

Building the SNCC Digital Gateway

*Geri Augusto, Molly Bragg, Bill Chafe, Charles Cobb, Courtland Cox,
Emilye Crosby, Kaley Deal, Karlyn Forner, John Gartell, Wesley Hogan,
Hasan Kwame Jeffries, Jennifer Lawson, Naomi Nelson, Judy Richardson,
Will Sexton, and Timothy Tyson*

Introduction

Karlyn Forner

It's one thing—I'm thinking from the university or institutional perspective—to consult with community people or movement veterans or activists. It's another thing to have them actually participating in it in an equitable way on ownership and decision-making and content.

—Charlie Cobb, SNCC veteran

There were times when this project slowed down because [the SNCC veterans] did not respond quickly enough. Because [the university partners] would do nothing until we said what we had to say, commented on it, directed it, do whatever we had to do. When they said scholar activists, they mean that in the fullest sense of the word.

—Judy Richardson, SNCC veteran

What makes this unique is not just the relationships with each other but the telling the history from the inside out and bottom up. We all know that it is not the norm.

—Courtland Cox, SNCC veteran

While there exists a rich body of literature about public history and shared authority, this chapter does not cite it. Instead, the collaboration between SNCC veterans, scholars, and archivists grew out of lived experience, as well as a collective willingness to try something and see it through. As Naomi Nelson, director of Duke University's Rubenstein Library, explained, "the 'literature' we consulted was not formal historiography, but the

DOI: 10.34314/wingodigital.00002

lived history of the Movement, the transfer of informational wealth from community organizers, and the hard-won insight of the movement veterans." The experiences of the movement veterans, scholars of grassroots organizing, and archivists committed to accountability framed the collaboration and guided the project through the challenges and opportunities along the way.[1]

In 2013 the Student Nonviolent Coordinating Committee (SNCC) Legacy Project, the Center for Documentary Studies at Duke University (CDS), and Duke University Libraries (DUL) formed a partnership to chronicle SNCC's historic struggles for voting rights and to develop ongoing programs that could contribute to a more civil and inclusive democracy in the 21st century.

During the 1960s, SNCC (pronounced "snick") became the cutting edge of the direct-action Civil Rights Movement, focusing on both political freedom and equal economic opportunity. SNCC was the only national, Southern-based civil rights organization begun and led primarily by young people. Its full-time student workers, "field secretaries," worked with local Black communities to help them organize and take control of their own lives. As SNCC activist and SNCC Legacy Project (SLP) member, Charlie Cobb, explained:

> At a deeper level than the immediate political concern with voter registration, SNCC's work was also about cultivating new local leadership and reinforcing existing local leadership. SNCC field secretaries did not see themselves as community leaders but as community organizers, a distinction that empowered local participants by reinforcing the idea at the heart of SNCC's work in every project that "local people" could and should take control of their own lives.

Movement veterans formed the SNCC Legacy Project in 2010 to preserve the history of SNCC's grassroots organizing work and to assist today's educators, activists, and students in ongoing struggles for self-determination, justice, and democracy. Three years later, SLP formed a partnership with Duke University that brought together SNCC veterans, noted civil rights scholars, library professionals, and students in a multi-faceted, multi-year project that sought to change the normative story of the Civil Rights Movement. The people sitting

DOI: 10.34314/wingodigital.00002

Figure 1.1: SNCC Digital Gateway Project Partners (from left to right); first row: Will Sexton (DUL), John Gartrell (DUL), Wesley Hogan (CDS), Karlyn Forner (DUL); second row: Jennifer Lawson (SLP), Geri Augusto (SLP), Charlie Cobb (SLP), Emilye Crosby (SUNY Geneseo), Judy Richardson (SLP), Hasan Kwame Jeffries (The Ohio State University); back row: Courtland Cox (SLP), Molly Bragg (DUL), Naomi Nelson (DUL), and William Chafe (CDS). Courtesy of the Center for Documentary Studies and the SNCC Digital Gateway Project.

at the table shared a common vision. They wanted to tell the story of SNCC's organizing from the bottom up and inside out—exploring SNCC's thinking and how their work at the grassroots affected how people organized to change history—and to make SNCC materials more widely accessible to students, teachers, activists, and citizens. "At the first meeting, we didn't even know where it could lead and what it could be, but there was that willingness and that interest and the trust," SNCC veteran Jennifer Lawson explained.

The collaboration's pilot website, *One Person, One Vote: The Legacy of SNCC and the Fight for Voting Rights,* launched in March 2015, and thanks to support from a three-year grant from the Andrew W. Mellon Foundation, the project partners were able to expand that work into the *SNCC Digital Gateway* website.

The *SNCC Digital Gateway* tells the story of how young activists in SNCC united with local people in the Deep South to build a grassroots movement for change. It unveils the inner workings and thinking of SNCC as an

DOI: 10.34314/wingodigital.00002

organization by examining how it coordinated sit-ins and Freedom Schools, voter registration and economic cooperatives, and anti-draft protests and international solidarity struggles. Profiles highlight individuals' contributions to the Movement; a timeline traces the evolution of SNCC's organizing; "Inside SNCC" pages delve into SNCC's internal organization; and a map highlights important sites of organizing.

Figure 1.2: Contemporary and veteran activists in conversation at the "Arts and Culture in the Movement" breakout session at the closing events of the SNCC Digital Gateway project at North Carolina Central University in Durham, North Carolina, March 24, 2018. Photograph by Kim Johnson. Courtesy of the SNCC Digital Gateway Project.

During all phases of the project, SNCC partners have been central in shaping the telling of SNCC's story. They have worked collaboratively with historians of the Movement, archivists, project staff, and students to weave together grassroots stories and primary source material and create new multimedia productions that illuminate this history for new generations. The perspectives of the activists are front and center throughout the website. In the "Our Voices" section, veteran activists explain important themes and ideas from SNCC's history in their own voices. The "Today" section then ties this

DOI: 10.34314/wingodigital.00002

history to the present, featuring contemporary activists' reflections on how SNCC's organizing informs their struggles today.

Beyond telling history from the inside out and the bottom up, the SNCC Legacy Project and Duke also sought to create a replicable model for partnerships between activists and scholars. Collaborations between activists and universities have a long, fraught history. "For SNCC, it's not unusual for people to misuse what we have done for purposes that go in another direction," SNCC veteran and SLP president Courtland Cox explained. A pattern of exploitive relationships with elite white institutions and scholars had created deep distrust among SNCC veterans.

To make their efforts transparent and of potential use to others, partners from SLP and Duke set out to formally document what made their collaboration between activists and the academy work. What follows is a working paper collaboratively written by sixteen partners of the *SNCC Digital Gateway* project. It lays out what project partners found to be the essential components for a successful partnership, one that's built on equitable relationships, mutual respect, trust, and a common vision. Copies of this working paper, as well as the longer unabridged version, can be found in the "Resources" section of the *SNCC Digital Gateway* website.

Figure 1.3: SNCC Digital Gateway logo. Courtesy of the *SNCC Digital Gateway* Project.

DOI: 10.34314/wingodigital.00002

Building Partnerships Between Activists & the Academy

This working paper was collaboratively written by the partners of the SNCC
Digital Gateway *project, including: Geri Augusto (SLP), Molly Bragg (DUL),
Bill Chafe (CDS), Charles Cobb (SLP), Courtland Cox (SLP), Emilye Crosby
(SUNY Geneseo), Kaley Deal (project coordinator), Karlyn Forner (project
manager), John Gartell (DUL), Wesley Hogan (CDS), Hasan Kwame Jeffries
(The Ohio State University), Jennifer Lawson (SLP), Naomi Nelson (DUL),
Judy Richardson (SLP), Will Sexton (DUL), and Timothy Tyson (CDS)*

Project Partners

It's possible, with the right people and the right place, to make things happen that
otherwise cannot happen.
—Bill Chafe, founder of the Center for Documentary Studies at Duke University

Activist Partners

Are organized.

The SNCC Legacy Project was established in 2010, following the 50th anniversary conference celebrating SNCC's founding. Within six months, the organization had a governing board, its own 501(c)(3) status, and the support of a
significant number of SNCC veterans. Its mission was to preserve the history
of SNCC's work and to assist today's scholars, activists, and organizers in
continuing the struggle for human and civil rights. The SLP's 501(c)(3) status
gave it an institutional equivalency in the partnership with Duke University
Libraries and the Center for Documentary Studies. SLP had established
ways to solicit feedback from SNCC veterans and could make decisions as
an organization. As a legal entity, SLP could enter into agreements with the
university, own copyright, etc.

DOI: 10.34314/wingodigital.00002

Have a clear purpose but are flexible on the means.

It was essential that the SNCC Legacy Project was clear and united regarding the purpose of and vision for the project. One of SLP's major objectives was to create new works to interpret and provide fresh perspectives on SNCC's ideas and experiences for a twenty-first century audience. Before entering into a partnership with Duke, the SLP Board had developed proposals for different ways to tell SNCC's history from the perspective of the activists themselves and how to pass their "informational wealth" on to subsequent generations. They brought this prior work into partnership with Duke. While SLP was clear on vision, they were also flexible about the means of carrying it out and embraced new opportunities that presented themselves throughout the course of the project.

Have strong relationships around which to marshal support.

Many movement veterans distrusted scholars. Too many, they felt, had failed to include the perspectives of the activists and gotten the story of the Movement wrong. Elite universities also had a long history of exploitive relationships with activists. "There was a lot of suspicion among members of our [SLP] Board about Duke and this relationship and questions of ownership and all of this," SNCC veteran Charlie Cobb explained. The SLP partners who were working with Duke needed to demonstrate to their board members, as well as the broader community of SNCC veterans, how the collaboration would be equitable and would get a more authentic telling of SNCC's story to a wider audience. SLP partners drew on the strong relationships that had developed within SNCC to marshal support as well as to diligently represent the interests of SNCC veterans throughout the collaboration. These efforts became easier as the project produced tangible work that won the approval of SNCC veterans.

DOI: 10.34314/wingodigital.00002

Figure 1.4: Naomi Nelson (DUL), Bruce Hartford (SLP), and Courtland Cox (SLP) at the collaboration's first meeting at Duke University, November 2013. Courtesy of the SNCC Digital Gateway Project.

University Partners

Have a history of valuing the stories of everyday people.

Beginning in the 1970s, the Duke Oral History Program had trained a generation of scholars that valued the voices of ordinary people and pushed the boundaries of what kinds of stories could be told. Over four decades, it produced forty-five Ph.D.s. Nearly thirty of their dissertations on grassroots activism were published, and eighteen of these won national book prizes, helping to change, significantly, the way historians write about the Civil Rights Movement. The program's commitment to everyday people in many ways paralleled SNCC's approach to grassroots organizing. Over time, its success created leverage and support in the university, which eventually led to the founding of the Center for Documentary Studies in 1989. By the time the SNCC Legacy Project approached scholars and librarians at Duke about a partnership, there was a strong base of people and institutions committed to local movement studies, as well as a favorable environment within the university for a project of this kind.

Have institutional will.

The SNCC Legacy Project found institutional will within Duke University in the form of people who were willing to commit to the project. Support

DOI: 10.34314/wingodigital.00002

from Naomi Nelson, the director of the David M. Rubenstein Rare Book & Manuscript Library; Wesley Hogan, the director of the Center for Documentary Studies; and William Chafe, founder of the Duke Oral History Program and the Center for Documentary Studies, and a former dean of Duke's Trinity College of Arts & Sciences, was essential in getting the project off the ground. They believed in the vision of the project, but more important, they were willing to put in the time and energy to bring that vision to fruition. Working together, they secured funds for the initial project and mobilized resources within their respective institutions, which was possible because the project aligned with the university's mission and programmatic goals.

Are flexible.

By entering into the collaboration with activists, university partners demonstrated an openness to nontraditional ways of working and creating knowledge. Two concepts common to the library and academic world—objectivity and efficiency—had to take a back seat in the partnership. Content produced for the website met rigorous citation standards, but it told history from the point of view of those who created it. The premise was that the input and insights of the activists were absolutely essential to getting the story right. University partners needed to accept that working in an equitable relationship with activists sometimes required more work and lengthy, ongoing, small-"d" democratic conversations. University partners at Duke were also flexible in the day-to-day work and committed to finding a way when potential roadblocks emerged. They were willing to restructure the project as they learned by doing, to bring in new collaborators as opportunities arose, and to undertake simultaneous but distinct projects to further the broader vision of the collaboration.

Shared Mission, Shared Values

There is a common set of values that the activists and the academics shared in this project that helped make it work.

—Hasan Kwame Jeffries, historian at The Ohio State University

DOI: 10.34314/wingodigital.00002

Part of the reason that the SNCC Digital Gateway was able to succeed was because project partners were committed to a common mission and held shared values. The veteran activists, archivists, scholars, and project staff were uniformly committed to telling SNCC's and the Movement's history from the bottom up and what they came to call "inside out"—that is, scholarship directed and created by those who lived it. Although there were disagreements about how to best implement this, there was never a question about what the primary purpose of the collaboration was and how the history needed to be framed.

Scholars whose work had earned the respect of the activists brought project partners together around a shared vision.

The civil rights scholars on the project were essential in forging the collaboration. Historians Emilye Crosby, Wesley Hogan, and Hasan Kwame Jeffries had a demonstrable track record of academic- and activist-approved scholarship. They had built trusting relationships with activists over the years. Throughout the collaboration, they mobilized this earned respect to bring the activist and university partners together around a shared vision.

SNCC's history of organizing—taking ideas, putting them into action, and finding solutions—infused the day-to-day work of the SNCC Digital Gateway project. A shared belief in the importance of the project pushed project partners to engage, problem-solve, persist, and make things happen. In many ways, this approach paralleled how SNCC approached its work in the 1960s. SNCC veteran Courtland Cox explained:

> When you think about SNCC at its essence, it was always trying to develop new ways and new methodologies of solving problems, and that's what it was. Whether you're talking about the Freedom Schools or whether you're talking about the MFDP [Mississippi Freedom Democratic Party], or things that didn't exist, we created it. And as I keep telling people, the basis of genius is what? Making sh*t up. So that's what we did.

DOI: 10.34314/wingodigital.00002

Beyond holding a shared vision, project partners could take ideas and put them into action, and project staff could follow through and get the work done.

As a group, project partners were willing to problem-solve and figure out ways to make things happen. People were "prepared to think about whether there are ways to get around the problems, even if they're outside of common practice," as historian Emilye Crosby explained. This openness to thinking about things in new ways and trying new approaches was essential to the project's success. The project regularly encountered new challenges and opportunities that weren't anticipated, but project partners and staff were able to adapt the project based on experience and need, solving problems and responding with flexibility. The project adapted and evolved organically over its four years. The final SNCC Digital Gateway website holds true to the vision laid out in the original proposal, but nearly all the specifics have been reimagined and refashioned to fit the shifting circumstances and new ideas the project encountered along the way.

An Equal Partnership

The early and unwavering commitment by partners at Duke University to having movement veterans participate in an equitable manner in all aspects of the project was essential to the collaboration's success. At the project's first meeting, the SNCC Legacy Project, Duke University Libraries, and the Center for Documentary Studies agreed that movement veterans were to be equitable partners in terms of ownership, decision-making, and content. This commitment was made real in a number of ways:

Governance

SLP, DUL, CDS, and scholars had equal representation and an equal say on the Advisory Board that oversaw governance for the project and the Editorial Board that was in charge of content decisions.

DOI: 10.34314/wingodigital.00002

Decision-Making

No decision was made without consulting the appropriate project partners, and most importantly, the movement veterans. The process could be slow and time-consuming, but it was critical to the project's success. As Naomi Nelson of Duke Libraries explained, "We've all been able to hold this idea in our head that everybody owns this project." At its core, it reflected SNCC's own commitment to small-"d" democracy and building consensus.

Ownership

Ownership was a primary concern for SNCC partners, as they were the creators of the history to be told on the SNCC Digital Gateway. In the first meeting, Duke Libraries and the SNCC Legacy Project agreed that their common goal was to create access to SNCC materials and get them out in the world. They moved forward with an agreement to make the material as open as possible via Creative Commons licenses and contract language prohibiting future paywalls or similar requirements. Copyrights for attributed new works created for the SNCC Digital Gateway would belong to the authors, while copyrights for unattributed new content would be owned by the SNCC Legacy Project. The authors and SLP then granted Duke non-exclusive, perpetual licenses to publish and provide access to the content using Creative Commons licenses. This creator-centric approach reflected SNCC values regarding the value of work and respecting the rights of the creators who do the work.

Memorandum of Understanding

In the first six months of the partnership, Duke University and the SNCC Legacy Project wrote a Memorandum of Understanding (MoU) to document their commitment to equitable ownership and participation in decision-making, as well as to open access. This was an important step in building trust early in the collaboration. It was important that SLP came into drafting the MoU with clear terms of what it wanted, as well as experience working with large bureaucracies. On the other side, Naomi Nelson of Duke Libraries, who

DOI: 10.34314/wingodigital.00002

was responsible for shepherding the agreement through the university's legal department, saw SLP's terms as reasonable and in alignment with Duke's aims and values. Despite university pushback, she was able to preserve the statements of joint copyright between SLP and Duke. Meanwhile, SLP was understanding of the need for Duke to include complicated legal language. This agreement helped create a basis of trust early in the collaboration.

The commitment to equitable participation helped build strong relationships among project partners and fostered a respectful way of working together. Scholars, archivists, and project staff were dedicated to carrying out the SNCC partners' vision. As John Gartrell of Duke Libraries explained to the SNCC partners, "We're always accountable to you all."

Figure 1.5: Charlie Cobb (right) in the SNCC Digital Gateway project room at Duke University Libraries working with Todd Christensen (left) and other members of the project team, November 2015. Photograph by Kaley Deal. Courtesy of the SNCC Digital Gateway Project.

Told from the Perspectives of the Activists

We were trying to make a very difficult conceptual switch and say that the people who made the history have vital insights, and we will not understand all of this other data that we have unless they're able to narrate and explain.

—Wesley Hogan, director of the Center for Documentary Studies

DOI: 10.34314/wingodigital.00002

From the project's earliest conceptions, the SNCC Digital Gateway had two primary purposes: to tell the history of SNCC from the perspective of the activists themselves and to pass their "informational wealth" on to subsequent generations. As the SNCC veterans saw it, the essential "how-to's" of the freedom movement had often been lost after each generation. The tactics and strategies of grassroots organizing have had to be found, discovered, and put together by each activist generation. The SNCC Digital Gateway would be a way to remedy this.

SNCC veterans' knowledge and experiences were crucial to the work. Traditionally, scholars have been the primary tellers of activists' stories. The name recognition of a handful of activists has given them the opportunity to tell their story in their own voices, but more often, scholars have been those who uncover the lesser-known stories and interpret them for the present day. While the makers of history appear as subjects, they rarely get to shape and interpret the story in a way that accurately reflects their experiences and understandings.

In the SNCC Digital Gateway Project, SNCC veterans took the lead in framing the story and shaping the content, both on the Editorial Board and as Visiting Activist Scholars (see below). The scholars on the Editorial Board were critical in determining content, but they played a supporting role in finding documentation, clarifying, and bringing to life the visions put forward by the SNCC veterans. The process for creating content ultimately drew on project partners' three different realms of expertise: new content was led by the activists and informed by the scholars, and its presentation was structured by the librarians. Together, the partners saw themselves as true partners in the production of knowledge, with SNCC veterans leading the way.

Building Trust

The trust factor is gonna happen over time. It's not gonna happen from jump. And it's through the work.

—Judy Richardson, SNCC veteran

You're gonna have to show me through actions.

—Courtland Cox, SNCC veteran

DOI: 10.34314/wingodigital.00002

Activist partners are involved in and guide the day-to-day work of the project.

One of the ways the project prioritized the knowledge and experiences of SNCC veterans was by creating the Visiting Activist Scholar position. In this capacity, SNCC veterans came to Duke's campus to guide the project staff and student project team in creating content, work for which they were compensated. The SNCC veterans provided on-the-ground oversight in the work of writing history and were people that SNCC Legacy Project members trusted to get the story right. They also created new content for the website—including audio, video, and written narratives—that told the history from SNCC's perspective.

The Visiting Activist Scholar position helped build trust between the activist and university partners. The first two Visiting Activist Scholars—journalist Charlie Cobb and filmmaker Judy Richardson—were SNCC veterans and members of the SLP Board and the project's Editorial Board. This was a strategic decision. Both Charlie and Judy were involved in the earliest conceptualization of the project and were already invested in its success. Their physical presence on campus and direct interactions with the project staff and team shaped the project work and helped assuage the concerns of the SNCC Legacy Project. "Their being on the project was a big, important issue because I knew there were going to be ups and downs, and everything wasn't going to be smooth," SLP chairman Courtland Cox remembered. "But if they were involved, I could feel that things were going fine."

Project staff are able to transform ideas into tangible outputs.

The project staff needed to have a range of skills to carry out such an expansive project. These included knowing the content, listening to project partners' wishes and ideas and incorporating them into the work, implementing tasks efficiently and effectively, problem-solving, and adapting to the shifting project needs. It was essential that the project manager and coordinator had the buy-in of the activist partners. They needed to prove that they could carry out project partners' visions and create an atmosphere of accountability. This was central to earning the trust of the activist partners and Editorial Board.

DOI: 10.34314/wingodigital.00002

Figure 1.6: SNCC Digital Gateway project partners after final joint meeting of the Editorial and Advisory Boards at Duke University, March 25, 2018. From left to right, first row: Wesley Hogan (DUL), Charlie Cobb (SLP), Judy Richardson (SLP), Naomi Nelson (DUL), Danita Mason-Hogans (CDS), Emilye Crosby (SUNY Geneseo), John Gartrell (DUL), Karlyn Forner (DUL), and Kaley Deal (DUL); back row: Jennifer Lawson (SLP), William Chafe (CDS), Geri Augusto (SLP), Courtland Cox (SLP), Bruce Hartford (SLP), and Molly Bragg (DUL). Courtesy of the SNCC Digital Gateway Project.

Over time—and through the work—the project staff demonstrated that they could transform ideas into tangible outputs that accurately reflected project partners' desires. They developed a process of asking targeted questions, listening closely, and creating concrete options for moving forward for the Editorial Board to choose from. Editorial Board members came to trust the project staff as good problem-solvers and synthesizers. They could feel confident that they could leave something unfinished or unsettled until the next time they got together and that the project staff would successfully pull together an option that everyone could agree on. The reliability and follow-through on the part of the project staff was important in building strong

DOI: 10.34314/wingodigital.00002

working relationships and trust. They approached the work with sensitivity and accountability, making sure that project partners were heard and that their concerns were addressed.

Project partners use a variety of strategies to deal with conflict.

Regular communication was central to keeping project partners on the same page and addressing conflicts before they arose. "We follow up. We touch base. We follow up. And something gets done," John Gartrell of Duke Libraries explained. Project partners were also adept at reading people and the nuances of situations. Many potential problems were averted because of ongoing side conversations between different project partners. Sometimes this involved one SLP member talking to another SLP member about a particular issue; or the project manager talking with a scholar and SLP member about how to best approach a pending decision; or the directors of Rubenstein Library and CDS consulting on how to manage conflicting expectations of activist partners and the broader university. These ongoing formal and informal conversations were instrumental in holding the project together.

Inevitably, conflicts arose in the work, and project partners discovered that sometimes the best way to move forward was to not deal with an issue head-on. It was a strategy of conflict avoidance as opposed to conflict resolution. Instead of insisting on complete agreement on vision or structure, project partners forged through impasses by focusing on the specifics of the work. "We started the work, and we came back to those sticking points in a piece-by-piece manner," project manager Karlyn Forner explained. Avoiding direct confrontations by moving forward on what project partners could agree on kept the project on track and leaving disagreements to be settled at a future date actually helped mitigate the conflicts.

A foundation of respect and trust, as well as steady progress, also helped project partners overcome moments of disagreement. The tenants of equitable partnership and shared vision were always bigger than the current point of contention. One-on-one side conversations smoothed the waters. Tangible options that reflected project partners' desires kept the work moving forward.

DOI: 10.34314/wingodigital.00002

Project partners also did not get caught up in the drama of hurt feelings. Despite differing opinions, everyone around the table agreed that the most important thing was telling SNCC's history. That shared vision of the project always took precedence.

As of this writing, the collaboration between the SNCC Legacy Project and Duke University continues its efforts to tell SNCC's history from the bottom up and the inside out, and to develop programs that contribute to a more civil and inclusive democracy in the twenty-first century.

Notes

1. For more information about the evolution of the collaboration, see Courtland Cox, Karlyn Forner, John Gartrell, Wesley Hogan, Jennifer Lawson, Isabell Moore, Naomi Nelson, "Archival Ties: The SNCC Digital Gateway" *Zapruder* 47 (September-December 2018).

DOI:.10.34314/wingodigital.00002

2

Archival Resistance to Structural Racism

A People's Archive of Police Violence in Cleveland

Melissa A. Hubbard

On November 22, 2014, twelve-year-old Tamir Rice was shot and killed by police officer Timothy Loehmann while playing with a toy gun outside the Cudell Recreation Center on the west side of Cleveland. Four days later, surveillance camera footage of Tamir's last moments was released to the news media. As these facts unfolded in the public eye, multiple narratives were operationalized to explain this tragedy. Only four months earlier, eighteen-year-old Michael Brown had been shot and killed by police in Ferguson, Missouri. Local residents there responded with protests and utilized social media to express their thoughts and feelings about the incident, leading to increased media interest in the case and a national conversation about police violence and racist policing. Tamir Rice's nationally publicized death immediately became a part of that story, often presented as disturbing evidence that police violence against Black people is worse than most white Americans had previously believed, and was part of a long history of structural racist violence. Writing for the *Washington Post*, Stacey Patton made a historical connection between the deaths of Black children and teenagers at the hands of police and the violent injustices of slavery and the Jim Crow era. Tamir Rice was one of several young people named in the essay, along with Emmitt Till, Jordan Davis, Darius Simmons, Trayvon Martin, Michael Brown, Aiyana Stanley-Jones, and Renisha McBride.[1]

At the same time, a parallel media narrative placed blame for Rice's death not on racist policing, but on the boy's background. On November 28, 2014, the *Plain Dealer*, Cleveland's major daily newspaper, published a story

DOI: 10.34314/wingodigital.00003

titled "Tamir Rice's father has history of domestic violence." In June 2015, the Associated Press released an article about Rice's death titled, "Boy with pellet gun warned by friend before police shooting," implying that Rice's own behavior was to blame for his death. When Tamir's mother, Samaria Rice, publicly called for Cuyahoga County prosecutor Tim McGinty to recuse himself from the investigation and prosecution of the police officers involved in Tamir's death, McGinty responded by claiming she was "economically motivated" rather than acting out of a desire for justice.[2]

While these narratives played out nationally, different stories could be told in Cleveland, where many residents know that Tamir Rice's death was not anomalous in the city but part of a long legacy of racist policing that frequently has violent and deadly consequences. In November 2014 when Tamir was killed, the Cleveland Division of Police (CDP) was already under investigation by the United States Department of Justice for improper use of force. The report on the two-year investigation described systemic excessive use of both deadly and "less lethal" force by the CDP, arguing that these practices emerged from multiple structural deficiencies within the department.[3]

Now we have three stories about Tamir Rice's death. In one, he is a symbol of a nation grappling with its ongoing legacy of racist violence, police reform, and accountability. In another, he is a boy raised in violent circumstances, perhaps doomed to a violent death. In the third story, he is one of many victims of an urban police force structured to produce violence. None of these stories are really about Tamir. Many records have been used to construct the stories above. One of the most important primary sources of Tamir Rice's death is the video of the shooting and its aftermath, in addition to official records created by the CDP and the U.S. Department of Justice. There are fact-based newspaper articles, some of which rely on firsthand reports from witnesses and family members. There are editorials appearing in every form of news media, most using one of the above stories as a frame. There are countless individual pieces of social media content created as individuals around the world publicly engaged in dialogue about Tamir's death. Separated from the context of his life and his community, records about Tamir's death can serve any of the larger narratives described above.

DOI: 10.34314/wingodigital.00003

This essay is about collecting records of police violence in Cleveland, the stories those records can tell, and how archives can be deliberately constructed to enable the creation of counter-stories that serve to challenge, disrupt, or complicate dominant narratives in productive ways. I began this essay by writing about Tamir Rice because what happened to him led me, then a new Cleveland-area resident and the Head of Special Collections and Archives at Case Western Reserve University, to get involved in *A People's Archive of Police Violence in Cleveland (PAPVC)*. *PAPVC* is a digital archive that collects, preserves, and shares the stories, memories, and accounts of police violence as experienced or observed by Cleveland citizens. The stories of archivists and librarians matter also when we construct historical narratives from archival records. Knowing who selected, organized, described, and preserved those records, and why, helps explain their full context. Everyone who worked on *PAPVC* had two primary goals: first to support the people directly affected by police brutality in Cleveland, and ultimately, to end police violence. These goals shaped both the process we engaged in and the decisions we made as we built the archive.

Overview of *A People's Archive of Police Violence in Cleveland*

In August of 2015, the Society of American Archivists (SAA) held its annual conference in Cleveland. Three months prior to that, archivist Jarrett Drake had issued a call on Twitter inviting those who were planning to attend the conference to join him in developing a service project that would help the communities impacted by police violence in Cleveland. Multiple archivists volunteered, and work on the project began immediately, resulting in A People's Archive of Police Violence in *Cleveland.*[4]

The idea for the archive did not originate with the archivists involved. Instead, we decided we would do anything the community needed, including manual labor or other basic tasks. After reaching out to Cleveland community groups about their needs, we connected with an organization called Puncture the Silence (PTS), a local chapter of the national Stop Mass Incarceration Network (SMIN), which had been organizing opposition to police brutality

DOI: 10.34314/wingodigital.00003

in Cleveland. After we explained what archivists do, PTS members suggested that we could help them create a web space for records they already possessed, in addition to serving as a repository for future oral histories and other new records of police violence in Cleveland. In addition to creating the Omeka-based website for *PAPVC* and populating it with existing content, archivists also partnered with PTS and other Cleveland activists to collect oral histories from individuals in neighborhoods affected by police violence, which were later added to the digital archive.

Since the original archive was created, the role of the *PAPVC* project as a site for community organizing and memory work in opposition to police violence has evolved. PTS members control the collection development choices, and they have focused on adding material related to local activism. Thus, the archive highlights not only the stories of those affected by police brutality, but also ongoing work opposing racism and structural violence in the criminal justice system in all its forms. While the current national narrative about resistance to police brutality often begins with mass protests held in Ferguson, Missouri, in 2014, that story renders invisible the grassroots work taking place in cities across the country and spanning decades. Just as those who live in Cleveland have long experienced racist policing, they have also resisted state violence by organizing primarily within those neighborhoods most affected. Viewing and listening to the records on *PAPVC* offers a glimpse into that longer history, contextualizing the current moment by placing it within a tradition of organized resistance that started long before national mainstream media began to engage in the recent focus on people of color victimized by the police.

The *PAPVC* project has also evolved to take on an educational aspect that arose from community requests. In one instance, a group of eighth grade students at a local school reached out to the *PAPVC* team asking for advice on how to organize against police violence as young people. In another, a teacher at the Cuyahoga County Juvenile Justice Center requested that *PAPVC* volunteers speak to her class of 18-year-old incarcerated students. When we met with the students, we talked to them about the project and invited them to record their stories for the archive if they wished to do so. Most declined, but

DOI: 10.34314/wingodigital.00003

they did engage in lively conversations about the role of policing in their own lives and how they believe the criminal justice system should change. These examples demonstrate that there are no clear boundaries around *PAPVC* as an "archive." It is a repository for records and a digital space for community memory, but it is also a political project that serves as one node in a web of ongoing local and regional organizing around systemic injustice. *PAPVC* tells many stories about the history of police violence and associated resistance, but it is also part of that story, created at a particular point in time and for particular political and personal reasons for those involved.

Dominant Narratives and Counter-Stories

The introduction to this essay was partially inspired by Richard Delgado's "Storytelling for Oppositionists and Others: A Plea for Narrative Legal Storytelling."[5] In that essay, Delgado presented stories told from different perspectives about the same event to demonstrate that there is a "war between stories" attempting to define and describe reality. Delgado argued that when the same stories are told over and over again, they become the dominant reality. Dominant groups often employ stories that reinforce oppressive systems and absolve dominant groups of responsibility for dismantling those systems. The Cleveland *Plain Dealer*'s choice to focus on Tamir Rice's parents' history of violence, despite the fact that it was irrelevant to Tamir's death, is an example of a dominant group story. Such framing suggests white people do not need to challenge racist police violence because Black families and communities are inherently dysfunctional, and Black male bodies are dangerous and doomed to destruction by police whose job is to keep white people safe. The author of the *Plain Dealer* article didn't have to explicitly write that Black men and boys are inherently dangerous, because that story is so common in American media that white readers would make the connection without prompting.[6]

According to Delgado, counter-stories can interrogate or challenge the dominant reality by exposing systems of oppression. The media narrative that situated Tamir Rice's death within a pattern of excessive police violence

DOI: 10.34314/wingodigital.00003

against Black men and boys is a counter-story. By piecing together multiple instances of unarmed Black people being shot and/or killed by police officers, and connecting those stories to the history of racist violence in America, some members of the media constructed a narrative suggesting that anti-Black racism was to blame for the violent deaths of these individuals. While this counter-story is powerful and has drawn attention to racist policing, it frequently cherrypicks incidents of police violence from around the country. By weaving a national narrative into these stories, it removes them from their local context, where solutions are most likely to be found.

In their article on *A People's Archive of Police Violence in Cleveland*, Stacie Williams and Jarrett Drake outlined the history of the relationship between the Cleveland Division of Police and the Black community, while also situating *PAPVC* within that history. By engaging directly with this local context, *PAPVC* resists both the dominant narrative that Black people are inherently violent and the counter-story that police violence is a national problem occurring in isolated incidents. Rather, the intervention highlights that police brutality is a problem that evolved locally over a long period of time in multiple locations across the country. *PAPVC* also enables the creation of multiple counter-stories. Additional records confirm racist policing and excessive use of force as longstanding structural problems in the Cleveland community, but this archive is unique in offering firsthand perspectives from those most affected by police brutality. Encountering the stories in *PAPVC* pushes those who engage with the archive to acknowledge that police violence is not an abstract problem to be solved, but rather a system that structures people's lives in Cleveland. Listening to individuals' accounts of their encounters with police violence allows one to develop an affective sense of the harm done by decades of racist policing that cannot be conveyed by secondary accounts.

At the same time, *PAPVC* tells stories about the history of resistance to racist policing in Cleveland, in both firsthand accounts and in records of PTS and other activist groups. Police violence received a great deal of national attention in 2014, but the story of resistance in Cleveland has changed over time, and has never disappeared, even when national media focused on other issues. Police brutality is a constant presence in the city of Cleveland, as is

DOI: 10.34314/wingodigital.00003

resistance to racist policing. Police violence is a complex structural problem that impacts lives in many ways, and it cannot be solved with individual reform efforts aimed at specific aspects of the structure. In discourse about the problem of police brutality, it is especially important to center the views of those who have been directly impacted by the problem and who have been working to solve it for many years. *PAPVC* allows users to understand how these multiple strands of violence and resistance are woven into individuals' lives as expressed in their stories, such as the oral histories found in the archive. *PAPVC* challenges those who seek an end to police violence to avoid the simplicity of replacing one dominant narrative with another, and instead to make room for multiple counter-stories that center on the lived experiences of those most affected. By prioritizing firsthand narratives, it avoids turning victims of police violence into symbols, and emphasizes their subjective experiences and interpretations. It also situates police violence within one particular city, acknowledging that the stories and histories told in other cities may have similarities but will not be the same. Police violence is a national problem, but if it is to be ended solutions must be local, grounded in history, and focused on justice and care for those affected.

Items from the Archive

The multimedia items included here reflect *PAPVC*'s emphasis on storytelling as an act of resistance. Many of the oral histories from the archive, like the one by Brenda Bickerstaff, weave personal narratives of repeated exposure to police violence along with expressions of a commitment to activism. Remembering lives lost is also an important theme. The image of a poster commemorating Tamir Rice is one of many such items that appear in *PAPVC*, along with commentary from activists about the lives and deaths of the people pictured. The last three items included here reflect the narrative and memory-work that Cleveland activists were doing prior to the creation of the digital archive. Those who resist structural violence and oppression have long told their stories as a way of galvanizing public support for their cause, and have also collected materials documenting the histories of their struggles as a means

DOI: 10.34314/wingodigital.00003

of maintaining evidence of their work and its impact. Digital or digitized versions of items representing this work are included throughout the archive. These items were donated by individual activists who had been maintaining them in their personal physical and virtual spaces. By viewing them alongside the oral histories and other narrative testimonies included in *PAPVC*, a visitor to the archive can develop a sense of the larger narrative of the long struggle against police violence in Cleveland.

#1   Oral history interview with Brenda Bickerstaff, describing her personal history with police violence, as well as her commitment to activism. A recording of the interview can be found here: http://archivingpoliceviolence.org/items/show/7

> Transcript: Okay, well first back in January 26, 2002, my brother Craig Bickerstaff was murdered by police on East 105th and Lee. July—retract that—back in 2012, March of 2012, I was wrongfully indicted by an officer, a detective by the name of Vincent Lucarelli. I have an investigation business as well. Was trying to get an individual out of jail. Apparently he was having a relationship with my client's girlfriend, and I found that out after—you know, once I got indicted. We pulled text messages and found out he was not only having, trying to have relations with her. He had been, had relations with other women. So they dismissed the case against me, and he was terminated from his job. July 26, 2015, my niece Ralkina Jones was found dead in the Cleveland Heights jail, and that is still under investigation. So unfortunately, our family has been—not, I won't say brutalized, but we've had some pretty tough experiences with the police. And it's just, it's a hard, it's a hard thing to deal with, especially me losing Ralkina now. And now she has to be on a poster like Craig because of the situation she went through. And she was arrested, however that wasn't the issue. The issue was that she died in their custody. And we're trying to find out why she died in their custody. Unanswered questions and things we went through when we were dealing with Craig. And it's just, it's just a hard thing to deal with. But I'm not going to give up on it . . . . I want people to be able to stand up. Don't be afraid. Don't be afraid to speak about it, because a lot of people are. Like today, we're right here on 105 and Saint Clair. I'm here because I've been a victim of it, my brother's been a victim of it, and now my niece has been a victim of it. And I've been a true advocate of this. And I want people to be able to be comfortable and speak about it and don't worry about any type of retaliation. I want them to come forward. Do not be afraid.

DOI: 10.34314/wingodigital.00003

#2   *Figure 2.1:* Poster remembering Tamir Rice, reading "Tamir Rice. Killed November 22 by Cleveland Police." Images of posters like this one honoring those killed by police appear alongside commentary written by longtime Cleveland activist Bill Swain in the *PAPVC* website.
http://archivingpoliceviolence.org/items/show/463.

#3   *Figure 2.2:* Palm card publicizing the People's Tribunal on Police Brutality, organized by Puncture the Silence in 2015. The need to provide ongoing access to videos of this event was the initial catalyst for creating *PAPVC*.
http://archivingpoliceviolence.org/items/show/141

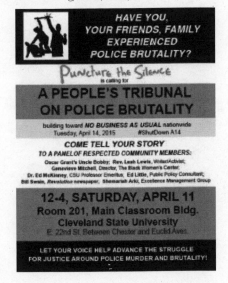

DOI: 10.34314/wingodigital.00003

#4   *Figure 2.3:* Photograph from a march protesting police violence in Cleveland.
       http://archivingpoliceviolence.org/items/show/294

#5   *Figure 2.4:* Clipping of a newspaper article about Puncture the Silence from the
       Cleveland *Plain Dealer. PAPVC* documents press coverage of local activism, as well as
       the activists' own perspectives.
       http://archivingpoliceviolence.org/items/show/307

DOI: 10.34314/wingodigital.00003

Communities, Individuals, and Institutions:
Building Archives Through Relationships of Care

PAPVC was founded through a collaborative process developed by the individual archivists and activists who chose to participate, and it has never been affiliated with any university or professional organization. Working without institutional support or constraints enabled us to put building relationships of care at the center of our processes for developing *PAPVC*. Ethical considerations were often at the heart of our conversations, as we built and managed the archive in collaboration with the PTS activists and other Cleveland community members, but we did not seek guidance from particular professional or academic codes of ethics. Instead, we tried to address the needs of those most affected and hurt by the problem we were addressing, to prioritize them, and to include those who had been seeking solutions to that problem far longer than we had. There is a growing body of literature about the application of ethics of care frameworks to library and archival practice. Michelle Caswell and Marika Cifor wrote about the need for archivists to activate radical empathy by situating themselves within a web of relationships of affective responsibility with record creators, the subjects of records, users of records, and the larger community.[7] Bethany Nowviskie argued that digital librarians and others engaged in digital humanities work should develop "an appreciation of context, interdependence, and vulnerability" and orient themselves toward "worldly action and response" rather than "objective evaluation and judgment."[8] These arguments cast the professional practitioner not as a distant, objective, unobtrusive observer, nor as a powerful expert arbiter of community needs, but as a subjective human fully embedded within and dependent upon various communities, responsible for developing relationships of care with other members of those communities.

Regardless of how an academic archivist views herself in relation to the communities she works with, she cannot control how those communities view and respond to her and to her position. Professions and academic institutions wield great power, and academic archivists often embody that power in their interactions with community members outside the profession or the university.

DOI: 10.34314/wingodigital.00003

In the very act of describing themselves as professionals with particular skill sets, archivists and librarians assert expert power, the ability to influence people because of perceived superior knowledge and skills.[9] Colleges and universities have a great deal of institutional power, shaping the communities in which they reside in profound ways. In community outreach work, academic professionals try to wield that power for the benefit of community members, but power can separate the professional from others in the community. It is often assumed in these relationships that the professional does not have the same needs as the "community." Relationships between universities and their local neighborhoods are often tense, for good reason.

These power dynamics are explored in the literature on the ethics of "participatory action research," a type of social science research that seeks to involve the subjects of research in the design, methodology, and execution of the project. Participatory action research developed as a response to ethical concerns about researchers attempting to study marginalized communities and causing harm through the use of methodologies that fail to fully account for the impact of the research on those communities.[10] Ethical dilemmas still arise in this type of research, however, particularly around communication, trust, consent forms, and power dynamics.[11]

We encountered all of these issues in the course of working on *PAPVC*. Consent forms for those who donated oral histories or other records to the archive were a particularly complex example. Consent forms required for IRB-approved research projects can be confusing to participants, actively limiting their understanding of the nature of the project and any risks involved.[12] Although we did not undergo any IRB approval process for this project, we were particularly concerned about consent because of the potential for police retaliation against those who chose to share their stories about police violence. We also wanted people to understand their individual rights related to copyright and the legal risks associated with statements that might be considered libelous. At the same time, we wanted to clarify what the archive would and would not do with donated records, and mitigate legal risk for the volunteers who created the archive. Stacie Williams, one of the archivists most actively involved in developing *PAPVC*, consulted a lawyer as we drafted the

DOI: 10.34314/wingodigital.00003

consent form, developing language to address all of those concerns. One PTS member strongly and repeatedly objected to the use of dense legal language in the form, arguing that it was confusing and so long that many were likely not to read it in full. This consideration became particularly complicated when we spoke to the incarcerated students in the Cuyahoga County Juvenile Justice Center. While all of the students were 18 and thus legally able to consent, we feared that they may have felt coerced to participate if they saw us as authority figures. We agreed to address these concerns by creating a "plain language" explanation of the consent form that we distributed along with the legal form for participants to sign. We also covered all of the issues described above in conversation, attempting to gauge participants' understanding as we answered all of their questions. We tried to emphasize that consent was no mere formality, but an agreement between the participant and *PAPVC* in which both parties had rights, responsibilities, and risks. I do not believe that any of the participants I worked with felt coerced to participate, or that they did not understand the terms of participation, but of course I must accept the ethical discomfort of never knowing whether that is completely true. I am certain that our conversations about consent led some potential participants to choose not to share their stories in the archive.

While operating *PAPVC* independently of institutional control enabled us to put relationships of care at the center of our decision-making processes, it was also important to consider the ethical implications of deliberately choosing to create and maintain a memory project without infrastructural and institutional support. Christine Paschild has argued that community archives may reinscribe the marginalization of the communities they document by maintaining their important records within sites that have limited resources and lack professional support.[13] By contrast, Bergis Jules noted that large collecting institutions such as academic library special collections are often beholden to donor interests, rendering them all but incapable of properly caring for and providing access to materials that don't fit "clean narratives of history" preferred by the donor class.[14] In writing about archives that specifically document human rights abuses perpetrated against people of color, Tonia Sutherland argued that by failing to document instances of lynching

DOI: 10.34314/wingodigital.00003

across the United States, mainstream collecting institutions have made it nearly impossible for families of victims to seek truth and reconciliation. This suppression of historical records of injustice grants "archival amnesty" to abusers and implicitly endorses violence against Black people.[15] If archivists today hope to do a better job of facilitating future investigations into abusive and racist policing and other ongoing human rights crises, we need to think carefully about the role of collecting institutions and professional archivists and librarians in building and maintaining collections related to violence.

Reflecting on my work with *PAPVC*, I find that engaging with community archives related to difficult or marginalized histories encourages us to think carefully about the boundaries between individual professionals, institutions, and communities. The individuals who created and maintain *PAPVC*, both the professional archivists and the community activists, are individually situated within multiple institutions and communities, and we brought those communities and institutions into dialogue with one another through our collaboration. In the case of *PAPVC*, the geographic coincidence of the Society of American Archivists (SAA) holding their annual conference in Cleveland served as the catalyst for the project. Although SAA was never formally involved as an institution, it provided justification for many professional archivists to travel to work on the project, and collecting oral histories for *PAPVC* became an informal activity that shaped the conference discourse. Just as professional associations helped to shape *PAPVC*, the archive has also shaped the profession. In 2016, I traveled with two of *PAPVC*'s community activists to speak at DPLAFest, a conference for the digital library and archives community. A group of *PAPVC* volunteers also spoke with graduate students in an Information Studies program at the University of California, Los Angeles.

In these ways, institutions provided space for productive dialogue between professional and community archivists, but in a way that reverses the typical power relationship. Community outreach projects are often developed as a way for powerful institutions to "give back" to local communities. In these cases, the community activists were offering their valuable perspectives based on lived experience to professional archivists and librarians. When we spoke at DPLAFest, the conference organizers paid for the community activists' travel

DOI: 10.34314/wingodigital.00003

expenses, but not for mine. In that situation, it was clear that their expertise as long-term activists grappling with issues of how to document violent and racist policing appropriately was valued by the DPLA community. They were the ones with something to offer to the institution, and the material conditions of the arrangement reflected that.

These situations can also dissolve the boundaries between overlapping communities in ways that can be productive for collaboration. Through my engagement with the activists, I learned more about the history and realities of Cleveland, which allowed me to become more embedded in the community. At the same time, they became members of the archival profession in some ways, learning new skills and contributing to professional discourse and education. Although *PAPVC* was developed with an ultimate goal of ending police violence, it had a secondary impact in the archival community by bringing in new voices and new ways of thinking about these kinds of memory projects.

I propose that when we think about archival custody and stewardship, we move away from the binary construction of institutional or community ownership and control toward thinking about an ecosystem of individuals, communities, and institutions that care for and use these materials. Each member of the system is connected to each other member, and all members of the system co-evolve. Just as a robust biological ecosystem has high capacity to support life in a complex web of ecological niches, a robust archival eco-system has a high capacity to support records, documentation, and memory in a complex web of communities and institutions. In many cases, collecting institutions may not be the right niche for any particular collection. However, institutions can provide resources to community archives in the form of professional labor, funds, administrative support, and space. Archivists who work in institutions that cannot support projects like *PAPVC* can still resist archival amnesty for oppressors by finding ways to use their professional skills to support community initiatives. In doing so, they may serve as a bridge between the "community" and the "institution," bringing the two into dialogue with one another about how all members of the system can support historical documentation in service of justice and care. Yusef Omowale argued that Western collecting institutions were developed as part of the colonial project, and thus

DOI: 10.34314/wingodigital.00003

reproduce colonialism when they acquire materials from marginalized communities, inscribing colonialism into the archive and projecting it into the future.[16] Projects like *PAPVC* enable us to think deeply about what values we hope to inscribe into the memory sites that we build, focusing on the futures that we hope to project forward.

Conclusion

PAPVC is an archive shaped by the community it documents, by the historical context of the subject it documents, by the personal and political motivations of those who developed and maintain it, and by the negotiated ethical frameworks used to guide decision-making as the archive came together. It is also an active site of political organizing and education in opposition to police violence and mass incarceration. As the needs of the Cleveland community and the activists maintaining *PAPVC* change, the archive itself will continue to change. It could not be so dynamic if the archivists and librarians involved had approached it using traditional modes of collecting to suit the needs of an institution and its primary user base. While *PAPVC* can serve as a historical record of police violence in Cleveland, its primary function is to participate in an active conversation that is both local and national in scope. Its independence from institutional control and standard professional practice is critical to enabling it to function this way. Institutional collecting often begins from a dominant narrative, with curators and archivists seeking records that support that narrative, or perhaps challenge it in specific ways. The goal of institutional collecting is usually to support the needs of that institution's users. The goal of those who created *PAPVC* is to mitigate the harm caused by police violence in Cleveland, and ultimately to end police violence in the city. No one who worked on the archive believes that it alone can accomplish those goals, but all decisions made in the construction of the archive reflect them. The choices made in building and maintaining the archive enable it to support the construction of narratives that challenge the dominant culture to make space for the voices, perspectives, and feelings of those affected by structural racist violence. We must understand police violence before we can end it, and the

DOI: 10.34314/wingodigital.00003

national media narratives about it are insufficient for deep understanding. *PAPVC* presents counter-stories that offer insight into the myriad ways that police violence shapes individual lives and communal spaces in Cleveland, as well as the long history of political resistance to racist policing in the city. Because it prioritizes those most affected and injured by police violence in Cleveland, and those most invested in ending it, the archive is not just a repository for records but a site of active historical narrative development, changing as necessary to support the stories that the community that created it wants to tell.

Notes

1. Stacey Patton, "In America, Black Children Don't Get to Be Children," *Washington Post*, November 26, 2014. https://www.washingtonpost.com/opinions/in-america-black-children-dont-get-to-be-children/2014/11/26/a9e24756-74ee-11e4-a755-e3 2227229e7b_story.html?utm_term=.f0ad2914480f.

2. Joy-Ann Reid, "Lawyer for Tamir Rice's Mother Blasts Prosecutor's Remarks," *MSNBC*, November 7, 2015. http://www.msnbc.com/msnbc/lawyer-tamir-rices -mother-blasts-prosecutors-remarks.

3. United States Department of Justice Civil Rights Division, "Investigation of the Cleveland Division of Police," Washington, D.C., December 4, 2014. https:// www.justice.gov/sites/default/files/opa/press-releases/attachments/2014/12/04/ cleveland_division_of_police_findings_letter.pdf.

4. Stacie Williams and Jarrett Drake have written extensively on *A People's Archive of Police Violence in Cleveland*. Please read their work for more information:
   Jarrett Drake, "#ArchivesForBlackLives: Building a Community Archives of Police Violence in Cleveland," *Medium* (blog), April 22, 2016. https://medium.com/ on-archivy/archivesforblacklives-building-a-community-archives-of-police-vio lence-in-cleveland-93615d777289.
   ———, "Expanding #ArchivesForBlackLives to Traditional Archival Repositories," *Medium* (blog), June 27, 2016. https://medium.com/on-archivy/expanding-ar chivesforblacklives-to-traditional-archival-repositories-b88641e2daf6.
   ———, "In Defense of Offense," *On Archivy* (blog), October 6, 2017. https:// medium.com/on-archivy/in-defense-of-offense-3ff6251df9c0.
   ———, "RadTech Meets RadArch: Towards A New Principle for Archives and Archival Description," *Medium* (blog), April 6, 2016. https://medium.com/ on-archivy/radtech-meets-radarch-towards-a-new-principle-for-archives-and -archival-description-568f133e4325.

DOI: 10.34314/wingodigital.00003

————, "Seismic Shifts: On Archival Fact and Fictions," *Sustainable Futures* (blog), August 20, 2018. https://medium.com/community-archives/seismic-shifts -on-archival-fact-and-fictions-6db4d5c655ae.

Stacie M. Williams, and Jarrett Drake, "Power to the People: Documenting Police Violence in Cleveland," *Journal of Critical Library and Information Studies* 1, no. 2 (April 23, 2017). https://doi.org/10.24242/jclis.v1i2.33.

————, "Building a Community Archive of Police Violence," *Rhizome* (blog), August 27, 2018. http://rhizome.org/editorial/2018/aug/27/building-a-community -archive-of-police-violence/.

5. Richard Delgado, "Storytelling for Oppositionists and Others: A Plea for Narrative Legal Storytelling," *Michigan Law Review* 87 (1989–1988): 2411–41.

6. For more on racist media narratives about black men and boys, see Patricia Hill Collins, *Black Sexual Politics: African Americans, Gender, and the New Racism.* (New York: Routledge, 2005).

7. Michelle Caswell and Marika Cifor, "From Human Rights to Feminist Ethics: Radical Empathy in the Archives," *Archivaria* 82, no. 0 (May 6, 2016): 23–43.

8. Bethany Nowviskie, "On Capacity and Care," *Bethany Nowviskie* (blog), October 4, 2015. https://nowviskie.org/2015/on-capacity-and-care/.

9. John R. P. French, Jr., and Bertram Raven, "The Bases of Social Power." In *Group Dynamics*, edited by Dorwin Cartwright and Alvin Zander (Evanston, IL: Row, Peterson, 1960), 607-23.

10. Ronald David Glass, Jennifer M. Morton, Joyce E. King, Patricia Krueger-Henney, Michele S. Moses, Sheeva Sabati, and Troy Richardson, "The Ethical Stakes of Collaborative Community-Based Social Science Research," *Urban Education* 53, no. 4 (April 2018): 503–31. https://doi.org/10.1177/0042085918762522.

    Ronald David Glass and Anne Newman, "Ethical and Epistemic Dilemmas in Knowledge Production: Addressing Their Intersection in Collaborative, Community-Based Research," *Theory & Research in Education* 13, no. 1 (March 2015): 23–37. https://doi.org/10.1177/1477878515571178.

    Anne Marshall and Suzanne Batten, "Researching Across Cultures: Issues of Ethics and Power," *Forum Qualitative Sozialforschung/Forum: Qualitative Social Research* 5, no. 3 (September 30, 2004). https://doi.org/10.17169/fqs-5.3.572.

11. Karolina Gombert, Flora Douglas, Karen McArdle, and Sandra Carlisle, "Reflections on Ethical Dilemmas in Working with So-Called 'Vulnerable' and 'Hard-to-Reach' Groups: Experiences from the Foodways and Futures Project," *Educational Action Research* 24, no. 4 (December 2016): 583–97. https://doi.org/ 10.1080/09650792.2015.1106958.

12. Gombert, et al., 589–90.

13. Cristine Paschild, "Community Archives and the Limitations of Identity: Considering Discursive Impact on Material Needs," *The American Archivist* 75, no. 1 (April 1, 2012): 125–42. https://doi.org/10.17723/aarc.75.1.c181102171x4572h.

DOI: 10.34314/wingodigital.00003

14. Bergis Jules, "Confronting Our Failure of Care Around the Legacies of Marginalized People in the Archives," *Medium* (blog), November 11, 2016. https:// medium.com/on-archivy/confronting-our-failure-of-care-around-the-legacies-of -marginalized-people-in-the-archives-dc4180397280.

15. Tonia Sutherland, "Archival Amnesty: In Search of Black American Transitional and Restorative Justice," *Journal of Critical Library and Information Studies* 1, no. 2 (2017): 1–23.

16. Yusef Omowale, "We Already Are," *Sustainable Futures* (blog), September 3, 2018. https://medium.com/community-archives/we-already-are-52438b863e31.

Works Cited

Caswell, Michelle, and Marika Cifor. "From Human Rights to Feminist Ethics: Radical Empathy in the Archives." *Archivaria* 82, no. 0 (May 6, 2016): 23–43.

Collins, Patricia Hill. *Black Sexual Politics: African Americans, Gender, and the New Racism.* New York: Routledge, 2005.

Delgado, Richard. "Storytelling for Oppositionists and Others: A Plea for Narrative Legal Storytelling." *Michigan Law Review* 87 (1989–1988): 2411–41.

Drake, Jarrett M. "#ArchivesForBlackLives: Building a Community Archives of Police Violence in Cleveland." *Medium* (blog), April 22, 2016. https://medium .com/on-archivy/archivesforblacklives-building-a-community-archives-of -police-violence-in-cleveland-93615d777289.

Drake, Jarrett M. "Expanding #ArchivesForBlackLives to Traditional Archival Repositories." *Medium* (blog), June 27, 2016. https://medium.com/on-archivy/ expanding-archivesforblacklives-to-traditional-archival-repositories -b88641e2daf6.

Drake, Jarrett M. "In Defense of Offense." *On Archivy* (blog), October 6, 2017. https://medium.com/on-archivy/in-defense-of-offense-3ff6251df9c0.

Drake, Jarrett M. "RadTech Meets RadArch: Towards A New Principle for Archives and Archival Description." *Medium* (blog), April 6, 2016. https:// medium.com/on-archivy/radtech-meets-radarch-towards-a-new-principle -for-archives-and-archival-description-568f133e4325.

Drake, Jarrett M. "Seismic Shifts: On Archival Fact and Fictions." *Sustainable Futures* (blog), August 20, 2018. https://medium.com/community-archives/ seismic-shifts-on-archival-fact-and-fictions-6db4d5c655ae.

French, John R. P., Jr., and Bertram Raven. "The Bases of Social Power." In *Group Dynamics.* Edited by Dorwin Cartwright and Alvin Zander, 607–23. (Evanston, IL: Row, Peterson, 1960).

DOI: 10.34314/wingodigital.00003

Glass, Ronald David, Jennifer M. Morton, Joyce E King, Patricia Krueger-Henney, Michele S. Moses, Sheeva Sabati, and Troy Richardson. "The Ethical
Stakes of Collaborative Community-Based Social Science Research."
Urban Education 53, no. 4 (April 2018): 503–31. https://doi.org/10.1177/
0042085918762522.

Glass, Ronald David, and Anne Newman. "Ethical and Epistemic Dilemmas
in Knowledge Production: Addressing Their Intersection in Collaborative,
Community-Based Research." *Theory & Research in Education* 13, no. 1
(March 2015): 23–37. https://doi.org/10.1177/1477878515571178.

Gombert, Karolina, Flora Douglas, Karen McArdle, and Sandra Carlisle. 2016.
"Reflections on Ethical Dilemmas in Working with So-Called 'Vulnerable'
and 'Hard-to-Reach' Groups: Experiences from the Foodways and Futures
Project." *Educational Action Research* 24, no. 4: 583–97. https://doi.org/10.1080/
09650792.2015.1106958.

Jules, Bergis. "Confronting Our Failure of Care Around the Legacies of Marginalized People in the Archives." *Medium* (blog), November 11, 2016.
https://medium.com/on-archivy/confronting-our-failure-of-care-around-the
-legacies-of-marginalized-people-in-the-archives-dc4180397280.

Marshall, Anne, and Suzanne Batten. "Researching Across Cultures: Issues of
Ethics and Power." *Forum Qualitative Sozialforschung/Forum: Qualitative Social
Research* 5, no. 3 (September 30, 2004). https://doi.org/10.17169/fqs-5.3.572.

Nowviskie, Bethany. "On Capacity and Care." *Bethany Nowviskie* (blog), October 4,
2015. https://nowviskie.org/2015/on-capacity-and-care/.

Omowale, Yusef. "We Already Are." *Sustainable Futures* (blog), September 3, 2018.
https://medium.com/community-archives/we-already-are-52438b863e31.

Paschild, Cristine. "Community Archives and the Limitations of Identity:
Considering Discursive Impact on Material Needs." *The American Archivist*
75, no. 1 (April 1, 2012): 125–42. https://doi.org/10.17723/aarc.75.1.c181
102l71x4572h.

Patton, Stacey. "In America, Black Children Don't Get to Be Children." *Washington Post*. November 26, 2014. https://www.washingtonpost.com/opinions/
in-america-black-children-dont-get-to-be-children/2014/11/26/a9e24756
-74ee-11e4-a755-e32227229e7b_story.html.

Reid, Joy-Ann. "Lawyer for Tamir Rice's Mother Blasts Prosecutor's Remarks."
MSNBC. November 7, 2015. http://www.msnbc.com/msnbc/lawyer-tamir
-rices-mother-blasts-prosecutors-remarks.

DOI: 10.34314/wingodigital.00003

Sutherland, Tonia. "Archival Amnesty: In Search of Black American Transitional and Restorative Justice." *Journal of Critical Library and Information Studies* 1, no. 2 (2017): 1–23.

United States Department of Justice Civil Rights Division. "Investigation of the Cleveland Division of Police." Washington, D.C., December 4, 2014. https://www.justice.gov/sites/default/files/opa/press-releases/attachments/2014/12/04/cleveland_division_of_police_findings_letter.pdf.

Williams, Stacie M., and Jarrett Drake. "Power to the People: Documenting Police Violence in Cleveland." *Journal of Critical Library and Information Studies* 1, no. 2 (April 23, 2017). https://doi.org/10.24242/jclis.v1i2.33.

Williams, Stacie M., and Jarrett M. Drake. "Building a Community Archive of Police Violence." *Rhizome* (blog), August 27, 2018. http://rhizome.org/editorial/2018/aug/27/building-a-community-archive-of-police-violence/.

DOI: 10.34314/wingodigital.00003

3

Harvesting History, Remembering Rondo

Marvin Roger Anderson and Rebecca S. Wingo

Marvin Roger Anderson has travelled all around the world and can't imagine a better place than the Rondo neighborhood in his home town of St. Paul, Minnesota. After college, law school, and the Peace Corps, he returned to Minnesota to earn an MA degree from the University of Minnesota's School of Library Science. In 1980, the Minnesota Supreme Court appointed him State Law Librarian, a position he held until retiring in 2002.

In 1982, along with a childhood friend, he co-founded Rondo Avenue, Inc. (RAI). RAI is a community-based nonprofit created to preserve and transmit the history, culture, and social impact of St. Paul's predominately African-American neighborhood of Rondo. He served as the Project Manager and now Executive Director of the Rondo Commemorative Plaza (RCP), the nation's first public memorial honoring communities destroyed by interstate freeway construction, which opened in July of 2018; he chairs the Rondo Center for Diverse Expression—a small gathering site and museum; he also chairs an organization called ReConnect Rondo that seeks to determine the feasibility of building a land bridge or "highway lid" over the section of I-94 that bisected the community of Rondo.

Rebecca S. Wingo is an Assistant Professor of History at the University of Cincinnati where she serves as the Director of Public History. She collaborated with Mr. Anderson on several public history projects (both digital and not) from 2015–2018 when she was the Mellon Postdoctoral Fellow in Digital Liberal Arts at Macalester College. What follows is the story of that collaboration.

DOI: 10.34314/wingodigital.00004

In the 1950s, the Minnesota Department of Transportation (MnDOT) began construction on a stretch of I-94 that would connect the downtowns of Minneapolis and St. Paul. Developers proposed two routes: a northern route that followed abandoned railroad tracks, and a central route along Rondo Avenue. Rondo Avenue was a wide, tree-lined boulevard that formed the main business district for the predominantly African American neighborhood. MnDOT chose the latter. Some residents took the lowball offer on their home and moved away; others fought through the legal system; still others sat on their front porches with shotguns and waited for police. MnDOT claimed homes and businesses under eminent domain, and displaced over 750 families and 125 businesses. Minority communities around the nation faced similar destruction and robbery at the hands of highwaymen.[1]

From 1900 until the early 1960s, African-American men and women of St. Paul built churches, established businesses, educated their children, and formed social clubs and other institutions that led the fight against the persistent racism and oppression they often encountered on their jobs and throughout the greater St. Paul environs. Despite the social, political, and economic odds stacked against them, the community that became known as Rondo survived and thrived until it became one of the many Black neighborhoods across America destroyed by the twin demons of urban renewal and freeway construction.

In her groundbreaking book *Root Shock: How Tearing Up City Neighborhoods Hurts America, and What We Can Do About It*, Mindy Fullilove writes, "starting in 1949, urban renewal and freeway construction swept America, bulldozing and demolishing over 1,600 Black neighborhoods causing inhabitants to suffer 'root shock,'" a "traumatic stress reaction related to the destruction of one's emotional ecosystem." According to Fullilove, "the experience of root shock—like the aftermath of a severe burn—does not end with emergency treatments but will stay with the individual for a lifetime. In fact, the injury from 'root shock' may be even more enduring than a burn, as it can affect generations and generations of people."[2] Rondo is one of these communities.

In 1982, community resident Marvin R. Anderson attended "Grand Old Day," a celebration of a neighborhood in St. Paul on the eastern end

DOI: 10.34314/wingodigital.00004

of Grand Avenue. An exuberant festivalgoer shouted, "Grand Avenue is the best neighborhood in St. Paul!" *No it's not,* Mr. Anderson thought to himself. *Rondo is.* Determined to best Grand Old Day, he teamed up with his best friend, Floyd Smaller, to form Rondo Avenue, Incorporated (RAI). They held their first annual Rondo Days festival commemorating their history and the vibrancy of their community in July 1983.

Ever since, the community has rallied under the cry "Remember Rondo!" and in 2015, during a Healing Ceremony at Rondo Days, the mayor of St. Paul apologized. "Today we acknowledge the sins of our past," Chris Coleman said. "We regret the stain of racism that allowed so callous a decision as the one that led to families being dragged from their homes creating a diaspora of the African-American community in the City of St. Paul."[3]

The stars aligned that following spring semester to reconstitute an old partnership between RAI and Macalester College. I (Rebecca Wingo) began my position at Macalester College just two weeks after Mayor Coleman's apology. As a postdoc in Digital Liberal Arts (DLA) on a campus where DLA didn't yet exist in any formal way, I focused my energy on developing a flagship course with longterm campus impact. My colleague in the history department, Amy Sullivan, was scheduled to teach an oral history course that semester and was exploring her options for potential community part-nerships. Our departmental chair played matchmaker, and Sullivan and I

Figure 3.1: Logo for Rondo Avenue, Inc. and the Rondo Days Festival.

DOI: 10.34314/wingodigital.00004

ended up approaching RAI together to propose a team-taught course called "Remembering Rondo: A History Harvest."

The History Harvest is a community-based, student-driven, collaborative digital archive. As the founders of the History Harvest at the University of Nebraska state, "It is . . . the shared experience of giving that is at the heart of the History Harvest concept. The project makes invisible histories and materials more visible by working with and within local communities to collect, preserve and share previously unknown or under-appreciated artifacts and stories."[4] The History Harvest recognizes that the bulk of historical artifacts are in private hands: history is in our basements, in our attics, on our mantles, and in that shoebox tucked under our beds. The History Harvest subverts the traditional role of archives, libraries, and museums by giving archival power back to the community. It builds upon the tenets of a shared authority.[5] At the Harvest, people bring their objects of significance, and then they take their artifacts back home where they belong. There is no acquisition. And unlike Antiques Roadshow, everything is valuable. This model is empowering from both the community and student perspective. The history classroom transforms into a lab in which the students act as liaisons, archivists, and public historians.

Our course objectives blended content-based learning with hands-on, methodological training in digital and public history:

- Students will become proficient in Minnesota's African American history and the history of urban development in the Twin Cities
- Students will use public history methods including oral history and archival management following Dublin Core standards
- Students will identify and become proficient in the necessary methods and technologies
- Students will develop mutually beneficial partnerships with local community groups

Though we already decided to use Omeka, an open-source archival management system developed by the Roy Rosenzweig Center for History and New Media at George Mason University, we required students to identify any

DOI: 10.34314/wingodigital.00004

additional technological needs and justify the technologies they selected. For instance, what would we use to edit audio and video, and why? What is the cost? Do we support the mission of the company? Why does it matter? Asking these questions allowed us to interrogate the power structures that undergird some technologies while simultaneously teaching students to become aware of their own digital agency.

During the event itself, the students thought carefully about the logistics. To avoid an assembly-line feel (check in, sign forms, get interviewed, digitize objects, goodbye), they arranged the Harvest stations along the walls. They set up long tables in the center of the room and provided lunch from a neighborhood BBQ joint, thereby funneling any money we spent back into the community. During lunch, the Harvest became secondary to cross-cultural, intergenerational conversations. The students built a lot of trust with the community members over that lunch, and the archive reflects those community members' generosity. It also happened to be Mr. Anderson's birthday, so we bought cake and had a real party.

Figure 3.2: Marvin R. Anderson (left) examines an artifact brought by Rondo community member Lester O. Myles (right). Photo courtesy of Macalester College.

DOI: 10.34314/wingodigital.00004

Figure 3.3: History Harvest participant Gerone Hamilton (left) reads a placard about the history of Rondo that lined the walls of the community center. RAI president, Ronald Buford (right), takes pictures with his phone. Photo courtesy of Macalester College.

Figure 3.4: A History Harvest student helps Estelle Hartshorn-Jones fill out paperwork about her artifacts. Photo courtesy of Macalester College.

DOI: 10.34314/wingodigital.00004

Figure 3.5: Rondo resident Joyce P. Williams sits for an oral history interview during the History Harvest. Photo courtesy of Macalester College.

Figure 3.6: A group of students and Rondo residents chat over lunch. Photo courtesy of Macalester College.

DOI: 10.34314/wingodigital.00004

Figure 3.7: A History Harvest student goes over paperwork with Rondo artist Seitu Jones. Photo courtesy of Macalester College.

Figure 3.8: Marvin R. Anderson explains the story behind a spoof *Ebony* magazine cover to Amy Sullivan. The magazine cover was a gift for his mother on her 100th birthday. Photo courtesy of Macalester College.

DOI: 10.34314/wingodigital.00004

Partner Perspective
What did you think about the first History Harvest?

Despite my involvement in the planning and preparation for the Harvest, this was a new concept for the community and to be honest there were those moments of normal apprehension—will it rain, did we get the word out, and, more specifically . . . will it work? However, by the time the first resident arrived and the process began, I was more relaxed, calmed, and filled with pride knowing that this group of gifted and dedicated people had assembled to listen, learn, and transcribe the personal treasures of the people of Rondo. I tend to be optimistic about matters and what I observed of the interactions among the participants over the course of the Harvest clearly validated this tendency and cemented my belief in the value of the story of Rondo to those who genuinely desire to hear and understand it.

—Marvin R. Anderson

The History Harvest is an inherently collaborative project. In addition to community collaboration, the course required extensive classroom and campus collaboration. By the third year, my colleagues and I had finessed and fine-tuned the following classroom teams:

- *Hospitality Team*: Responsible for greeting people, making sure contributors go to all the Harvest stations, entertainment, and catering.
- *Registration Team*: In charge of making sure that the contributors understand and sign the release forms and organizing the artifact labeling process for the other teams.
- *Artifact Team*: Conduct short interviews with the contributors about their objects. Sample questions: "What does this object mean to you? Why did you bring it today? How does it tell your story of Rondo?" Unless the contributor opts out, these interviews are recorded, edited, transcribed, and uploaded to the archive with the object.
- *Digitization Team*: In charge of photographing 3D and fragile objects, or scanning 2D objects. (During busy moments, scanning creates a bottleneck, so the photographer can photograph even the scannable items more efficiently.)

DOI: 10.34314/wingodigital.00004

- *Oral History Team (optional)*: The first year, Sullivan and I ran a successful oral history booth. We had enough volunteers to cover this element of the event. However, we do not recommend trying to coordinate the Harvest and the oral history booth unless team teaching.

The work of all of these groups dovetailed to create a seamless experience for the contributor. The team you don't see here is the Outreach Team mentioned in the *History Harvest Handbook*. Outreach is too much work for a handful of students—as we learned through trial and error (mostly error). We suggest instead categorizing types of outreach suitable for the community and dividing the labor among all students. When Dr. Crystal Moten led the second History Harvest with Rondo, she divided students into teams suitable for the Rondo community: churches, businesses, and organizations and public spaces.

We also received support from campus collaborators, including Macalester's librarians, archivist, Civic Engagement Center, history department, and individual professors who volunteered their time and students. For example, three students and Morgan Adamson, a professor teaching a documentary studies course, volunteered to shoot b-roll and run the oral history booth. The history department later found the funds to pay Adamson's students to create a mini-documentary about the Harvest that they could include on their résumés and RAI could feature on their site. One student from Professor Eric Carroll's photography class also volunteered for the entire day, so I found a willing Rondo resident to feature in her final portrait project. Carroll and several of the volunteer students showed up for the second and third years as well.

The History Harvest fires on all cylinders for a school with a mission like Macalester. It aligns itself with community-engaged, experiential learning; it supports civic engagement and the students' desire for social justice; and it is an outward-facing model that defines public history as history co-created with the public. Our first History Harvest was a roaring success—so much so that RAI invited Macalester to run a second harvest in 2017. And a third in 2018.[6]

The History Harvest was the first step in developing a longer partnership with RAI because it established trust. For example, members of the

DOI: 10.34314/wingodigital.00004

Partner Perspective

What did you look for when establishing this partnership?

The stories of Rondo are deep, very wide, and filled with a mixture of remembrance of the joy of having lived during Rondo's heyday–but also anger, sadness and depression having witnessed its destruction and demise. These stories are not to be taken lightly, so the first three boxes for me to check were: (a) the depth of understanding about Rondo's unique history; (b) the level of advance preparation; and (c) the clarity of the course objectives. Once I was assured that these had been fully and comprehensively addressed, the road to a successful partnership was laid.

—Marvin R. Anderson

community and RAI were excited by the outcome of the Harvest but they worried about losing control of the artifacts, since the archive was hosted by Macalester. As a result, I worked with RAI to set up a Reclaim Hosting account where they installed their own instance of Omeka and we transferred the archive. It now lives at RememberingRondo.org.[7] Even the digital artifacts reside in Rondo.

Building trust included a number of factors, including invitations to the classroom, investment outside the classroom, and open communication about the partnership. Our classroom had an open-door policy for any Rondo community member. They were welcome in class any time, and did not need to notify us they were coming. No one took us up on this offer, but that wasn't the point. Implementing and maintaining transparency was key to developing trust. Giving people the option to visit the class actively demonstrated that we had nothing to hide.

Furthermore, we invited some community members into the classroom to talk about their experiences. Deborah Montgomery, a prominent Rondo citizen, visited with us every year. Montgomery was from Rondo and, through her activism, found herself serving on the national board of the NAACP before she had even graduated from high school. She marched on Washington and Selma, and was both the first African American and first woman to serve on St. Paul's police force. She was a city planner, local politician, and educator. Where possible, we found the funds to provide community speakers like

DOI: 10.34314/wingodigital.00004

Montgomery with an honorarium. We recognize that communities aren't an endless supply of generosity that scholars can mine at will with no reciprocity or compensation.

Sullivan, the students, and myself also invested time outside the class-room. The Harvest was not a one-and-done event. For example, students attended community programs and fundraisers. They wrote cards to all the participants thanking them for their time and directing them to the archive. After the first year, I also set up a booth at Rondo Days with a wireless hotspot so that people could explore the archive on site. We may have only had five visitors that day, but the members of RAI saw us there and appreciated what we were trying to do. In many ways, that was more important.

We also gave RAI an out at nearly every phase of the project. Before we taught our first Harvest class, we presented the syllabus and proposed an event date to the RAI board. Sullivan and I included Paul Schadewald, the Associate Director of the Civic Engagement Center at Macalester College (a center devoted to building partnerships), in all the meetings with RAI. As contingent faculty, Sullivan and I were not guaranteed to be at Macalester for the longevity of the partnership with RAI. Schadewald was the long-term contact for the organization, which helped ameliorate the board members' concerns about working with us. We received unanimous approval but we emphasized that RAI could withdraw at any time if the partnership stopped being equitable, productive, or valuable. RAI had fewer reasons to trust us than not, so they appreciated that, too.

The History Harvest was essentially "step one" for Macalester and RAI. The organization is actively seeking ways in which they can preserve their history and claim their digital identity. The care Sullivan and I took to make sure the Harvest was co-creative rather than extractive opened up opportuni-ties to collaborate with RAI on other affiliated public and digital history com-munity engagement projects. These projects included a course on mapping, directing a student research project on the Reconnect Rondo land bridge, and overseeing interns for the Rondo Commemorative Plaza. Mr. Anderson didn't just open a binder and let me choose which projects interested me. Each additional project and responsibility was equal parts trust-building exercise and serendipity.

DOI: 10.34314/wingodigital.00004

Mapping Rondo's Businesses

While Mr. Anderson loved the History Harvest and wanted to run the event again, he also wanted a map of historic Rondo businesses to visualize the vibrancy of the business district along Rondo Avenue. Before highway construction, Rondo Avenue was the heart of the neighborhood's economy. It had to be. Most white business owners outside of the neighborhood banned Black citizens; as a result, Rondo had to be self-sustaining in order to provide all the services its residents needed. When the city built I-94, it undermined the economic ecosystem of the community. The timing of Mr. Anderson's request was perfect—I just so happened to want a new course.

There is a printed poster of Rondo neighborhood landmarks and businesses available for purchase through the Minnesota History Center. Sullivan and I bought our students copies so they could become familiar with the neighborhood, but we couldn't find the map-maker, Jim Gerlich, anywhere on the internet to save our lives. Gerlich doesn't really do the computer thing. Then, he heard the radio spot about the History Harvest that Mr. Anderson and I did on Minnesota Public Radio's *All Things Considered*, and he came— with an armful of maps.

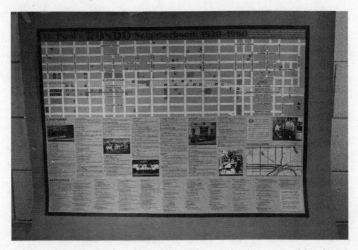

Figure 3.9: Photograph of Gerlich's poster of Rondo businesses and landmarks from 1920–1960 at the History Harvest in 2016. The lighter color down the middle of the map represents the highway.

DOI: 10.34314/wingodigital.00004

We invited Gerlich to the History Harvest class and he told the students about his research process. He went through all the business ads in the community newspapers from 1920–1960. He explained that limited space on the poster meant that he only included the businesses by the decade. In the process of producing the map, he actually identified a stretch of Rondo Avenue by the capitol that hadn't been destroyed by the highway; he and Mr. Anderson petitioned to have the street name restored. At the end of class, Gerlich showed me the two CDs and jump drive he was using to preserve his map. I promised to explore better options. He handed me the cardboard envelope and told me that those were his only copies. I asked if he minded if my students made a digital version. He offered us all his research files.

In the spring 2017 semester, my students and I made a map of the historic businesses in Rondo. We talked about civic technology and explored our options. The students chose ESRI Story Maps. A free version of the software

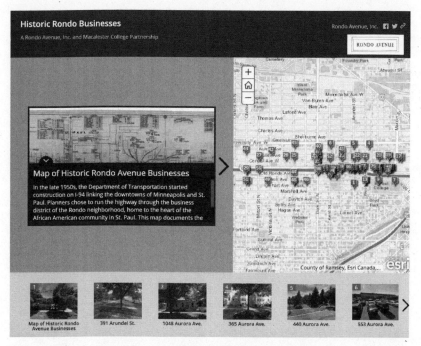

Figure 3.10: Screenshot of the map of historic businesses in Rondo (1920–1960) generated by Macalester students in 2017.

DOI: 10.34314/wingodigital.00004

is available for creating digital maps, and since items are added to the map via spreadsheets, it's also easy to use. RAI can host the project without paying for an expensive ArcGIS license and can edit the spreadsheet with relative ease. After processing what felt like *miles* of newspaper microfilm, the map now lives at RememberingRondo.org alongside the History Harvest.

At the end of the semester, I gave Gerlich some options about what we might do with his scholarship. He decided to donate the map to the Ramsey County Historical Society. When I facilitated his donation, I also donated my students' project and research files.

> ### Partner Perspective
> #### How has the map been useful to your work?
>
> *By the end of 2019, three businesses with deep Rondo ties will be offering food, beverage, and gathering services for those living within the Rondo community and throughout the entire city. A number of us have taken note of these developments and we wanted to show our appreciation to the proprietors for taking the risk inherent in opening any business, and more so in food and beverage service. Our idea was to come up with a gift that had a common theme but also features unique to each establishment. After a while, I thought of Jim Gerlich's map and its comprehensive listing of the type of businesses with the same functions from Rondo's past as those we are going to honor. We thought a picture would be worth a thousand words and would better describe what we have planned. We'll be asking an artist to prepare a poster combining the images of cooks, servers and patrons of the places from the Gerlich map with the images from the students' research into a current map indicating the physical location of the honorees—it's going to be great!*
>
> —Marvin R. Anderson

ReConnect Rondo

Then, in another stroke of serendipity, a geography student intern at the Rondo Community Land Trust (RCLT), Anna Dolde, set up a meeting with me. Mr. Anderson told RCLT about the map my students built and RCLT was interested in our findings. Dolde was a stellar student and Mr. Anderson wanted to find some way to employ her as an intern on ReConnect Rondo, a project proposing a land bridge over the highway. The bridge would have

DOI: 10.34314/wingodigital.00004

mixed-income housing, senior living, shops, parks, and maybe even the St. Paul farmer's market. It would also reconnect the bifurcated neighborhood. Earlier that week, my dean emailed me to tell me about some unclaimed undergraduate research funds for community-based projects. He thought I might have something in mind. And here was Mr. Anderson telling me he wanted an intern, and Anna, the undergrad with the expertise. Dolde spent the summer forming the Housing Committee and doing site visits to other land bridges across the country.

Partner Perspective

What is ReConnect Rondo, and why is it important?

ReConnectRondo's (RCR) mission is the realization of a Rondo Land Bridge (RLB) to reconnect communities proximate to I-94 in the Rondo neighborhood of St. Paul. RCR is a community development organization established to maximize opportunities for business, economic, and social development. RCR's goal is to persuasively shape transportation policy for the RLB to create opportunities that uplift the public health, economic, housing, and social conditions of the Rondo communities. With the construction of the land bridge, a new Rondo Boulevard will be built as the major walkway of the bridge. At roughly four blocks long it can only be a symbol of the original 21-block length of old Rondo. Nevertheless, there will be shops, cafes, offices, and housing that will enable a new generation of people to collect memories for subsequent History Harvests many years into the future.

—Marvin R. Anderson

Rondo Commemorative Plaza

Mr. Anderson and RAI were also involved in developing the Rondo Commemorative Plaza. The plaza has twenty-four permanent panels telling the history of Rondo and the stories of its present. Rondo is the landing site for many immigrants in the community, including Hmong, Somali, Eritrean, Karen, Oromo, Ethiopian, and Vietnamese people. They also have stories to tell and the plaza will give them space to do so, but Mr. Anderson was on a crunched timeline and needed immediate text writers for the panels. I offered to oversee four interns—a historian, two geographers, and an artist.

DOI: 10.34314/wingodigital.00004

Together, we created two of the panels. One of our panels profiles the Rondo Avenue/Dale Street intersection that was the heartbeat of the business district; the other profiles a house taken by MnDOT. The house—a firmly middle-class home with many well-maintained improvements—was owned by the Galloway family. The students used archived eminent domain files to develop mathematical equations assessing the monetary value lost in the neighborhood houses, but they also interviewed displaced resident Nate Galloway in an attempt to describe the intangible values lost.

Partner Perspective

What does the Rondo Commemorative Plaza mean to the community?

The Rondo Commemorative Plaza opened in July 2018. Brick pavers, cleverly built-in benches, and a long exhibit wall that spans the decades of Rondo's story—including the stories of today's Karen, Hmong, Oromo, and Somali residents—surround a grassy mound that symbolizes both the old neighborhood's resting place and the dreams that continue to rise amid its ruins. Atop the knoll are pieces of the granite curb that once lined nearby streets.

At the south end, a pergola shades a platform where singers and musicians can perform, and an installation of chimes by local artist Seitu Jones can be played with hammers. Each chime is dedicated to one of the 18 north-south streets that crossed Rondo, and each hammer bears the inscription of a notable family or resident from the old neighborhood. A tower with a lighted beacon stands at the northeast corner of the park, visible to drivers passing by on I-94. It is our hope the plaza will help rekindle the spirit of Rondo, bringing people of all backgrounds together.

—Marvin R. Anderson

Working with the Rondo community has been one of the most rewarding and transformative experiences of my academic career. My students feel the same. Though working with RAI has been productive, *listening* to RAI has been generative. The History Harvest was our litmus test for the partnership. The moments of specific engagement were just as important as sticking around afterward to see if there are other ways to partner with the community. If we in the academy are going to truly break down the barriers between

DOI: 10.34314/wingodigital.00004

Figure 3.11: A view of the Rondo Commemorative Plaza from the north. The photographer would have been standing on Old Rondo Avenue. Photo courtesy of Morgan Sheff.

Figure 3.12: A view of the Rondo Commemorative Plaza from the south. In the foreground is the art installation of chimes representing historic streets designed by Seitu Jones. Photo courtesy of Morgan Sheff.

DOI: 10.34314/wingodigital.00004

the public and access to scholarship, we need to empower citizen scholars and include them in the planning process. When we parachute in and leave, we replicate the same systems that marginalized the community in the first place.

There is no one recipe for developing a sustainable partnership. If I had to boil down what made the partnership between RAI and Macalester so fruitful, I would identify three things: 1) mutual respect which ultimately begat trust, 2) flexibility, and 3) the people. So much of the partnership is a result of the individuals involved. If Mr. Anderson didn't like me, none of this would have happened. The reverse is probably also true—but everyone likes Mr. Anderson.

> ### Partner Perspective
> #### What do you think made our partnership so successful?
>
> *Clearly the advance preparation provided by Professors Wingo and Sullivan, along with the clarity of the class objectives and willingness of the students to engage the project with "gusto," were important elements that contributed to the success of the History Harvest. In addition, there were a couple of factors from a personal basis that deserve mention. I truly found the professors to be authentic in their proposal, transparent in their strategy, and genuine in their desire for a positive outcome for all concerned, which led to the success of our partnership.*
>
> —Marvin R. Anderson

A lot of things happened after that first History Harvest. When I set up the booth at Rondo Days in July, half of our students came—during their summer break. In 2016, Sullivan and I invited a History Harvest student and Mr. Anderson to co-present with us at the Imagining America conference. It was standing room only. People are hungry for this type of scholarship and pedagogy, in part because it's relevant. In the wake of alarming realities like the local murder of Philando Castile—a son of Rondo—by a police officer in July 2016, Rondo's history is also the history of our present. Black Lives Matter protestors shut down the highway at Lexington Avenue, the western boundary of the neighborhood—the same highway that still cuts through Rondo. That symbolism is hard to ignore, and not lost on my students. In this

DOI: 10.34314/wingodigital.00004

context, "Remember Rondo" is best understood as both a rallying cry and a warning.

It's hard to describe Marvin Anderson's charisma. He has been fighting for recognition of what happened to Rondo for longer than I have been alive. To be in the presence of that kind of determination and passion is humbling. During a community meeting about the development of a land bridge to reconnect the bifurcated community in April 2018, Mr. Anderson delivered the opening remarks. "They say there are two important days in your life," he said. "The day you are born and the day you realize why you are born." There is no higher calling for Mr. Anderson than empowering his neighborhood and establishing RAI as a model for other communities traumatized by urban development.

Mr. Anderson is 70-something years old,[8] and he's thinking about what happens when he's gone. If you ask him what he hopes the outcome of all his work will be, he'd tell you that he hopes to find someone from Rondo to take his place, and maybe he'd have a park on top of the highway posthumously named after him. As for Jim Gerlich, the mapmaker who doesn't "computer," he still works with Macalester students on a handful of his own

Figure 3.13: Melvin Carter, Jr. at the 2016 History Harvest.

DOI: 10.34314/wingodigital.00004

research projects. He spends a fair portion of his retirement energy running a philanthropic youth organization in North Minneapolis, one of the neighborhoods to which the Rondo citizens relocated in the 1960s. And Chris Coleman, the mayor who apologized to Rondo? He retired. In his stead St. Paul elected Melvin Carter III, a grandson of Rondo. His father came to our first History Harvest.

Notes

1. See Eric Avila, *The Folklore of the Freeway: Race and Revolt in the Modernist City* (Minneapolis: University of Minnesota Press, 2014); P. E. Moskowitz, *How to Kill a City: Gentrification, Inequality, and the Fight for the Neighborhood* (New York: Bold Type Books, 2017); Richard Rothstein, *The Color of Law: A Forgotten History of How Our Government Segregated America* (New York: Liveright Publishing, 2017); and Christopher W. Wells, *Car Country: An Environmental History* (Seattle: University of Washington Press, 2012).
2. Mindy Fullilove, *Root Shock: How Tearing Up City Neighborhoods Hurts America, and What We Can Do About It* (New York: Ballantine Books, 2004).
3. Allen Costantini, "Rondo neighborhood gets apologies for I-94," *lohud,* July 17, 2015.
4. "About," *The History Harvest.* Accessed November 18, 2016.
5. Michael Frisch, *A Shared Authority: Essays on the Craft and Meaning of Oral and Public History* (Albany: SUNY Press, 1990) and "From A Shared Authority to the Digital Kitchen, and Back," in *Letting Go?: Sharing Historical Authority in a User-Generated World,* eds. Bill Adair, Benjamin Filene, and Laura Koloski (Philadelphia: Pew Center for Arts and Heritage, 2011), 126–137.
6. Dr. Crystal M. Moten directed both the 2017 and 2018 History Harvests. I provided consultation expertise for the 2017 History Harvest only, and Moten developed new strategies to keep community interest fresh for the 2018 History Harvest by working directly with the elders' clubs and partnering with a group of local high schoolers.
7. There are many people to thank for the successful transfer of the archive, including RAI's web guru, Sharon Kennedy Vickers, and Macalester College's digital scholarship specialist, John Meyerhoffer.
8. Come on. It's rude to ask.

DOI: 10.34314/wingodigital.00004

Works Cited

Avila, Eric. *The Folklore of the Freeway: Race and Revolt in the Modernist City*. Minneapolis: University of Minnesota Press, 2014.

Costantini, Allen. "Rondo neighborhood gets apologies for I-94." *lohud*, July 17, 2015.

Frisch, Michael. *A Shared Authority: Essays on the Craft and Meaning of Oral and Public History*. Albany: SUNY Press, 1990.

Frisch, Michael. "From A Shared Authority to the Digital Kitchen, and Back." In *Letting Go?: Sharing Historical Authority in a User-Generated World*. Edited by Bill Adair, Benjamin Filene, and Laura Koloski, pp. 126–137. Philadelphia: The Pew Center for Arts and Heritage, 2011.

Fullilove, Mindy. *Root Shock: How Tearing Up City Neighborhoods Hurts America, and What We Can Do About It*. New York: Ballantine Books, 2004.

Moskowitz, P.E. *How to Kill a City: Gentrification, Inequality, and the Fight for the Neighborhood*. New York: Bold Type Books, 2017.

Rothstein, Richard. *The Color of Law: A Forgotten History of How Our Government Segregated America*. New York: Liveright Publishing, 2017.

Wells, Christopher W. *Car Country: An Environmental History*. Seattle: University of Washington Press, 2012.

DOI: 10.34314/wingodigital.00004

4

"Send Out a Little Light"

The Antioch A.M.E. Digital Archive

Julia Brock, Elayne Washington Hunter,
Robin Morris, and Shaneé Murrain

Introduction

Julia Brock and Robin Morris

Digital community engagement relies on building and sustaining relationships with a particular public. Sometimes, as in our case, a digital project is
not necessarily the most valuable and enduring outcome. What does matter
is that a past is uncovered and examined, and reflexive partnerships between
institutions make that possible: both history and society are thus served in our
projects. This chapter about the *Antioch A.M.E. Digital Archive* is a study in
the challenges and successes of digital community engagement.[1] The archive
is a growing compendium of records (texts, images, and three-dimensional
objects) about the church, originating with service-based work by staff at the
University of West Georgia and Agnes Scott College along with the articulate
vision and community-based work of church members. In this chapter, our
project members reflect on building and sustaining the archive, emphasizing
the material process of working in collaboration with each other. Contributors,
each of whom authored her own section of the chapter, consider the practical
and ethical realities of work grounded in living partnership and inflected by
digital technology. We hope to describe a kind of praxis that will avail in other
contexts. In the conclusion, we offer milestones that we missed along the way
that may help others who are undertaking similar collaborative work.

Our labor is framed by a number of commitments: to ethical, public
work; to emerging practices in our field; to critical assessment of power

DOI: 10.34314/wingodigital.00005

dynamics at play in university-community partnerships; to the value of working with and training students; and, above all, to telling the history of Antioch A.M.E. Church. The project might be classified as digital public history, or something distinct from digital humanities and digital history, what Sharon Leon notes as "formed by a specific attention to preparing materials for a particular audience—to address their questions, to engage with them, to target a real conversation with the public about a particular aspect of history."[2] The project is also informed by community archiving, an emergent practice in the archival field in which archivists act in consultative roles, and historic artifacts and records continue to be stewarded by the communities in which they matter most.

The *Antioch A.M.E. Digital History Project* is a community-generated repository of artifacts, images, oral histories, and documents that trace the history of the church in concert with its 150th year celebration in 2018. The church, which today thrives in Stone Mountain, Georgia, was the first African American church founded in Decatur, near Atlanta. Since its founding, Antioch has been engaged in ministering to the spiritual welfare of its congregants while also acting as a cultural and social bulwark—from serving as a place of education for newly freed men and women in 1868; speaking publicly against the Atlanta Race Riot in 1906; hosting lectures in Black history in the 1930s; ministering to AIDS patients in the 1980s; and today, through its Social Action Committee, focusing on pressing community issues. The church has been a force of gravity in the community, drawing parishioners for services, weddings, funerals, holiday meals, and homecomings. Despite this role, and its historic place in the heart of downtown Decatur, church records have not been housed in institutional repositories. Instead, members of its congregation preserved records and recorded histories of the church, which they saved and stewarded in family homes and the church itself. Those preservationists are the reason this archive exists.

The project began under the initiative of church members. In early 2015, church member Tigner Rand approached Julia Brock, newly arrived at the University of West Georgia's Center for Public History, about beginning an oral history project. Rand was the church's newsletter author and

DOI: 10.34314/wingodigital.00005

had attempted to find information about the history of the church. He came upon the work of public historian David Rotenstein, who has documented the effects of gentrification and urban renewal in Decatur, particularly the perilous consequences for the once-thriving Black community that surrounds the town.[3] Rotenstein's work offered the inspirational clue for Rand in his search for the past, and Rotenstein encouraged Rand to actively document the history of Antioch by recording the memories of elderly church congregants.

Brock's conversation with Rand began with an interview project as one outcome, but funding options required us to broaden our view. The most likely starting place for support was Georgia Humanities (GH), our state National Endowment for the Humanities (NEH)-affiliated organization, which offered small programming grants for history and humanities projects but only rarely funded oral history projects. The requirements of the grant, including a public program and the addition of a humanities scholar, shifted our plans to an event-based celebration of church history. We devised a History Day program at the church during its original homecoming month in July (a new homecoming celebration was added to the church calendar in September to recognize its move to Stone Mountain in 1996). We created a programming committee: church members Elayne Washington Hunter and Calvin Washington, siblings whose family had been connected to the church since the nineteenth century; Robin Morris, a history professor at Agnes Scott College who joined as our humanities scholar; and Elyse Hill, an African American genealogist.

We began building components of the project before our event in July. As a project team, we wanted to capture the strong intergenerational population of the church. To that end, we planned and conducted an intergenerational oral history day to bring the children and the elders of the church into con-versation. On a Saturday morning, Morris trained about eight middle-and high-schoolers in oral history methods. Unfortunately, we were not able to record interviews since we had not gotten out the word sufficiently to ensure a strong elder presence on that day. Thankfully, a couple of elders did join the group later and shared memories of holidays and baptisms. In the future, we might do training one week, and then include the children to a greater extent

DOI: 10.34314/wingodigital.00005

in the History Harvest with an oral history booth. We also want to record the youths' own recent memories of the church to highlight that the congregation is now building its seventh and eighth generations.

The History Day program, which took place in July 2016, had two goals: to offer guidance for interested church and community members in preserving family and church records, and to digitize church records in the form of a History Harvest.[4] University of West Georgia archivists Shaneé Murrain and Blynne Olivieri led a session on preserving documents and photographs, while Elyse Hill offered a workshop on African American genealogical research. In addition, Larry Rivers, a historian at the University of West Georgia, gave a talk on the history of the A.M.E. Church, particularly focusing on Antioch's development within that larger narrative.

The History Harvest yielded the records that Rand, Hunter, and Washington hoped to locate—photographs, documents, and objects that illuminated the church's rich past. In the months leading up to the History Day program we scanned church members' collections and built a small cache of digital reproductions. During the event we continued our scanning and photographing, thanks to a number of UWG public history graduate students and interns.

History Day proved a success, drawing well beyond church members to those from the community. Over fifty people attended, mostly church members but also other public historians and community members working to document African American history in Dekalb County. Most church members responded to the day with enthusiasm. One respondent to a post-event survey said, "I really enjoyed the day," and that only "longer sessions and break-out sessions with [the] experts" would have improved it. Another said the day was "very comprehensive, detailed, and thorough!"

Some members who attended were wary of the project's goals and outcomes, and expressed mistrust at the participation of the mostly white UWG group of staff and students. A woman whose family was rooted in the church assumed that we were there to scan records in order to make a profit from their collection. Although this was never our aim, this points to a well-founded fear based in a history of white exploitation of communities of color.

DOI: 10.34314/wingodigital.00005

The woman went on to question why the church, or even her family, could not run an archive without the help of a predominantly white institution (PWI). This highlights a key issue of privilege and community partnerships: saying "yes" to a partnership without questioning whether a PWI was the most appropriate partner for the church. Our first interface as public historians with a community partner is often consultative; when we are considering what projects to move forward, it is critical to think not only about our standing commitments and resources but whether or not we are truly serving the community partner.

The critique of the church member also raised the issues of ownership and control over access. The physical objects remained in the hands of their original stewards, but the digital reproductions were another story. Consent forms first reflected the risk-averse nature of the university. Donors signed over copyright of the scans to the University of West Georgia, the institution that would house and manage them. But as Leon argues, public historians have to consider the "use and reuse" of digital content—in this case, it is important to add (as others have elsewhere) that we must confront the ethical implications of reuse.[5] The digital archive made it so donors did not have control over how their material was used on the web. After History Day, we attempted to remediate the lack of control by adopting a Creative Commons licensing structure on the consent forms. So far we have employed this language in oral history consent forms, though we have not scanned additional items and thus have not used the updated permissions form for digitization. Those who donated objects and papers for scanning consented that the material would be publicly accessible on the web, while the physical artifacts remain in personal collections.

By the end of summer 2016 we had enough of a collection to begin building the digital archive. As Sheila Brennan has argued, "Doing any type of public digital humanities work requires an intentional decision from the beginning of the project that identifies, invites in, and addresses audience needs in the design, as well as the approach and content, long before the outreach for a finished project begins."[6] With the church members as a primary audience in mind, Brock chose Omeka, created by the Roy Rosenzweig Center for

DOI: 10.34314/wingodigital.00005

History and New Media at George Mason University, as the platform on which to build. It met several requirements for our use: it is free and open-source; has a user-friendly interface students can easily learn and use; has a structured metadata schema for archival objects; and includes features that allow for community interaction. Graduate and undergraduate students played an important role in researching and adding metadata to individual items in the Omeka database, using guidelines from the Digital Library of Georgia (DLG). The site is poised to be indexed in the DLG, which also serves as a content hub of the Digital Public Library of America, which will allow for greater discoverability of the archival material.

We continued our work to some extent after History Day, aided by new leadership in the church. In 2017, Pastor Vandy C. Simmons accepted an assignment to lead Antioch. Rand and Calvin Washington facilitated an introductory meeting of project team members and Simmons shortly after his arrival. At this meeting, church leaders introduced Simmons to the long history of his new church home and asked for a blessing to pursue the project. Pastor Simmons has brought a new vibrancy to the congregation and continues the legacy of community engagement.

We learned after building the digital archive, however, that even when community-institution relationships are strong and the digital product is a resource for the public, that public may not always know about, or use, the creation. Though we do have visitors to the site, we've had no one upload additional items, nor comment on content (the ability to do both are prominent features of Omeka). The lack of engagement with the site can only be the fault of the project team—after History Day and the initial excitement of the collection, the team ebbed in its work. This break was due to other professional and personal demands, not to lack of interest. We are currently regrouping and considering new ways to widely share this virtual space.

Still, we continue to think about how to make the site more robust. One avenue is to link the archive to the church's current ministry. The church records Sunday services for congregants unable to attend in person, for example. Church A/V volunteers then upload these videos to YouTube. We wondered about historical sermons as we built the archive: what did the congregants hear about voter registration or racial violence? What did they

DOI: 10.34314/wingodigital.00005

hear about Jim Crow or Massive Resistance or Atlanta's own Martin Luther King, Jr.? While we have not found old sermons, future researchers can know what congregants heard in 2018. They will be able to link to the video—with the words and presentation—to hear the sermons of this era. The church, for example, has recently been active in hosting political candidates, such as gubernatorial candidate Stacey Abrams, and documentaries that explore current disenfranchisement of voters of color.[7]

We also continue to attend special events and record contemporary history on the site. We try to keep up with scanning flyers for the numerous social and community events the church hosts. In the summer of 2018, Antioch hosted a community Meet the Candidates Forum in anticipation of the primary elections. They invited candidates for all state and local offices and opened the doors to the entire community. Morris and Brock attended the event and, in addition to learning more about the candidates, took photographs for the record. Church members have also expressed the desire to collect "history as it happens," and this documentation effort has become another way to build the site.

In January of 2019, Antioch project team members were fortunate to attend the Sustaining Digital Humanities (DH) Workshop at Georgia Tech University. Faculty and graduate students based at the University of Pittsburgh's Visual Media Institute led the two-day workshop, which trains digital humanists to implement the Socio-Technical Sustainability Roadmap in order to plan strategically for a project's lifespan.[8] This workshop was invaluable for helping us articulate goals and a plan for moving forward. We use the conclusion of this chapter to reflect on these goals and how the workshop brought to light the steps we missed in the beginning stages of our work.

During the workshop, the team listed all of those that were part of the project's life—from the web server host to the funders to the important role of undergraduate and graduate students. One of our partners who contributed invaluable intellectual and practical framing is assistant professor Shaneé Murrain of the University of West Georgia's Ingram Library. As mentioned before, Murrain and her colleague Blynne Olivieri of the Annie Belle Weaver Special Collections offered a workshop at the Antioch History Day on preserving family and church records. But Murrain continued to play a role after

DOI: 10.34314/wingodigital.00005

the summer of 2016 in helping project team members understand a turn in archival practice with regards to ownership and belonging. The digital archive thus relied upon consultation with Murrain, whose practice is committed to equity and transparency. She now offers a brief meditation on the practice of community archiving.

Figure 4.1: University of West Georgia University Archivist Shaneé Murrain talks with a participant of the Antioch A.M.E. History Day in July 2016.
Courtesy Mark Greenberg.

Figure 4.2: Genealogist Elyse Hill gave a workshop on family history research at the Antioch A.M.E. History Day in July 2016. Courtesy Mark Greenberg.

DOI: 10.34314/wingodigital.00005

Figure 4.3: Julia Brock, Tigner Rand, and Robin Morris led an oral history workshop with the Young People's Department at Antioch A.M.E. church in April 2016. Courtesy Robin Morris.

Figure 4.4: University of West Georgia public history students talk with Sharon Youngblood, a long-time member of Antioch A.M.E. at History Day in 2016. Ms. Youngblood allowed students to scan a souvenir program of the 1960s church ground-breaking in its second location in downtown Decatur, Georgia.

DOI: 10.34314/wingodigital.00005

Figure 4.5: A black and white photograph of the original 1874 Antioch A.M.E. Church wooden building. The photograph also features Antioch A.M.E. Church members. Courtesy of Sylvia Clarke via the Antioch A.M.E. Digital Archive.

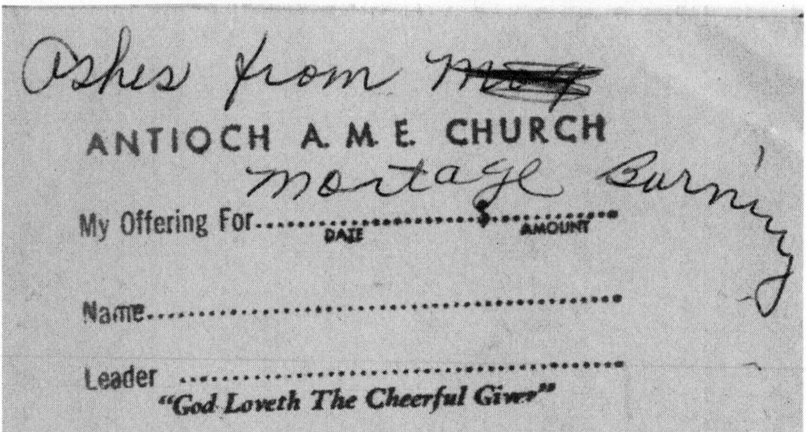

Figure 4.6: A church envelope holding ashes from a mortgage burning ceremony in 1981. Courtesy of Barbara Lowe via the Antioch A.M.E. Digital Archive.

DOI: 10.34314/wingodigital.00005

Figure 4.7: Historian David Rotenstein documented the 2014 destruction of the last church building that Antioch occupied. Courtesy of David Rotenstein via the Antioch A.M.E. Digital Archive.

Figure 4.8: Elayne Washington Hunter.

DOI: 10.34314/wingodigital.00005

Community Archiving

Shaneé Murrain

Who tells the story of Black Church life? How that story is told, through years of written and published documentation, oral testimonies and artifacts, is partially informed by both the archivist and the archive. For me, archivists don't tell the story of Black Church life; the records and the communities they come from do. The Black Church is the expert on Black Church life.

Part of the work of community archives concerns changing the narrative of African American collections that often are not seen as on par with other materials related to American history collected by majority institutions, like PWIs. Pushing against this notion has been an uphill battle for many of us in the archival world, but it needs to be taken as seriously as other resources. We are now working to provide comparable access to these holdings; to build these collections at a similar pace to other holdings; and to use them in our research, scholarship, and teaching. Herein lies the question: what do we want to remember and how do we tell the story? Who is silenced? Why? Who articulates competing and contested memories? Why? Where is the glory in only telling certain stories? How can archival institutions operate in such a way as to communicate that the Black Church is relevant—that it does still, and will always, matter?

One method attends to the role of time and season in the community. A year is measured differently in the church and the academy. The liturgical calendar gives structure and momentum to people's lives by directing a church's organization around seasonal and occasional events such as deaths, anniversaries, weddings, birth of children, and changes in leadership. Throughout this experience collaborating with one church and one community member, we found managing expectations about time and success have been crucial to developing genuine relationships. The transactional nature of relationships in academia is often motivated by momentum: an effort to meet deadlines, receive proper credit for a groundbreaking research discovery, or achieve tenure are different measures of success than what occurs outside academia. The church and the academy are alike in that the work of

DOI: 10.34314/wingodigital.00005

individuals has greater purpose. The difference is the reward. In the academy careers are elevated, while in the church the people are celebrated. This ethos is important to recognize and critique in community archives.

Complete independence from the traditional archive is complicated by various forms of power. While community archives interrogate the functions of narrative, authority, and memory in our collection development policies, these collections are not created and sustained without financial support. The *Antioch A.M.E. Digital Collection* project is led by tenure-track faculty and librarians from PWIs that have the resources to support a host of projects beyond a community preservation workshop. In an article written for a series on community-based archives, Yusef Omowale argues, "If we are to restore and document our humanity, we must refuse the spectacle for the everyday. The archive has privileged the spectacle to our detriment."[9] In primary documents produced by African American associations and church bodies we see congregations participating in constructing their own stories and revisiting them throughout the life of the community.

This community archives project is designed to showcase how churches and universities can work together to preserve African American history, and invite intergenerational dialogue and storytelling via oral history. In a genuine effort to build relationships with churches, workshops such as History Day act as community gathering spaces. Community members are empowered by participating in the planning and collection of their stories as they deem appropriate. They also facilitate the preservation of these stories by building a local archive representative of the people and free of the traditional institutional repository. Breaking from traditional roles in archives, we are creating relationships rather than bringing collections in. Absorbing stories is not the only way to build archival collections.

The communal work of preserving the church's historical records can deepen our understanding of identity as an ever-evolving conversation with the past and within ourselves as educators within the academy.

DOI: 10.34314/wingodigital.00005

A History Ministry

Elayne Washington Hunter and Julia Brock spoke on a September afternoon. Prompted by questions from Brock, Hunter reflected on the history of Antioch and the dynamics of the project. As with any interview, the questions and answers are shaped by the agenda of the interviewer, the identities of the interviewer and interviewee, and the relationship of the two. Brock transcribed Hunter's responses below.

We are on our fifth generation of membership at Antioch. My great-grandfather was James Fowler and he was one of the founding members and one of the first stewards at the church. On every cornerstone of our churches, of the buildings, the edifices, someone from my family has been there. The church on Marshall Street—my grandfather's name was there. The church on Atlanta Avenue—my father was there. My brother is on the current stone. My grandchildren are members now.

The church was in Decatur and had been there since the 1860s; we are the oldest church for people of color in the city of Decatur. I remember that there was a page in the Decatur history that was dedicated to our church. I always heard that as a child growing up. I remember as a child that Mrs. Lorena Kemp kept the history of the church; she was the church historian. Prior to this project coming together a couple of years ago the church celebrated every year in July until we moved over to Stone Mountain. We moved to Stone Mountain in October and so the pastor at the time, who was our pastor for twenty-three years, changed the anniversary date to October. Growing up in the church I remember that the celebration of the anniversary was in July.

We need more attention paid to the history of our church from our administration, from our leadership, from our pastor, and from the current officers. Since our church moved over to Stone Mountain it has changed so much. The people who run the church, the people who are the leadership of the church, they come from all different spaces and places and times. Before, when we were literally in Decatur, the majority of the people who were leaders in the church came from Decatur. They had an allegiance to the church. That doesn't really exist anymore because we were a church of 150

DOI: 10.34314/wingodigital.00005

people that became a church of nearly 2,000 people. You can imagine how the dynamics changed.

It's important for us to know our history. I think it's important for the children to know it. Our country is what it is based on the history of the country and I feel the same way about the church. Our church is where we are and who we are based on our history. I think that our history contributed to the community in a way that some churches did not. That needs to be known. I just think about when I learned some of the things that we uncovered, just the mere fact that these people were slaves before 1865 and three years later they founded a church, and that church became a school and a meeting place. You know, it leaves me in awe. I'm just awestruck based on the fact that my family was a part of that. Not that we dwell on our past but where are we without it? It's important for us to document our history every place that we can because it's worth somebody knowing about it.

Our project began when Dr. David Rotenstein took note of who we were. He is a historian who wrote an article about what was happening with urban renewal in the city of Decatur and how this church was getting pushed over to the side. Tigner Rand communicated with myself and my brother—so that's how I think we all got started. There was money available through the Georgia Humanities that funded us to do our history day project. That's how we started meeting and uncovering.

I was excited by the project because we might be able to let the world know Antioch, where we came from and how we got where we are. I thought that we were going to be able to even draw in people who had an affiliation to the church who were gone away from it. We were going to be able to bring those people back and have some conversation with them about Antioch. Some families who had been affiliated with the church for a long period of time did not go with the church when it left for Stone Mountain. They are very few families now who were affiliated with the church from the beginning.

At the History Day in July of 2016, I thought that the presentation that was done by Dr. Larry Rivers was the core of the entire day. I was in awe as to how he took the history of Richard Allen and brought it all the way to Decatur, Georgia, and Stone Mountain. That's how I felt sitting there—I

DOI: 10.34314/wingodigital.00005

felt like, wow, this has come all the way from Philadelphia to Atlanta. Also, the fact that people brought archival information to us. Some of them, I was surprised that they still had it. That's what intrigued me about the day. I wish, however, that we had had more people in attendance.

We planned the day well. I was happy about how we advertised and marketed it. I don't think we could've done anything differently that particular day that would have changed anything. The church members who came were happy to contribute. One of them, though, was very negative about the whole project. She seemed to have thought that we had hooked up with white people who were going to make a whole lot of money off the church and that she wouldn't be a part of that money-making deal. But it was not like that and I do not think that we communicated it that way. I just think that she came in with that negativism and kept it while she was there, and verbalized it.

We need to have another History Day and I'd like for us to get the current membership more involved. When I say "involved" I mean more knowledgeable. I think we have the capability of doing that. It amazes me that our current bishop of the district is really interested in having all of our local churches deal a lot more with social action and be a lot more community-based. I feel that Antioch started out that way and so I do not want to see us lose that. I'd like for us to continue our project. I really wish that we would have been more involved with the sesquicentennial, happening right now.

I'd like to see a history ministry in the church because the history is a rich history. You have the missionaries, for example, and they do work with the homeless and caring for the community. The history committee would focus on the past and constantly record our history as it's happening. Nobody is really recording the current history and tying it all together with where we used to be to where we have come to be. I think that's what the ministry can be involved in. I think it's almost a given that we end up there based on our early beginnings.

Had it not been for our relationship with University of West Georgia and Agnes Scott College and college students we would not have uncovered as much as we actually did. I think it's having somebody to be able to do some of the work, someone who is knowledgeable about projects like this,

DOI: 10.34314/wingodigital.00005

knowledgeable about history and historical reference points. Someone who has contacts that we can grab and use to help us along our way. I think we should develop a mission statement so that we know where we want to go and what our mission is as a committee or ministry. From there, we should continue our relationship with these colleges and universities. The students, young people, they are learning a lot every day in school, and for them to be able to apply some of that to our history is important. Even the techniques and the exposure—all of that, to me, is important for students.

I think that the best things that have been done in this country have been done through collaboration. I just feel that we don't stand alone. Had the possibility of the project not come to our attention we probably would just be going on and on and never even thinking about it, other than it being a passing thought—as opposed to it becoming a project. I personally do not think there are any drawbacks to partnering with universities.

I don't think that race affected our partnership. We're an African American church and we have a history that started when our forefathers were brought here as slaves. And so, based on that alone, there is a racial side or aspect to what we're actually doing here. But otherwise I don't. I think that people are prejudiced from all different sides and from all different angles . . . I don't think that's going to die out; I think that people are going to be prejudiced no matter what and no matter who's involved in the project.

Conclusion

The *Antioch A.M.E. Digital Archive* is, in many ways, an example of a successful community-institution partnership. Project partners created a shared vision to address a need of the church, and carried out plans with the help of experts and supporters. The outcome is not only an accessible digital archive but an ongoing relationship between church and institution partners. Both undergraduate and graduate students worked as part of the process, which means that the project also served as training for young public historians. Finally, the process we used and the project we created has become a model for church partnerships championed by Georgia Humanities, our funder, and shared by us at conferences and public talks.

DOI: 10.34314/wingodigital.00005

Ours, like so many projects, is also weighted by the burdens we encounter: personal priorities change, key partners move to new jobs, and a lack of clarity about new directions stymies progress in any direction. Though we are all committed to the project's future at the time of this writing, we are still a work-in-progress as we decide upon future directions. In the following paragraphs, written after a brainstorming session at the Sustaining DH Workshop, we address what we hope other project teams will take as lessons from our process and what we see as key contributions of our work and the future of the project.

The Sustaining DH Workshop brought us together again in January 2019 after a few months' ebb in project work caused by Brock moving to the University of Alabama. Using the Socio-Technical Sustainability Roadmap (STSR), workshop leaders guided a room full of digital humanists through a step-by-step process to identify the assets of our projects and how we might sustain both the partnerships and the digital infrastructures or datasets we are building and preserving. The workshop allowed our team to have rich discussions about our process to date and about the meanings we give to the project.

First, to the pieces we missed. We came together as a group of people with a common goal: to preserve and share the past. We learned that we liked each other—we enjoyed our meetings, which were often fueled by homemade baked goods, storytelling, and laughter. But we never assigned formal roles to project members, something that was asked of us as part of the STSR. That exercise was clarifying. We determined, for example, that Calvin Washington Hunter served as not only a church liaison but as coordinator of project meetings and additional project members (we have decided to bring in new partners from the church congregation); Elayne Washington Hunter focused on public relations opportunities within the church; Julia Brock primarily managed the infrastructure of the Omeka site; Robin Morris would continue to work as project consultant, providing support for programming and resources available at her institution; and Tigner Rand would continue to develop outreach opportunities within and outside of the church and provide technical support. Though we had been working in these specific ways for the life of the project, articulating roles was incredibly helpful for making discrete plans for future work.

DOI: 10.34314/wingodigital.00005

We also confronted the distance between who we hoped our audience would be (for the archive, in particular) and who actually used the site. In our imagining, users of the site would include those interested in the history of Antioch; in Black Church history; and in the history of Decatur. Those users might be church members, K-12 teachers, and researchers, for example. In reality, the project team members currently make up the primary users of the site, in addition to the occasional visitor from the church. Facing this reality made us think hard about what steps to take in order to connect more users to the site itself.

Finally, we created a timeline for attending to digital sustainability. These actions, based on the STSR, are in some ways common sense—backing up data, storing data responsibly, and creating access tiers to the site and records for project team members. But the curriculum also encouraged us to think about the lifetime of our project. How long do we imagine its life to be? How will we retire the site when the time comes? The workshop leaders ask that project teams revisit the STSR modules every three years to ask and answer similar questions.

This workshop, then, was inestimably helpful and we left after two days with written documentation of our work and a clear, if modest, plan to move forward. Actions include student-created exhibits on the site to interpret the archive's contents, continued outreach to the church to build interest in the site, meeting with the pastor once again to remind him of our work, and a clear plan for digital preservation. We also agreed to plan for the site's eventual retirement; we imagine one possibility could be archiving the information at the Atlanta University Center Archive or somewhere that has robust collections in Black history (though we have *not* approached any institution about this). Perhaps just as important, our time together allowed us to reflect out loud on what our project has meant to us personally and what we think it means in a wider sense. These are the points we want readers to understand:

First, this project did not take a lot of money. We started with a grant of $2000 and drew from our own labor and that of our students to create and build the site. We urge those who want to engage in similar projects to know it is possible to do so starting with little in the way of a budget. As this went

DOI: 10.34314/wingodigital.00005

to press, Morris received a small grant from Agnes Scott College to develop a Spring 2020 class for advanced history undergraduates to scan material from the church photographer's collection and to conduct additional oral histories. The grant also funds rideshare transportation for students to attend at least two church services to meet the community whose story they will be telling. Finally, students will use the Omeka feature of digital curation to create online exhibits using the site's archive.

Second, ours is one model of creating a community archive without removing objects from their owners, though we must make a critical note. Yusef Omowale sees a danger in "institutionally approved ways to do community-based memory work, with attending certification, funding, awards/ recognition, and accountability." He urges us to "refuse attempts at incorporation which will only further alienate our communities from themselves."[10] In our case, this means at minimum we need to continue to acknowledge the power dynamics of workers at historically white institutions asking for permission to digitize and make accessible the records of a displaced (but not annihilated) community of African Americans. We need to be honest about how these projects benefit the academic partners and the institutions they represent—through promotion and tenure, through the PR possibilities that this project presents of "community engagement", and in potentially bettering town-gown relationships. We then need to confront parity. What does the partnering community receive in return? Is it enough to preserve its past in small ways or is something greater owed?

Finally, our work is fundamentally built on the expertise of the community; we relied upon the archival and historical work of generations of church members. It was their labor that allowed us, too, to look for revelations in the corpus of accumulated material. The archive tells of the systematic removal of a community, but one that thrives, though different in constitution from its historic membership. We learned about twentieth century Black life in downtown Decatur, and that property and business ownership created a thriving Black neighborhood in the heart of the city. We learned that the church was and is a center of community life and social activism. Antioch, as Hunter said as we were discussing this conclusion, "was a church that helped

DOI: 10.34314/wingodigital.00005

the community become what it did." The members of that church helped the
Antioch A.M.E. Digital Archive to become what it did.

Notes

1. The title comes from a description of Antioch A.M.E. Church by its historian, Lena Harper, in 1957: "In 1868 at the close of the Civil War, everywhere ruins and discouragement among the people, Antioch A.M.E. began
   to send out a little light to the people of Decatur." Lena Harper, "The History
   of Antioch A.M.E. Church, 1957 July 14," *Antioch A.M.E. Digital Archive*,
   accessed September 23, 2018.
2. Melissa Dinsman, "The Digital in the Humanities: An Interview with Sharon
   M. Leon," *L.A. Review of Books*, July 10, 2016.
3. David Rotenstein, "Antioch's Eyes (Updated)," *History Sidebar*, January 29,
   2014.
4. Robin Morris learned of the History Harvest idea from a presentation by
   University of Nebraska-Lincoln at a professional conference of historians.
5. Sharon M. Leon, "Complexity and Collaboration: Doing Public History in
   Digital Environments," in *The Oxford Handbook of Public History*, ed. James B.
   Gardner and Paula Hamilton (New York: Oxford University Press, 2017),
   60; see Jack Daugherty and Candace Simpson, "Who Owns Oral History?
   A Creative Commons Solution," in *Oral History in the Digital Age*, ed. Doug
   Boyd, Steve Cohen, Brad Rakerd, and Dean Rehberger (Washington, D.C.:
   Institute of Museum and Library Services, 2012).
6. Sheila Brennan, "Public, First," in *Debates in the Digital Humanities*, ed.
   Matthew K. Gold and Lauren Klein (Minneapolis: University of Minnesota
   Press, 2016).
7. Antioch A.M.E. Church, "Celebrating Women, Character, Courage And
   Commitment," March 31, 2019. The Antioch A.M.E. Church runs a
   YouTube channel, which hosts the archive of Sunday sermons, Wednesday
   night Hour of Power programs, and other church programs.
8. The very supportive leaders of the workshop were the Visual Media Institute's director Dr. Alison Langmead and graduate students Aisling Quigley
   and Chelsea Gunn. Learn more about VMI and the Socio-Technical Sustainability Roadmap.
9. Yusef Omowale, "We Already Are," *Medium* (blog), September 3, 2018.
10. Omowale, "We Already Are."

DOI: 10.34314/wingodigital.00005

Works Cited

Antioch A.M.E. Church. "Celebrating Women, Character, Courage And Commitment," YouTube video. March 31, 2019. https://www.youtube.com/watch?v=bOeUMJPIpZw.

Brennan, Sheila. "Public, First." In *Debates in the Digital Humanities*. Edited by Matthew K. Gold and Lauren Klein. Minneapolis: University of Minnesota Press, 2016.

Daugherty, Jack and Candace Simpson. "Who Owns Oral History? A Creative Commons Solution." In *Oral History in the Digital Age*. Edited by Doug Boyd, Steve Cohen, Brad Rakerd, and Dean Rehberger. Washington, D.C.: Institute of Museum and Library Services, 2012.

Dinsman, Melissa. "The Digital in the Humanities: An Interview with Sharon M. Leon." *L.A. Review of Books.* July 10, 2016.

Leon, Sharon M. "Complexity and Collaboration: Doing Public History in Digital Environments." In *The Oxford Handbook of Public History*. Edited by James B. Gardner and Paula Hamilton, 44–68. New York: Oxford University Press, 2017.

Omowale, Yusef. "We Already Are." *Medium* (blog), September 3, 2018.

Rotenstein, David. "Antioch's Eyes (Updated)." *History Sidebar.* January 29, 2014.

DOI: 10.34314/wingodigital.00005

5

Seen and Heard

Using DiCE to Reconnect Communities and Enrich History Pedagogy

Amy C. Sullivan

Two Case Studies

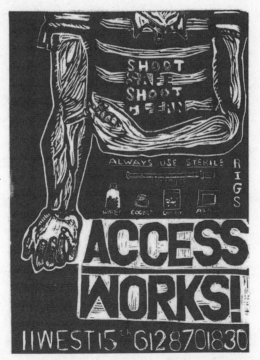

Figure 5.1: Shoot Safe, Shoot Clean was a promotional print created for Access Works in the early 2000s, artist unknown. The print was digitized at "Harm Reduction in Minnesota: Chronicling Our Origins," May 6, 2017 in Minneapolis, MN, now part of the Women with a Point and Access Works Harm Reduction Archive, Lee Hertel Collection.

DOI: 10.34314/wingodigital.00006

Figure 5.2: Artifacts from Camp Scott, an Oklahoma Girl Scout camp open from 1928–1977, digitized at the Camp Scott History Harvest. The plastic bag contains ashes from a 1970s campfire at Camp Scott, saved by Girl Scout Joni Kinsey.

Introduction

I was introduced to the History Harvest concept at Macalester College when Rebecca Wingo and I co-taught a public/oral history course that centered around the first *Remembering Rondo History Harvest.*[1] In the two years following, student research assistants and I hosted two more: one with people who worked in harm reduction programs for drug users in Minneapolis, Minnesota, and one with baby boom-era Girl Scouts in Tulsa, Oklahoma, whose summer camp closed after a tragedy. Despite the obvious differences between the two groups, they had some powerful things in common. Their histories had not been acknowledged, even among themselves. During both events, I witnessed how the very act of coming together made meaning of their stories and allowed them to see their place in a bigger narrative.

DOI: 10.34314/wingodigital.00006

The gathering itself was as important as the final digital archive. For these participants, being seen and heard by historians and each other helped them articulate important experiences that had been silenced by more dominant narratives. Before the History Harvest, the 1980s and 1990s-era harm reduction advocates felt the history of their hard-earned and difficult work was rendered invisible and unacknowledged in the midst of the current opioid crisis. After a horrible tragedy that forced their camp to close suddenly in 1977, the Girl Scouts' deep love of the place and its traditions was silenced; for decades, their history at the camp was overshadowed by sadness, and it too went unacknowledged. The process of digitizing personal artifacts and stories together in one room validated their histories and reconnected them with each other, some after decades had passed. The emotional content and complexity of their stories and related artifacts was a win for history pedagogy as well. The students gained interpersonal skills and were profoundly touched by the experience; they learned to be good listeners in the oral history tradition and engaged in higher levels of intellectual and emotional empathy, well beyond the bounds of classrooms and academic texts.

At first glance, harm reduction providers and lifelong Girl Scouts may seem as different as any two groups could be, but both of their stories involved trauma, loss, and invisibility. I wondered, how might we make their histories not just visible but valuable? And how can we best embody empathy and understanding when the communities we are engaging have experienced trauma, loss, and marginalization? When interacting with traumatic events, the methods and theory of oral history are particularly useful in projects such as these.[2] By placing empathy and listening at the center—as essential aspects of history-gathering—the History Harvest model has the ability to preserve even emotionally complex histories that are often lost, fraught, and contested. For these two communities, the History Harvest was a powerful way to validate and preserve their histories.

DOI: 10.34314/wingodigital.00006

Harm Reduction in Minnesota: Chronicling Our Origins
May 6, 2017
Minneapolis, Minnesota

Figure 5.3: Screenshot of a Facebook Event page for "Harm Reduction in Minnesota: Chronicling Our Origins," held on May 6, 2017 in Minneapolis, MN. The Women with A Point matchbooks were used in the invitation to attract attention and were among the first artifacts digitized that day.

Equal parts nervous and excited accurately described the emotions of my three students on the day of our History Harvest in May 2017, broadly shared and advertised as "Chronicling Our Origins: Harm Reduction in Minnesota." Aside from one community contact person I met by phone, we had no idea who might show up to our quickly planned History Harvest on that sunny Saturday afternoon in Minneapolis. I was nervous, too, especially since our team of five could have been easily overwhelmed if even half of the 140-odd people who said they were "interested" on our Facebook Event page showed up. In one afternoon, we hoped to gather artifacts and oral histories from a loose cohort of people who worked in the field of harm reduction in Minnesota: current and former outreach workers, harm reduction advocates, and social service professionals who worked with injection drug users and others at risk for contracting HIV or hepatitis since the 1980s. What kind of history would come from this gathering? What new evidence would we discover? Would active drug users show up, too? How might that go?

By phone a month earlier, I had connected with Sue Purchase, a well-known harm reduction service provider who lived in Colorado but who would soon be visiting Minneapolis. In 1996, she founded what was likely the first women-centered needle exchange in the U.S., Women with a Point. Later renamed Access Works and serving any gender identity, the storefront nonprofit thrived in Minneapolis for nearly a decade.[3] The organization's

DOI: 10.34314/wingodigital.00006

roots began in the midst of the AIDS/HIV epidemic some years after research-ers discovered that injection drug users were also among those at high risk for contracting the disease. Although needle exchanges (also called syringe access) and condom distribution continue to be important public health interventions, the history and principles of harm reduction have remained mostly hidden from the public. Since Sue Purchase knew many people in the Twin Cities area with experience and knowledge about its early history, both locally and nationally, she offered to connect us with her former colleagues. We hoped some of them would show up to our impromptu History Harvest.

In a few hours that day, Rebecca Wingo and I, along with my students Samantha Aamot, Sara Ludewig, and Zachary Malett, interviewed, pho-tographed, and scanned over eighty objects from eighteen participants. Several of these included short-form interviews with individuals and groups. Through the course of the afternoon, we learned that many of the attendees had provided life-saving health services to drug users more than twenty years before the current opioid epidemic refocused attention on harm reduction.[4] For some, many years had passed since they last saw each other. Any nervous-ness we felt as outsiders to this community dissipated quickly—the event had the relaxed feeling of a reunion, and they were eager to have their contribu-tions documented and acknowledged. And yes, some active injection drug users arrived and participated enthusiastically. Everyone shared powerful stories about their work in the early days of harm reduction, when they took risks and worked creatively to help keep some of the most marginalized people in society safer and healthier.

The contributions of these participants added an entirely new com-ponent to *The Minnesota Opioid Project*, an oral history collection and digital archive that I am creating to document the social, cultural, and treatment-re-lated changes occurring as a result of the opioid epidemic in Minnesota, a state world-renowned for its drug treatment model.[5] The "Minnesota Model" centers on total abstinence from drugs and alcohol, and the Twelve Step program is the core of its treatment protocol.[6] The staggering death rate from opioid overdoses, combined with a new demographic of users (suburban, rural, white), has slowly begun to change entrenched drug treatment pro-tocols and shifted public discourse and policy a bit more toward the harm

DOI: 10.34314/wingodigital.00006

Figure 5.4: Group photo of some of the attendees at the Harm Reduction History Harvest. Sue Purchase, the community contact for this event, is in the front row, far right. Amy Sullivan is in the back row, far right.

reduction model, one that focuses on reducing harm and meeting each person "where they are at," a common harm reduction slogan. Prior to the recent dramatic uptick of opioid misuse, early proponents of harm reduction led the way in overdose prevention at the height of the HIV/AIDS epidemic. Most who attended the event represented an earlier and lesser-known history of the people who cared for injection drug users who were at great risk for contracting HIV and other bloodborne pathogens. Although history scholarship about the early HIV/AIDS epidemic is robust and growing more so, the plight of injection drug users has remained as marginalized as drug users themselves. We intervened in this absence.

We discovered new tangents and histories regarding what the larger philosophy of "harm reduction" means to the people who have devoted their careers to it, in contrast to how the media and others have most recently deployed the term as a catch-all for saving people from opioid overdoses with the opioid antidote naloxone (brand name Narcan). Participant Lee Hertel expressed the sentiment of being left out of the history and unappreciated by the movement eloquently and powerfully in this audio file. Rather than sit

DOI: 10.34314/wingodigital.00006

down with an interviewer, Hertel took the list of interview prompts we had provided, borrowed a recording device, and answered them all in a mono-logue. Listening to it together a few weeks later, my students and I were deeply moved.

Julie Hooker was another History Harvest participant who addressed the layers of stigma drug users experience, even long after they have quit using. Now the CEO of her own harm reduction, trauma-informed, outpa-tient treatment center in St. Paul, she wanted us to document a 1998 news-paper story that she thought was intended to share her successful recovery from drug use and the work she had done to help others in recovery access stable housing. Instead, the story misquoted and marginalized both her and her housemate at the time, Nancy Ham. More than twenty years later, and even as accustomed to the ubiquitous judgmental language about drug users as she is, it still stung.

In her interview, Hooker shared with Purchase stories about the stigma she faced in early recovery and afterwards, despite the important work she was doing to help other people improve their lives. Next to a small picture of Julie is the caption: "Julie Hooker, a former alcoholic, drug abuser, and prostitute, has opened several homes in the area to support single women who were substance abusers." Instead of focusing on the great work she and others were doing to create housing for people seeking to rebuild their lives after chronic drug use, the reporter focused on the women's pasts. Holding the newspaper article, she explained,

> The second house that we opened took front-page news. This woman—it's a terrible picture of her—her name is Nancy. She was also a working girl. . . . This article started off saying we had lost the only detox center, they had run out of money. . . . Then I think on this next page, I love this one [quoting the story]: "Julie Hooker ignored laws, defied probation rules, and generally bucked authority during her 'insane' existence." Insane is in quotes which means I said it. I never said that. It wasn't insane. It was a little chaotic but it wasn't insane. Then, [quoting]: "even now she resents the notion of anyone telling her what to do." It got really a little odd. . . . "It's the inmates running the asylum." All these weird things that I never did say.[7]

DOI: 10.34314/wingodigital.00006

Figure 5.5a and b: Julie Hooker brought this 1998 Salem, Oregon *Statesman Journal* article to digitize, saying, "The point of saving that article was really to showcase not so much the Oxford House piece of it but how society looked at people like me."

Hooker's story about surviving chaotic drug use and her tenacity despite stigma added emotional content to the public health measures of harm reduction. Her story also reflected how the shared lived experiences of people who came to work in and promote harm reduction have shaped important protocol and policy changes.

Another group of participants at the event revealed a previously hidden history of collaboration between several youth-centered street outreach programs in the 1990s. Since 1994, several Minneapolis-based nonprofits combined forces for street outreach that coordinated their respective staff

DOI: 10.34314/wingodigital.00006

Figure 5.6: This StreetWorks backpack, circa 1993, belongs to Susan Phillips. The patch was designed and silk-screened by a young Minneapolis artist, Marcus Foster, for outreach workers' backpacks and jackets so homeless youth could easily identify them on the streets.

and resources in order to provide a near-constant presence on the streets for homeless youth. Donning backpacks with a special patch that the youth could easily recognize, StreetWorks provided housing and health information, personal hygiene supplies, bus passes, socks, and other useful items.[8] Thus, the history of homeless youth in the 1990s emerged as yet another new path to pursue in the history of harm reduction. It dovetailed with the history of HIV/ AIDS, with coordinated social work outreach models, and with social justice organizations—including IV drug users. From this experience we learned that keeping our event's focus welcoming to all resulted in previously unknown and undocumented histories.

The open nature of the event also attracted people new to the field but who had little opportunity to meet the people who worked in education and outreach long before they had. For Stephanie Devich, full-time counselor and harm reduction trainer for Valhalla Place, a methadone clinic, the event provided her with an opportunity to finally meet some of the harm reduction pioneers whom she had long admired, while at the same time having her current artifacts documented for the collection.[9]

DOI: 10.34314/wingodigital.00006

Reflecting on the History Harvest, Purchase said she was "in awe of and grateful for this project, because it not only recognizes and highlights our work, but it will serve to educate and guide future harm reduction efforts for others." She credits the experience of being interviewed for the oral history collection with "reconnecting her to former friends and colleagues," and more important, "it led me back to my early work with women, who were the reason I started working in harm reduction. There was a need to serve women who weren't being served back then, and there still is great need today. Moving forward, I want to be part of claiming our stories as our own, in our own words."[10] The digital archive connects harm reduction staff and activists with their shared history; it validates their groundbreaking human rights and social justice work, a fact often overlooked even in the midst of the current opioid epidemic.

I Remember Camp Scott: A History Harvest and Songfest
March 25, 2018
Broken Arrow, Oklahoma

Nearly a year after the harm reduction event, I had the opportunity to organize, with the help of my former students turned research assistants, Samantha Aamot and Sara Ludewig, a History Harvest with self-described "old Girl Scouts." The women of Camp Scott had experienced a significant loss and a trauma that required years for recovery. Organized for Girl Scouts in eastern Oklahoma who had been active during the 1950s, 1960s and 1970s, this event was also shared online in a closed Facebook group with fewer than one hundred members. Established in 2008, the page enabled the group members to reconnect with each other, post photos, and reminisce about a place that no longer existed. The forty-nine-year-old, 400-acre Camp Scott closed on June 13, 1977 after the devastating sexual assaults and murders of three young campers by a male intruder on the first night of the camp's summer season. A months-long manhunt and criminal trial ensued without a conviction, and the case remains unsolved to this day. The dozens of women and girls present that night dispersed into their own lives to deal with the trauma however they could. The story's notoriety among true-crime buffs

DOI: 10.34314/wingodigital.00006

Figure 5.7: A typical Camp Scott scene from the mid-1970s at a counselors' tent. Forthcoming in the *I Remember Camp Scott Girl Scout Archive*, Joni Kinsey Collection.

and the media created a protective culture of silence among the Girl Scout council and Camp Scott survivors.[11] With the camp property forever lost and the tragedy overshadowing their best memories, at least four generations of young women were disconnected from the place and from each other as the decades passed.

Although a few small gatherings had occurred in the ten years prior to this one, the History Harvest in 2018—forty-one years after the camp closed—functioned as a long-overdue reunion. Many of the attendees had not seen or spoken to each other about the tragedy and its impact on their lives. Despite the camp's tragic ending, they gathered that day to celebrate the delightful and positive force Girl Scouting provided them.

The Camp Scott History Harvest and Songfest was one part of my ongoing multimedia collaboration with Michelle Hoffman, the goodwill

DOI: 10.34314/wingodigital.00006

ambassador for Girl Scouts' healing from "Camp Scott," now shorthand for
a very specific tragedy in Oklahoma. Hoffman and I met for the first time
in 2008. Both of us are lifelong Girl Scouts, active mostly in the 1970s and
1980s. While we did not know each other then (she was 15; I was 10), we were
both present at Camp Scott on the night of the murders. When Hoffman
was in her mid-forties, after years of personal work processing the impact the
trauma had on her life, she decided she wanted to help her Girl Scout sisters,
many of whom had fallen out of contact. She considers herself a facilitator for
those in the Girl Scout community who might want to talk about the impact
the tragedy had on their lives, such as the closing of the camp, the criminal
and subsequent civil trial, and especially the mental health issues and undi-
agnosed cases of PTSD among her Girl Scout sisters. She feels she "has a
responsibility to facilitate as much healing about the tragedy as possible."[12]
She has done this with great success. Hoffman not only rekindled old friendships and crossed painful emotional barriers between the victims' families and
Girl Scout staff and survivors, but also reconstituted a dispersed and broken
community of women, almost single-handedly. While she understands that
the silence in the Girl Scout council about the murders afterwards became
ingrained as a protective measure to preserve Girl Scouting—as well as their
understandable fear of sensationalist media attention—that history of keeping
silent was also a big part of the reason that it took more than a decade of
cajoling to assemble the women who loved Camp Scott into a private home
for singing, reminiscing, and documenting their *good* memories of camp.

Hoffman performed a role similar to Sue Purchase's role in the harm
reduction community; Hoffman was the community networker for the "I
Remember Camp Scott" History Harvest. She had previously hosted several
informal get-togethers, mostly centered around singing together, but due to
the increasing numbers of women on the private Facebook page, we hoped
this one would be the largest. We were not disappointed. More than thirty
women attended over the course of the afternoon. My undergraduate student
research assistants, Samantha Aamot and Sara Ludewig, helped set up the
digitization stations in a private home made available to us by a Girl Scout
and Camp Scott alumna. We used the office area to set up the scanners and

DOI: 10.34314/wingodigital.00006

Figure 5.8: Four Camp Scott alumna looking at an album together. Left to right: Michelle Hoffman, Linda Henderson, Annette Marquardt, and Janet Cairns.

laptops, the entryway for participants to display and share their artifacts, and a sunny spot for photographing objects. The family room served as the main gathering space and singing area, and the house soon filled with nonstop songs and laughter.

The preciousness of their camp memories was evident in the ways they had preserved them: scrapbooks, special boxes, photo albums, and tins packed with various mementos filled the entryway. It quickly became clear that we were going to have to hustle to get everything the Girl Scouts brought documented. At the end of the day, we counted more than 350 individual items from a dozen women. Fortunately, we had two librarians from Oklahoma State University helping the three of us that day, and a few other volunteers jumped in when we realized we might not get to everything.

We had hoped for group interviews in the same kind of format that happened easily at the harm reduction event, but the pull to sing camp songs together overrode our plan. At one point, we had to cajole them one by one

DOI: 10.34314/wingodigital.00006

Figure 5.9: Student research assistant Samantha Aamot taking pictures of artifacts at the "I Remember Camp Scott" History Harvest in Broken Arrow, OK, March 2017.

to come describe their artifacts and photos for the digitization process. Being flexible and nimble with our plan and time constraints versus the personality of the group (think: herding singing cats) turned out to be an asset for us, though we did leave with a pile of papers and objects to digitize at a later date. Again, Aamot and Ludewig had to simultaneously practice patience and empathy while also efficiently documenting, listening, and organizing. The collections were rich indeed, and worth the scramble to collect them all.

Joni Kinsey, an art history professor from Iowa, brought ashes from a campfire that she had held on to, despite their degradation with the piece of foil they had been wrapped in (*Figure 5.1*). An Oklahoma Girl Scout tradition

DOI: 10.34314/wingodigital.00006

Figure 5.10: As participants entered the house, they put their special artifacts on tables in the entryway.

was that on the last night of a camp session ashes would be collected and saved until the next time Girl Scouts gathered around a campfire. These ashes represented the ongoing continuity of Girl Scout friendships over time, symbolized by putting the old ashes into the next one. Kinsey attended Camp Scott for eight summers and for the first four wrote in a handmade diary about her time at camp. She later transcribed the diaries into a Word document and brought both the diaries and the transcript along. Besides the punctual reporting of young Joni, reading about these two consecutive days at camp reveals so much about the history and culture of Camp Scott:

> **Mon., June 15, 1970**
> Woke up at 6:45. Breakfast and kapers. Rested until after lunch (after swimming). Lunch. Rest period. Got no letters. After rest period we hiked to Sycamore Valley. We canoed and cooked Cowboy Stew and French bread. Delicious! Hiked back and stopped at the graveyard. Read some of the tombstones. Carolyn is very mean. Bed.

DOI: 10.34314/wingodigital.00006

Tues., June 16, 1970

Woke up at 6:30 because Arapaho gave us a surprise breakfast. Good but not filling. Kapers. All Camp Kapers. We swept the craft hut. I have heat rash all over my back. Lunch. Rest period. We had an extra long rest because we are going on a bird hike with Smitty tomorrow morning. We did archery. I hit the target! Wupper. We had a Chocolate Dip, alone. Told ghost stories and had Somemores [sic].

Figure 5.11: Joni Kinsey's handbound Camp Scott diaries, 1969–1972.

Linda Henderson, a social worker from Oregon, brought a generous collection of personal artifacts to share. She also brought along her teenage daughter, a Girl Scout herself, who jumped in and helped us scan photographs. After they returned home, Henderson shared what the event meant to her after decades of very limited contact with her Girl Scout sisters.

> It felt like no time had gone by and that the feelings of love and friendship were just as strong. These friends understand what wonderful experiences we shared for years. They also understand the great loss, pain, and trauma of the tragedy whose force separated and isolated us. I felt satisfied in a way I have not felt since the tragedy. It was so healing to feel the strong connections of our bonds and our love of our shared positive and happy experiences.

DOI: 10.34314/wingodigital.00006

I loved that we shared items and memories that documented our community before the tragedy. I loved our community beforehand. It was like we reclaimed the happiness and hope we knew. I like remembering what a wonderful community and place we shared and how positive it was for young girls, for my friends, for me. It was amazing to touch and see items that we all understood, that brought back such loving, fun, and happy memories. Pictures, letters, clothing, songbooks, notebooks brought back wonderful memories. I like knowing that not only did we remind ourselves together, but the collection will be open and preserved for the public.

And just to be together again. It's hard to convey how the tragedy created such isolation and pain and how healing it is to be together again.[13]

Figure 5.12: Linda Henderson brought nearly seventy artifacts to the History Harvest. This is one page of her CIT notebook, made by her when she was a Counselor-In-Training at Camp Scott in the mid-1970s. The book has many sections on various camp tasks, first aid, botany, recipes, and arts and crafts projects. This page is of the knots section and is meticulously drawn.

Jeanne Barrett was another participant who had a lifelong connection to Camp Scott. She had been a camper, a counselor-in-training, a camp counselor, a Girl Scout leader, and an assistant camp director from 1968–1976.

DOI: 10.34314/wingodigital.00006

She was deeply dedicated to Girl Scouting, as her sentiments about the event conveyed:

> It is a challenge to express the depths of my soul that were touched by this gathering. This was a harvest, a human harvest of rich friendships, memories, the melding of voices in song, and the shared appreciation for a place loved—more than loved—a place and an experience that is a part of our DNA. The many formative years I spent in scouting were blessed with Camp Scott's natural beauty and guided by the lofty goals of those in leadership positions that came before me to teach responsibility ("ability to respond"). We have learned so much together, accomplished so much together, and grieved over the loss of shared loved ones over the years.
>
> A sense of our strength and connection as a community was evident after all these years in this example: during certain songs, conversations came to a halt, and all of us spontaneously joined in the song, in the shared voice. Then as quickly as conversations paused, they began again at the end of the song.
>
> Digitizing the breadth of activities and the goals for the campers allows Camp Scott to be represented by its loved ones—not the media. It allows the beauty of the experience to live on, though the property itself has and continues to return to nature. It gives us the opportunity to share this rich experience with the future.[14]

Barrett voicing the importance of the camp being represented by "its loved ones—not the media" put the whole History Harvest effort into one poignant phrase for me. The camp itself was a geographic victim of the murders that has yet to be memorialized. This digital archive project may well be the only way it can be remembered by the Girl Scouts who loved it and by others interested in the history of Girl Scouts at Camp Scott. Over several years, under Hoffman's leadership, interactions on the private Facebook page drew this group of women together and made the development of their virtual collection possible. The process of sharing their artifacts with each other and a few strangers was cathartic; they spoke of their childhood and teen camp experiences, reconnected joy to the place they lost, and sang their hearts out. Their gratitude to us for organizing the event and creating the archive was constant throughout the day and into the evening hour when we wrapped up

DOI: 10.34314/wingodigital.00006

Figure 5.13: Jeanne Barrett, seen here as a teenaged Girl Scout, at a fall camping trip with her troop, mid-late 1960s.

and went out to dinner. Again, as with the harm reduction community, my students were incredibly moved by the stories and the participants' affable generosity with us.

The digital archive, *I Remember Camp Scott*, is hosted by the Oklahoma State University Library in Stillwater, Oklahoma. The archive is currently being created by Sara Ludewig, now a graduate student in history and library science at the University of Maryland. We hope that the archive will reestablish the nurturing, empowering, and positive history of the camp before the tragedy and reconnect a community of women and girls estranged by a

DOI: 10.34314/wingodigital.00006

trauma and decades of silence. Before going their separate ways that evening, the remaining group of about ten women stood in a circle and sang the three songs that ended each day at camp. They left that event with their connections to each other revived and redeemed.

A DiCE Pedagogy of Emotions

The History Harvest model is an effective tool for engaging students in the process of history research, interviews, and archive creation. The entire process might be the closest that history teaching comes to having a "lab" environment for students. Learning how to use digital technology tools seems imperative for any job students pursue in the future. Because my two former students had some classroom experience with the History Harvest, which was followed by work on the Minnesota Opioid Project, they were quickly able to bridge skills from their undergraduate years with scholarly work just after graduation—an opportunity that connected them with local history beyond the classroom, with living people, and outside of the archives.

While my eyes were still somewhat fresh to the History Harvest experience, their eyes were fresh to the entire process of history-making, oral history, and artifact gathering. As a result of these experiences, they learned first-hand that history can be a collective process, one that empowers communities to document their own place in historical moments. I also delighted in reading Aamot's reflection on History Harvests in which she referred to herself as a historian. I have a hunch that being involved in digital community engagement projects sped up the process of claiming her vocation. She also described how it made history-making an active experience:

> One of the things the History Harvest model uniquely presents a historian with is the opportunity to interact with individuals who relate their lived experience in their own words as you assist in the recording and digitizing process. It allowed me to actively practice empathy as a historian. While in the past I had participated in this passively by engaging with text, I now understood it actively through interacting with people.[15]

DOI: 10.34314/wingodigital.00006

Figure 5.14: Sara Ludewig, center, conducting a group interview and looking at artifacts participants brought to the Harm Reduction History Harvest in Minneapolis, May 2017. Left to right: Deb Holman, Sara Ludewig, Mary Morris, and Gayle Thomas.

Not only that, Aamot realized and articulated the profoundly different experiences involved when doing archival research and oral history in community-based projects. Her comment that she learned "how to practice empathy as a historian," suggests that emotional intelligence was yet another aspect of the History Harvest model that could be highlighted and explored. How much empathy should a historian have, and under what circumstances is it best employed? Although empathy is central to my own scholarly pursuits in history and teaching, I had not imagined it was possible to "teach" empathy as part of history research until Aamot shared this.

The other student, Sara Ludewig, participated in three History Harvests. Ludewig articulated the immediate rewards of interacting with community members and the power of collecting artifacts and stories based on what the participants deemed important.

> The History Harvests I have worked on changed my perspective on how historians experience and archive the past. I got to be an active participant in the preservation of history by listening to people's experiences and

DOI: 10.34314/wingodigital.00006

> documenting the artifacts they wanted to represent them. There's some-
> thing really striking and tangible about hearing the story behind an artifact
> directly from the person whose life it impacted.[16]

In an increasingly siloed and polarized world, her surprise at the way these
two communities opened themselves to our projects makes an even stronger
case for how a History Harvest can bridge all kinds of communities. Ludewig
concluded, "I was also amazed by how readily and warmly each community
welcomed our engagement with their history."[17] In this context, documenting
people's stories and objects with their participation is a kind of intellectual
service work for the past, the present, and the future.

The impact that digital community engagement projects have on the
next generation of historians and humanities scholars has a lot to do with
how faculty mentors model best practices with the communities we research.
By empowering students to be sensitive, responsive co-creators in the event
preparation and final archive creation, they have the opportunity to stretch
themselves, to engage more fully with the often complicated and emotional
process of making meaning from stories and artifacts that might not fit into a
more well-known or well-documented history. The act of listening to a person's
story while interacting with tangible pieces of their lives and memories profoundly deepens students' connections to history, place, and community.

The success of History Harvest projects like these also depends on the
ability of all parties involved—history practitioners, archivists, and participants—to foster and maintain trust throughout the process. Does the community remember the event with sentimental regard? Do they respect and
admire the way the event unfolded and how it looks in its final digital form?
In these two cases, they did. The events themselves engendered feelings of
fondness and pride, and the resulting archive, if successful, should do the
same. While it may seem scary or even awkward to consider approaching
communities that may appear fragile, marginalized, and invisible, everyone
learned something valuable during these two events. The participants were
seen and heard. Students felt a larger sense of purpose and meaning through
their contribution to the project. By the way they conducted themselves, with
kindness and genuine interest, they learned how to make a technical and

DOI: 10.34314/wingodigital.00006

rather boring digital process into something meaningful for the participants. Although shared histories of trauma, isolation, and geographic disruption were common to these two community engagement projects, we observed that what people shared at the events did not focus solely on upsetting, disruptive, or alienating times in their lives. The overriding emotion in the collective sharing of artifacts, stories, and comradery? Joy.

Notes

1. See Chapter 3, and Wingo and Sullivan, "Remembering Rondo: An Inside View of the History Harvest," *Perspectives* (March 1, 2017).
2. Mark Cave and Stephen M. Sloan, *Listening on the Edge: Oral History in the Aftermath of Crisis* (New York: Oxford University Press, 2014).
3. I am currently writing a chapter about the history of Women with a Point in my forthcoming monograph about the history of the opioid crisis in Minnesota. *When 'Rock Bottom' is Death: Reckoning with Opioids in the Rehab State* is under contract with the University of Minnesota Press (Fall 2021).
4. Don C. Des Jarlais, "Harm Reduction in the USA: The Research Perspective and an Archive to David Purchase," *Harm Reduction Journal* (2017): 14-51.
5. Sullivan, *When 'Rock Bottom' is Death: Reckoning with Opioids in the Rehab State* (University of Minnesota Press, forthcoming, 2021).
6. For more on the Minnesota Model, see William L. White, *Slaying the Dragon: The History of Addiction Treatment and Recovery in America* (Bloomington: Chestnut Health Systems, 2014), 261–278.
7. Julie Hooker, "Interview with Sue Purchase." *Women with A Point & AccessWorks*, accessed May 6, 2018. http://amycsullivan.net/wap/items/show/87.
8. Susan Phillips and Sarah Gordon, "Interview with Sarah Gordon and Susan Phillips," *Women with A Point & AccessWorks*, accessed May 6, 2018. http://amyc sullivan.net/wap/items/show/86.
9. Stephanie Devich, correspondence with Amy Sullivan, May 7, 2018.
10. Sue Purchase, correspondence with Amy Sullivan, May 6, 2018.
11. Amy C. Sullivan, "What Fear Is Like: The Legacy of Trauma, Safety and Security After the 1977 Girl Scout Murders" (PhD diss., University of Illinois at Chicago, 2013).
12. Michelle Hoffman, email correspondence with Amy Sullivan, May 2, 2018.
13. Linda Henderson, email correspondence with Amy Sullivan, May 2018.
14. Jeanne Barrett, email correspondence with Amy Sullivan, May 2018.
15. Samantha Aamot, email correspondence with Amy Sullivan, May 2018.
16. Sara Ludewig, email correspondence with Amy Sullivan, May 2018.
17. Ibid.

DOI: 10.34314/wingodigital.00006

Works Cited

Wingo, Rebecca S. and Amy C. Sullivan. "Remembering Rondo: An Inside View of the History Harvest." *Perspectives* (March 1, 2017).

Cave, Mark and Stephen M. Sloan. *Listening on the Edge: Oral History in the Aftermath of Crisis.* New York: Oxford University Press, 2014.

Des Jarlais, Don C. "Harm Reduction in the USA: The Research Perspective and an Archive to David Purchase." *Harm Reduction Journal* (2017): 14-51.

Sullivan, Amy. *When 'Rock Bottom' Means Death.* University of Minnesota Press, forthcoming, 2020.

White, William L. *Slaying the Dragon: The History of Addiction Treatment and Recovery in America.* Bloomington: Chestnut Health Systems, 2014.

DOI: 10.34314/wingodigital.00006

6

Everyday Life in Middletown

The Archive as Community

Patrick Collier & James J. Connolly

Most human experience goes unrecorded and uncontemplated. Eating, commuting, daydreaming, internet-surfing, tooth-brushing, and the like constitute the largest portion of daily life, yet until recently these moments have attracted relatively little attention from scholars. Over the past twenty years, academic interest in the realm of the everyday intensified. Animated by questions about consciousness, power, and agency, scholars seek to understand the degree to which everyday life may constitute a realm of personal autonomy—in which we make our own decisions about what to eat, what to wear, or which route to take to work—or a sphere in which social imperatives and the determinations of race, class, and gender exercise their subtlest and most profound influence. The larger aim of such work is to document and explain the modes of perception, consciousness, and affect that characterize everyday life. It examines the dynamics of agency and conformity, self-determination and ideology, as they play out through mundane activities, within and against the structures and patterns evident in broader, more discernible cultural elements. If any consensus has emerged from this work, it lies in the sense that the everyday is the arena in which social, economic, and ideological forces collide with, shape, and meet resistance from the idiosyncratic and unruly energies of the individual's body, psyche, and bank of experience. Everyday routines, Rita Felski writes, "are neither unmediated expressions of biological drives nor mere reflexes of capitalist domination but a much more complex blend of the social and the psychic."[1]

DOI: 10.34314/wingodigital.00007

The goals of the *Everyday Life in Middletown* project (*EDLM*) derive from this body of scholarship. Since 2016, the *EDLM* team has collected, shared, and analyzed day diaries and other commentary from residents of a small Midwestern American city. Our core aim is to capture the moods, emotions, and ordinary doings that escape the attention of social scientists looking at broad trends or journalists who train their sights on major political and cultural events. Unless recorded, these experiences will be inaccessible to future historians; part of the project's purpose is to establish an archive of the everyday. But *EDLM* also serves a more immediate civic end: to make visible and comprehensible the complexities of human experience that are obscured when we focus on the latest partisan disputes or the distractions of mass culture. The various forms of resistance, accommodation, coping, and subversion that ordinary people employ, even if different in their particulars, constitute a common ground worthy of exploration.

EDLM is fundamentally a collaboration between scholars and community members in which both benefit. Its archive is accessible on an open-access website [*Figure 6.1*] and attached to a blog, where diarists and other community members are invited to engage with and comment on the diaries. The project thus constitutes a collaborative community writing project that emerges in dialogue among the diarists and us, the project creators. We identify shared "diary days" and prompt the volunteers to "record what you do, and what you are thinking and feeling as you do it." Documenting the shared set of experiences that emerge, and creating a space for reflecting upon them, offers a modest antidote to the fevered, technology-fueled polarization of the present day.

By focusing this archival experiment in a single city, *EDLM* resists the delocalization and abstraction of community that the explosion of online communication and media consumption has created. "Middletown" refers to Muncie, Indiana. It is the name that Robert and Helen Lynd gave to this small eastern Indiana city they first made famous in *Middletown: A Study in American Culture* (1929), their seminal ethnographic account of American urban life during the 1920s.[2] Their careful attention to the rhythms and details of domestic experience, work, and leisure prefigured the more recent

DOI: 10.34314/wingodigital.00007

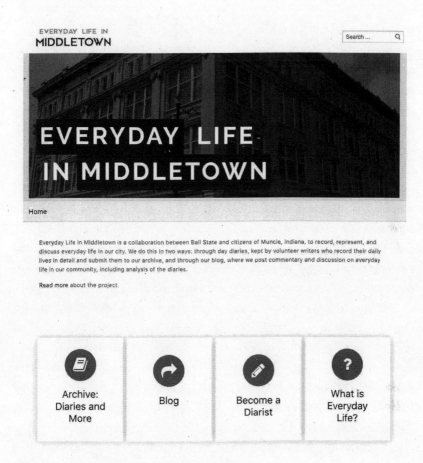

Figure 6.1: Homepage for *Everyday Life in Middletown.*

scholarly interest in everyday life. *Middletown,* the first of the Lynds' two Muncie-based projects, remains a classic social science investigation and has inspired an abundance of follow-up research and reporting on Muncie. Most recently, such work has focused on the city's transition to a post-industrial community divided by class, race, and politics. *EDLM* represents an attempt to continue but also reinvent the tradition of "Middletown Studies."

To sustain our vision of the archive as a collaborative expression of the community, we use digital tools and formats that empower our volunteers and readers to shape the project. Ideally *EDLM* will become a popular online

DOI: 10.34314/wingodigital.00007

destination where participants encounter both the commonalities that unite them and the challenges their neighbors face, and where they take a role in shaping the project's scholarly output. The interactive features of online communication—blogging, comment sections, tagging, and visualization tools—help make this possible. This orientation revises the traditional lens of Middletown Studies, which has customarily adopted a detached, anthropological gaze. The knowledge created by *EDLM* is generated by citizens in dialogue with scholars and each other.

Creating a publicly accessible platform in which people share personal experiences generates challenges involving accessibility, privacy, and legal liability. In what follows, we explain the project's conceptual foundation, describe the digital tools and methods it employs, document the creativity it fosters among participants, and review how we have addressed the problems that have arisen through the early stages of this developing project, which resides at the intersection of community engagement and digital scholarship.

Origins of the Project

Everyday Life in Middletown evolved from a 2016 undergraduate seminar at the Virginia B. Ball Center for Creative Inquiry. Fifteen students, led by professor and *EDLM* founder Patrick Collier, collected day-diaries and assembled them into an archival and scholarly website and made the documentary film *Everyday Melodies*. These initial diaries are now part of the *EDLM* archive. In a second phase, the Center for Middletown Studies and Ball State's Digital Scholarship Lab jointly supported the ongoing collection of day diaries, the development of a more robust web archive, the creation of a prototype of visualization tools that permit users to query the assembled texts, and the production of a forthcoming podcast. The *EDLM* project staff have now collected more than 200 day diaries and responses to directives (questionnaires) written by more than 50 volunteers. The project's long-term goal is to export this model to other communities, creating a network of open-access sites for the documentation and exploration of everyday life in the contemporary United States, with particular emphasis on distinct regional conditions.

DOI: 10.34314/wingodigital.00007

The questions about everyday life that inform *EDLM* arose as a major theme among intellectuals at the end of the nineteenth century and have only reemerged in recent decades. They emerged from a sense that modernity—that historical complex of industrialization, urbanization, technological change, rising literacy and its effects on media and cultural production, and movements towards greater democracy and self-governance—had radically transformed daily existence. Prompted by the midcentury work of Henri LeFebvre and Michel de Certeau, more recent scholarship has produced a widening body of research and theory about the ordinary. It examines the formation and circulation of moods, the nature of affective states, the avenues through which agency and possible futures appear or are foreclosed, and the "tactics" (to borrow a term from de Certeau) that people employ to cope with and resist prevailing social and cultural regimes.[3] As this plethora of scholarship suggests, the study of everyday life has found new energy in our own era of economic, political, and media disruption, as it did amid the political upsets of the early twentieth century.[4]

The British Mass Observation project, itself a collaborative experiment in theorizing and mapping the everyday, is the principal model for *EDLM*. Launched in 1936 by a small group of recent Cambridge graduates, Mass Observation responded to a perceived crisis of public discourse, the most extreme manifestation of which was fascism. The group launched an "anthropology of ourselves"—a determined tuning-in to everyday life in the hope that an alternative collective consciousness could be forged from its materials. They recruited thousands of British citizens to compile day diaries and respond to surveys about everyday life while also enlisting a corps of "mass observers" who took notes on such cultural events as "all-in" wrestling matches and nights in pubs. They published a half-dozen books and assembled a massive archive (now digitized and available via subscription) covering the 1930s and 1940s.[5] After a mid-century hiatus, Mass Observation re-launched in the early 1980s at the University of Sussex and continues to gather "directives" focusing on everyday life from a national panel of 500 ordinary citizens.

DOI: 10.34314/wingodigital.00007

The archive as community engagement

Like Mass Observation, the *EDLM* archive makes the ordinary available to exploration. Its assembled diaries, as well as a scattering of photographs and drawings and sets of responses to directives (short questionnaires), offer insights into core concerns of everyday life scholarship, including moods, the large and small anxieties that define daily life, and the self-help, future-oriented outlook that seems so pervasive in contemporary culture.[6] Other themes that have emerged organically in the diaries include people's relationships with their pets, interactions with and attitudes toward media, foodways (including frequent doses of guilt about overeating and fast-food consumption), and caregiving. The emerging picture of shared everyday concerns among largely disconnected neighbors thus begins to sketch out a portrait of ordinary life in Muncie at this historical moment.

The project's emphasis on community collaboration takes it beyond conventional ethnography or opinion polling. Diary writing spurs creativity, activated through attentiveness to everyday life. Having volunteers write for our blog, in addition to submitting diaries, gives them a voice in the analysis of the primary materials they generate. We also gather input on the project's form and direction through frequent email correspondence and periodic focus groups with volunteers. Thus our writers' primary creativity, as embodied in the diaries, also fuels meta-creative acts of two kinds. The first is reflection upon the diaries and the project via dialogue between us, the project creators, and the volunteers, which we discuss below. The second is the literary-critical work of reading the diaries as creative and social texts, performed in blog posts on the archival website and—more rigorously—in scholarly writing.

Seeking this dialogue with contributors and framing the archive as a collaborative artwork breaches the subject/object divide that vexes social science and which must be transcended if the study of the everyday is not to become yet another field in which experts issue generalizations about the objectified lives of others. Otherwise, as Felski argues, "everyday life" threatens to become a term "deployed by intellectuals to describe a non-intellectual relationship to the world." Whether thus posited as an "inauthentic, gray,

DOI: 10.34314/wingodigital.00007

intellectually impoverished" sphere or, more generously, as a utopian "area of authentic experience"—the everyday can be reduced to a distant, even exotic realm where academics do fieldwork, like the early anthropologists.[7] For these reasons we enlist the diarists to help shape policies and develop initiatives. As important, everyone on the *Everyday Life in Middletown* staff—we as co-directors, as well as graduate or undergraduate assistants—contribute diaries on every submission date. The project thus does not treat the volunteers as "subjects" or everyday life as a stable object of study. At its core the project is a collaborative writing of the everyday, seeking to create connection and commonality, at the primary level of the diaries themselves and the secondary level of commentary.

This collaborative ethic requires thorough and wide-ranging engagement with the community. The project does not have a single institutional partner but numerous partners with varying stakes in it. Our primary stakeholders, of course, are the fifty-four local volunteers who share their thoughts and feelings. Although their diaries are posted anonymously, with identifying and sensitive information removed, there is still some risk in conveying their experiences in this manner. We have also joined with a range of groups and institutions to share our project and invite feedback. We have done public talks for local groups ranging from a poverty alleviation agency to civic clubs. We have purposefully staged events in the city's poorest neighborhoods in the hope of attracting the interest of a wide cross-section of the city. Most recently, we have entered into an arrangement with the Muncie Public Library to hold diary-writing sessions at its various branches. All of these events allow us to share our early insights, get feedback, and recruit new diarists. We have also set up recruiting tables at local coffee shops, stores, and the annual county fair. Each year, we hold a focus group with diarists and website users to get input about how to engage them more fully, and to discuss new directions.

Digital Aspects

While such face-to-face engagement is essential, digital tools and methods are vital to broadening *EDLM* participation and making it truly public. On the

DOI: 10.34314/wingodigital.00007

most basic level, the project is an open-source web publication. The diaries
are published within weeks of their submission, creating relatively immediate
and friction-free engagement. An original stimulus for Mass Observation,
the project that most closely resembles *EDLM*, was the impulse to turn the
anthropological gaze inward, toward "ourselves." It aimed to give voice to
its volunteer participants, ordinary people who rarely drew the attention of
journalists and historians. But its analog methods required that for the most
part those voices were filtered through the interpretive lens of the project's
leaders in reports and essays.[8] *EDLM*'s digital character creates opportunities
for community dialogue around everyday life experiences that a paper-and-
print archive cannot provide.

Another advantage of the project's digital nature is the capacity it provides
to accept and share volunteer contributions in various formats. Most of our
submissions have been written diaries submitted via email, but we have also
received photographs and drawings. We plan to use this affordance to greater
advantage as we broaden the diversity of our volunteer writers. Diary writing
is mainly a practice of educated, middle-and upper-class people, which has
limited the diversity of the *EDLM* cohort. The archive's digital nature, though,
would allow us to solicit and share audio and video submissions from those
disinclined to write. This ability also presents a partial solution to the digital
divide between well-to-do and poorer citizens—a problem any digital project
focused on community engagement must take into account. A significant
portion of Muncie's population is impoverished. While a growing number of
poor Americans have a smartphone and home access to the internet, the class-
based technology gap remains substantial.[9] *EDLM*'s digital character ensures
that anyone with access to a relatively inexpensive smartphone can participate. Older residents less comfortable with new technologies are invited to
submit handwritten diaries, which a project staffer collects in person. And, as
noted above, we have recently partnered with the Muncie Public Library—a
key point of access to digital resources for poor residents—to plan a series of
diary-writing events at their branches—another step to ensure that technological barriers do not inhibit participation.[10]

DOI: 10.34314/wingodigital.00007

As the archive grows and evolves, the capacity of individuals to simply read and absorb its many and varied elements diminishes. As a result, it is important that the website offer some initial interpretation to emphasize the project's values and aims, and also provide alternative routes through the assembled material. The project blog serves this purpose, as the project's public face. Blog posts make initial, provisional sense of the copious detail contained in the diaries, but the blog is also a forum for discussion. *EDLM* founder Collier has to date written most of the blog posts, identifying themes, quoting from and linking to some of the most interesting submissions (and thereby creating pathways into the archive), and engaging, in layman's terms, with the theoretical concepts that undergird everyday-life studies. We have also published featured diaries in their entirety, with short, interpretive introductions. Further, diarists are invited to contribute blog posts, and we are recruiting others in the community who have expressed interest and support for the project to write entries about their experience of reading the diaries. Ultimately we would like the blog to move in this multi-voiced direction, becoming the primary venue for discussion of everyday experience in our community and for input on the project. In this way, not only the assemblage of the archive but its interpretation are conceived as collaborative, community projects. And since the website provides immediate access to the primary data—the diaries—anyone can assess the evidence upon which blog posts or more formal scholarship about the project rests, yet another way in which *EDLM* resists the observer/observed dynamic of much academic work.

We hope the blog will generate interest, persuading readers of the value of everyday-life study and inviting them to engage with the archive in detail. But as the archive grows, it becomes unwieldy and potentially off-putting to users. This problem will only increase over time. In its founding period, Mass Observation struggled with the plenitude of data. A plan for four books based on participant observations in Bolton, known as "Worktown," yielded just one title as the organizers sagged under the sheer weight and diversity of the archive.[11] At *EDLM*, after five diary collections of about 200 diaries, simply noting and indexing themes by hand has begun to reach the point of diminishing returns. Tools for searching, identifying themes, and visualizing

DOI: 10.34314/wingodigital.00007

the language and sentiments of its documents will not only make the archive more navigable for scholars but, we hope, will empower nonacademic users to develop their own interpretations.

To deal with the plenitude of data, we have developed a suite of tools that users can employ to identify themes, issues, or patterns evident in diaries. The simplest is a basic Boolean search tool that permits users to locate diaries and blog posts with specific words or word combinations. A tagging system indexes specific themes and topics covered in the diaries, directive responses, and blog posts, enabling users to engage quickly with material relevant to issues such as caregiving, dreams, or religion (*Figure 6.2*). More ambitiously, we have begun to develop a suite of text analysis tools to create new ways of conceiving the archive. Using RStudio, a development environment for the R statistical analysis package, a project staff member produced a prototype that permits text analysis and visualization, including word count, n-grams, and sentiment analysis (*Figure 6.3*). The prototype incorporates diary text from three of the appointed days (November 14, 2017, February 4, 2018, and April 27, 2018). Visualizations can be organized according to gender, date, and, potentially, other metadata elements we collect when diarists volunteer for the project.

Figure 6.2: Image of tags list for *Everyday Life in Middletown*, with the number of times each tag is used.

DOI: 10.34314/wingodigital.00007

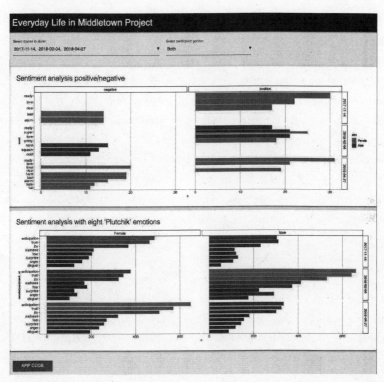

Figure 6.3: Graphs of sentiment analysis using *EDLM*'s text analysis tool, with both positive/negative and Plutchik emotions scales. Results are separated by male and female.

This trial version will form the template for a more sophisticated, flexible set of visualizations that can help discern patterns within the archive. As the archive grows and the percentage of it that can be reasonably read diminishes, such tools will spur users to more focused reading and sampling.

Creativity

All of these developing, provisional means of engagement with the archive are consonant with our vision of the project as a collaborative, creative endeavor. We offer not a social science database but something more like a participatory public art project. Creativity is the hallmark of the project thus far:

DOI: 10.34314/wingodigital.00007

volunteers have made free use of the latitude offered in our broad, standard diary prompt, "Tell us what you do, and what you are feeling and thinking while you do it." Participants have made the project their own. The diaries are shot through with inspiration, humor, satire, and formal experimentation. Submissions have included long, poetic diaries, illustrations, and imagined dialogues with future readers. And the project has begun to foster dialogue among community members. One particularly creative diarist submitted a blog post riffing on another volunteer's diary; we offered the original diarist the opportunity to respond, which she embraced. The aim is a playful and artistic *pas de deux* in which the writers sample, riff on, and "re-mix" each other's diaries. In the following section, we offer a sampling of ways in which the project has sparked creativity, insight, and attentiveness in our writers.

Speaking to the future

The significance of the ordinary is not self-evident to nonacademics, nor even to academics unfamiliar with everyday-life studies. But the idea of creating a record of today's world for future scholars is easy to grasp. In various ways, diarists have framed their contributions as addresses to a potential future reader. One writer, narrating a visit to his children's day care to pay the monthly bill, frames the substantial cost as a political issue and expresses hope for change. "I can only hope that by the time you're reading this we've arrived at a place socially where a different system of preschool and after school care has been determined." Another writer takes a more satirical view in his darkly funny, formally creative writing. In his diaries, the main body is a largely neutral, concise account of daily activities; but he appends footnotes that situate the day's events in historical and political context for an imagined future reader. There he registers sharp, often funny protests about inequality, political inertia on climate change, the media-saturated landscape, and more. "I hope that from your future socialist paradise you can look upon our patriarchal capitalist dystopia with compassion," he writes, discussing the strange looks he gets when he describes himself as a house-husband to his academic wife. He chaffs our reflexive belief in progress in a footnote remarking on his

DOI: 10.34314/wingodigital.00007

head cold: "A 'cold,' or rhinovirus, is a viral infection that I trust no longer exists in your brave future, as it was no longer supposed to exist in ours 50 years ago." Turning more serious, the writer, having complained about the sticky, humid September weather in the main text, adds in a footnote: "I can hear you laughing bitterly as you read my complaints about the heat, but the effects of climate change are in the early stages of manifesting themselves, and those of us who can still remember cool autumn days miss them dearly . . . . If you're there, reading this, you know what happens next. I wish I had greater faith in your existence."

Life-writing

As a long-established writing genre, the diary carries strong associations of self-reflection and stock-taking. As Philippe Lejeune has written, "The diary offers a space and time protected from the pressures of life. You take refuge in its calm to 'develop' the image of what you have just lived through and to meditate upon it, to examine the choices to be made."[12] For many *EDLM* diarists, recording the day evokes a desire to place it in context of a larger life narrative. One of our most prolific and creative diarists frequently reflects on his coming-out as a gay man, his divorce, the repressive setting in which he was raised, and the lingering fear of harm and repression, made acute by today's political climate. "Yet, as a gay man, I have spent much of my life trying to evade, elude capture, detection, have learned to keep a low profile, fly under the radar, be a people pleaser," he writes on Nov. 14, 2017.

Here details of ordinary life provide occasions for reflection and threads in a fuller embroidering of Diarist A29's life story. Diarist A29 is, moreover, the most striking example of someone who has made the diary project his own. He works by recording spoken notes during the day, then spends, often, several weeks fashioning these into formally inventive diaries of up to twenty-five single-spaced pages, with prose interspersed with photos, subheadings, quotations from song lyrics, and more. While his commitment is uncommon, many writers, more modestly, use the day diary to relate the present to the past and the future. Planning a move to his southern home state, a diarist

DOI: 10.34314/wingodigital.00007

frets that he may have missed his chance by coming to Muncie for school and
his first job. "Granted I don't regret any of my decisions thus far, but there
is a price to be paid for them," he writes. Another writer, attending winter
commencement at Ball State, notes that these ceremonies predictably trigger
memories of her first marriage, bookended by her undergraduate and Ph.D.
graduations. As this cyclical memory recurs, she notes the gradual change in
its emotional weight. "I felt like my graduation day from Ph.D. school was a
defining moment in knowing I was done with the marriage and feeling the
confidence to make that choice. These thoughts are more neutral than they
used to be."

Creative noticing and play

In conversations with us, volunteers have noted that the practice of keeping
a day diary causes them to tune in acutely to everyday activities. One writer
recorded this phenomenon on Feb. 4, 2018: listening to his iPod on shuffle
while doing dishes, he lists the songs and the thoughts they spur, then observes:
"I recognize around this point that the diary is making me notice more details
than usual." The diaries not only promote this assertive noticing but record
it for posterity—another benefit our writers have observed. In our last focus
group meeting, a volunteer remarked that the *EDLM* project has "given us a
gift. We wouldn't have these records of our days" otherwise; he envisioned
looking back on them and sharing them with his children years hence.

Channeling this assertive noticing into diary form has spurred creative
play. On Feb. 4, 2018—the first diary day of the project's current phase—
Diarist A29 presented two diaries: one in 10,250 words, and one in 16 words:
"Sing. Dream. Wake. Play. Die. Fuch. Stuff. See. Eat. Write. Hear. Read.
Watch. Tend. Sleep." These words become subject headings for the longer full
diary. Another writer experiments with a more fragmentary, condensed form.
This concise diary is arranged in isolated sentences, centered on the page to
suggest a poem, some recounting events, some thoughts, without paragraphs
or transitions. The fragments compress the feel of the day, and many details,
into a short 420 words. Rather than presenting the day as a continuous narrative it crystallizes it into discrete events, thoughts, and feelings:

DOI: 10.34314/wingodigital.00007

"The children in my house need to make better choices."

"Just because you didn't cause the problem doesn't mean you can't do some-thing to fix it."

"Starting a non-profit is running a business, so are you ready for taxes, accounting, employees, grant writing? No."

"I have to think about the 19th century, Walt Whitman awaits."

"Brain-dead, overtired, I feel a need for food that borders on survival-level urgency."

Diary as therapy

Such creative diary-keeping activates both the expressive and the reflective elements of the diary as a genre. Overlapping these functions is what might be called the therapeutic function, in which writers air and reflect on personal problems with significant emotional weight. While the public nature of the *EDLM* diaries might seem to discourage candor about intimate, emotional problems, other factors may in fact encourage it, including the anonymity of the diaries' publication and the openness that probably characterizes someone willing to participate in the project. It's tempting to speculate, as well, that the prospect of an audience beyond the self increases the sense of relief that expressing pain, loneliness, or grief in writing affords. Several writers shared feelings of sadness or depression around the holidays in diaries from December 15, 2018, including a grandmother who reported crying in a store at the sight of gifts that would be appropriate for estranged family members: "While walking to find soup, I think about all the missed holidays I've had with my granddaughters and how sad I am. I feel like I wear a mask most days." Another volunteer, in the most emotionally powerful set of diaries the project has collected, has voiced and processed her grief in the two years since her grown son died of a drug overdose, leaving her to care for his young son. The diaries constitute a version of what Lejeune calls a "crisis diary," and they record an array of fugitive emotional states: from depressed, over-whelmed, hopelessness . . .

DOI: 10.34314/wingodigital.00007

> I am awake and not altogether willing to do this project. . . . The enormity of
> the problems seem insurmountable. . . . Today I am tired. I'm sick and tired.

. . . to reverence, as she tunes into her grandson's expression of his grief:

> I was still looking at my phone, checking important stuff. He said, Gramma,
> I have a cold rock right here in my belly. It tells me that daddy is just nowhere.
> I got up and went over to the tub and leaned in to say "Will you tell me that
> again?" I wasn't sure that I was listening. He said it again. My mind went
> into a flurry like the snow this morning. I wanted to take a video so that I
> could remember it exactly as it was in this moment.

Such clear-eyed facing of painful facts sometimes resolves, later in the day, in
clarity and forward-looking re-commitment to her own happiness and health.
More than once, such regatherings reference the role of the diary itself in
bringing things into focus:[13]

> This has been a meaningful exercise for me today. I appreciate the notion of
> being mindful of every action that I take. I am pretty sure that my happiness
> is the direct result of my internal response and external reaction to circum-
> stance both past and present.

At its most ambitious, *Everyday Life in Middletown* strives to be a remedy to
social isolation and an alternative to the endless streams of online reading
and writing that express the worst impulses seeking expression in our political
moment. Thomas S. Davis has traced a similar drive towards "reconciliation" in the original Mass Observation, among the political upsets of the late
1930s and the onset of World War II.[14] If it is too utopian to view *Everyday
Life in Middletown* as a project of social reconciliation, or too early to claim
success, the diaries quoted in this section suggest that, at least on an individual level, the project is benefiting the citizens of Muncie, Indiana, who are
participating in it.

Challenges

The project faces a number of challenges, from the difficulty of reaching
its loftiest aims of community building to the banal complications of digital

DOI: 10.34314/wingodigital.00007

publishing. Building a website alone does not generate engagement, so we continue to devise online and in-person strategies to generate diary writing and to invite readers to the archive. Striking a balance between accessibility and long-term preservation has also been more complicated than expected and has informed our choice of web platforms. Most significant, there is a substantial editorial process involved in collecting and sharing this often-intimate material, one that involves both ethical issues and strategic choices about dissemination. These concerns occupy the largest share of our day-to-day work on the project.

We learned quickly that an "if-you-build-it-they-will-come" approach to the project's website was insufficient. Initial traffic was modest, drawing some local interest and user responses but not as much as desired. We went through several versions of the project site, drawing upon informal user feedback as well as a more formal user-experience review to make it simpler and more accessible. We employ social media, primarily Twitter and Facebook, to draw attention and drive traffic to the site, as well as to provide another portal through which the project's online audience can offer commentary and interpretation. These efforts have yielded some fruit according to analytics, but the work of attracting users to the site and making it easy and appealing to use remains a major focus.[15]

Tension between providing access and ensuring long-term preservation has also been an issue. During the focus group with our diarists, it became clear that our initial platform and content management system, Omeka, was not sufficiently inviting. Key elements, such as the blog and discussions of everyday-life theory, had to reside on another website, separate from the archive, which became unwieldy. More important, without substantial and (given our resources) costly customization we could not make the diaries easily readable on mobile screens. Even Omeka Everywhere, a mobile application, is designed in a manner that emphasized metadata over the diaries themselves. Our users told us they most wanted to be able to read the diaries easily on their phones and tablets and to bypass metadata. As a result we shifted to WordPress as the principal site for reading our diaries. It presented them clearly on mobile screens and facilitated the tagging and linking that we

DOI: 10.34314/wingodigital.00007

employ to cultivate interaction with the material. We continue to maintain the Omeka site, however, because it permits us to develop robust metadata that follows Dublin Core standards. This facilitates long-term preservation and access to the material by making it readily transferable to an archival repository. Academic researchers and designers may eventually find the more extensive metadata useful for deeper investigations or more complex visualizations of the material.

Perhaps the most time-consuming element of managing *EDLM* is its editorial process. Publishing material about our volunteers' private actions, thoughts, and emotions raises questions about privacy and legal liability. We therefore vet diaries carefully and flag potentially troublesome passages for review and possible excision. These might include exceptionally personal disclosures, material that reveals personal information about diarists' friends, family, or acquaintances, or potentially libelous criticisms. We often consult individual diarists for clarification or permission to include specific language or even whole sections of a diary. We sometimes suggest small revisions. No full names are used, only initials, and we remove other identifying information. Of course, all participants sign releases, and we emphasize that they must choose how much of their personal lives or thoughts they wish to reveal. Nevertheless we seek their okay for passages that may touch on sensitive topics or seem overly revealing.

Everyday Life in Middletown remains a work in progress. The archive is growing steadily, and we expect to continue collecting diaries for several more years. Over the longer term, we aim to expand *EDLM*'s geographic reach. We purposely zeroed in on a single community initially for both substantive and practical reasons. The most obvious was one of scale: exploring everyday life in a single place seemed less daunting than attempting a broader project. We also wanted to take advantage of Muncie's history and reputation as a site of social research. The degree to which communities like Muncie—a Midwestern Rust Belt city—became a focus of political discussion during the 2016 presidential campaigns also made a project centered here seem timely. Most significant was our sense that concentrating on one place made it more feasible to cultivate a genuine sense of commonality based on ordinary daily

DOI: 10.34314/wingodigital.00007

experiences, in an age when people seem increasingly prone to sort themselves into (largely online) political and cultural silos. As a next step we intend to export this model to other communities, arranging collaborations with libraries and educational institutions that will create digital commons for their cities and towns. These local initiatives will form a network of linked sites where the everyday is explored.

Digital tools and resources make such an expansion possible without sacrificing the collaborative approach that animates *EDLM*. Creating a linked set of online digital archives will facilitate sharing of data and methods while still keeping projects at a scale where participant input can be meaningful. More important, the lessons we have taken from building an online commons for sharing and exploring the everyday, especially around issues of access, collaboration, and privacy, will provide a model not only for similar endeavors in other communities, but for many kinds of scholarly projects in which community members create content.

Notes

1. Rita Felski, "The Invention of Everyday Life," *New Formations* 39 (1999): 21.
2. Robert S. Lynd and Helen Merrill Lynd, *Middletown: A Study in Modern American Culture*. New York: Harcourt, 1959 [1929].
3. On "tactics" see de Certeau, *The Practice of Everyday Life* 29-42. Key early-twentieth century texts include Walter Benjamin, "On Some Motifs in Baudelaire," in *Illuminations: Essays and Reflections,* ed. and introd. Hannah Arendt (New York: Schocken, 1968): 155-94; Georg Simmel, *On Individuality and Social Forms*, ed. D. Levine (Chicago: The University of Chicago Press, 1971).
4. Important examples of this work include Lauren Berlant, *Cruel Optimism* (Durham: Duke University Press, 201); Kathleen Stewart, *Ordinary Affects* (Durham: Duke University Press, 2007); Ben Highmore, *Ordinary Lives: Studies in the Everyday* (New York: Routledge, 2011) and *Cultural Feelings* (New York: Routledge, 2017).
5. Nick Hubble, *Mass Observation and Everyday Life: Culture, History, Theory* (New York and Houndmills: Palgrave Macmillan, 2006). The original Mass Observers were also inspired in part by the Lynds' *Middletown* volume.
6. See Berlant, *Cruel Optimism*.
7. Felski, "The Invention of the Everyday," 16.
8. Mass Observation tried to subvert such power relations by quoting heavily from primary documents and designing books with a surrealism-inspired, montage

DOI: 10.34314/wingodigital.00007

aesthetic. See Mass Observation, *May the Twelfth: Mass Observation Day Survey* (London: Faber and Faber, 2009, 1939).

9. Monica Anderson, "Digital Divide Persists Even as Lower-Income Americans Make Gains in Tech Adoption" (Pew Research Center, 2017).

10. "Public Libraries and Technology: From "Houses of Knowledge" to "Houses of Access" " (Pew Research Center, 2014).

11. On the unmanageability of the everyday as archive, and Mass Observation's particular challenges with it, see Ben Highmore, *Everyday Life and Cultural Theory: An Introduction* (New York: Routledge, 2002): 24, 96–105.

12. Philippe Lejeune, "How Do Diaries End?" *Biography* 24, no. 1 (2001): 99–113.

13. Lejeune, "How do Diaries End," 107.

14. Thomas. S. Davis, *The Extinct Scene: Late Modernism and Everyday Life* (New York: Columbia University Press, 2016), 27-67.

15. Our analytics measure the number of hits and time on site.

Works Cited

"Public Libraries and Technology: From 'Houses of Knowledge' to 'Houses of Access.'" Pew Research Center, 2014. Accessed June 1, 2019.

Anderson, Monica. "Digital Divide Persists Even as Lower-Income Americans Make Gains in Tech Adoption." Pew Research Center, 2017. Accessed June 1, 2019.

Davis, Thomas S. *The Extinct Scene: Late Modernism and Everyday Life*. New York: Columbia University Press, 2016.

de Certeau, Michel. *The Practice of Everyday Life*. Berkeley: University of California Press, 1984.

Felski, Rita. "The Invention of Everyday Life." *New Formations* 39 (1999): 15–31.

Highmore, Ben. *Everyday Life and Cultural Theory: An Introduction*. New York and London, Routledge: 2001.

Lejeune, Philippe. "How Do Diaries End?" *Biography* 24, no. 1 (2001): 99–113.

DOI: 10.34314/wingodigital.00007

7

Mobilizing Digital Stories

Collaborating to Educate and Engage
a Local Public in Realities of Homelessness

Allison Schuette, Megan Telligman, Liz Wuerffel

What happens when several nonprofit agencies invite university partners and a regional museum to educate the local public about homelessness? How does this collaboration put a digital story collection to work?

In 2015, four nonprofit agencies that work to end homelessness in Porter County, Indiana, approached the *Welcome Project* at Valparaiso University—a regional, first-person, digital story collection—about collaborating on what became known as the *Invisible Project*. The purpose of this project was to raise awareness of homelessness in the county and break down stigmas that people experiencing homelessness face.

On any given day in Porter County (population approximately 170,000 with a median household income of $64K); 160 individuals are homeless. Many in the region don't recognize their situation because these individuals, predominantly women and children, don't conform to traditional stereotypes of homelessness.

The *Invisible Project* aimed to depict those who experience homelessness as neighbors, fellow residents deserving of recognition and respect. Staff members from the Porter County Museum, professional photographers, as well as students and faculty in graphic design, collaborated with the *Welcome Project* and the nonprofit agencies to create a mobile exhibit that makes visible the reality of homelessness in Porter County through first-person stories, art, and infographics. Simultaneously, the audio and video stories collected by the *Welcome Project* were published online.

DOI: 10.34314/wingodigital.00008

By September 2017 the exhibit had visited eighteen sites and now resides permanently at one of the nonprofit agencies. The online stories have been viewed/listened to over 2,000 times, and several stories have aired on Lakeshore Public Radio, which broadcasts to the Chicagoland area and five counties in Northwest Indiana for a potential audience of more than two million listeners.

Background

"Roof Over Your Head"

> *I got to experience homelessness, I got to experience living on others'–I got to experience all that, so it gave me more respect for people who are out there homeless, that they're not in this alone.*[1] (See Appendix A for a full transcript.)

The way retired Housing Opportunities Chief Executive Officer Caroline Shook remembers it, Rachel Niemi, then executive director of Dayspring Women's Center, came to her with an idea.[2] Niemi, a licensed clinical psychologist, had been encouraging her clients to write down their stories, in part to help them process their experiences of homelessness, in part to encourage others who would come after them. What would happen if their stories were shared more widely? What if they were accompanied by portraits? Could some of the stigmas around homelessness, addiction, and mental illness be publicly challenged with these intimate glimpses into people's lives?

Shook liked the idea but found herself skeptical; she had an MBA, not an MFA. Even after Elizabeth Allen, Project Coordinator for the Porter County Coalition for Affordable Housing, organized a meeting in 2015 with Liz Wuerffel and Allison Schuette, Valparaiso University professors and co-directors of the *Welcome Project*, Shook says she "didn't get it." *Why would university faculty be interested? Where was this going to go?*

What Shook didn't know was that the *Welcome Project* had been developing a digital story collection practice poised to help these agencies realize their vision. For the previous five years, Wuerffel and Schuette had been working with students, faculty, and staff on campus, interviewing campus members

DOI: 10.34314/wingodigital.00008

about when they felt like they belonged and didn't belong and editing these hour-long interviews into short audio and video stories for their website. During this time, they also partnered with their colleague Elizabeth Lynn, founder of the Center for Civic Reflection, to apply the Center's facilitation practice to their stories (see Appendix B).[3] In classrooms, meetings, workshops, and presentations, participants were led into a deeper understanding of a particular storyteller's experience and further led to consider how we can live well together with and across our differences. The *Welcome Project's* model could be adapted to help the nonprofit agencies meet their goals of raising awareness and breaking down stigmas by depicting those who experience homelessness as neighbors, fellow residents deserving of recognition and respect.

Two and a half months later, the planning team had grown. Wuerffel had brought in colleagues Yeohyun Ahn from the communication department, who would dedicate a graphic design class to creating a poster series for the project, and Aimee Tomasek from the art department, who volunteered to photograph clients. Mignon Kennedy, director of Gabriel's Horn Homeless Shelter, had begun helping Niemi identify clients willing to share their stories. Megan Telligman, then coordinator of the Porter County Museum, had started working closely with Wuerffel and museum staff member Jacob Just to design and later build a mobile exhibit to house the stories, portraits, posters, and infographics.

That's when Shook said, "I got it."[4]

The Practice

"one kind of intervention is the intervention of listening."

—Anna Deavere Smith[5]

Typically, we frame our work on the *Welcome Project* as a practice in community engagement, but a research methodology that takes listening as its primary tool has evolved out of our work and undergirds it. This highly qualitative method involves three practices—interviewing, editing and facilitating—each of which employ different kinds of listening, each of which were

DOI: 10.34314/wingodigital.00008

valuable for the *Invisible Project*. (For a fuller discussion of our methodology, see Appendix C.)

Interviewing, with its focus on asking people what they've experienced and what they think about those experiences, *listens to learn and to establish trust*. Sometimes this requires breaking down the one-sided quality of the interview situation. Schuette, for example, often shared moments from her own life with the clients of the nonprofits to help them understand the source of her interest and to encourage them to see how they had the authority of their own experiences. This often generated confidence in the interviewees, who sometimes wondered what they had to share or what was of value in what they shared.

Editing, with its focus on revisiting the interview to sound out those stories that are important to the interviewee and to the mission, *listens to identify and interpret*. Because a single ninety-minute interview will produce several three-to five-minute stories, an editor's first job is to listen again. The ethics here are paramount. As we transcribed the interviews of those who had experienced homelessness, we sought to identify areas of concern for the inter-viewees. Obviously, this practice still requires interpretation, but listening for repetition and recurrence, or for the cadence by which a client demonstrated emotional investment, meant the editors could get closer to representing what the interviewees wanted others to know.

Facilitating, with its focus on bringing participants into a story for whose telling they were not originally present, *listens to prepare and to guide*. Facilitators, in preparing to lead a discussion, listen to and review an edited story. They attend to those parts of the story that resonate and provoke, and at the same time prepare questions that will help participants interpret the story (see Appendix B). This initial preparation lays the groundwork for facili-tators as they shift, during the actual conversation, into *listening to guide*, an act that ultimately aims to both connect and challenge participants. Facilitators want to create meaningful engagement for participants with the storyteller and with each other, to help participants recognize the ways in which they interpret, and to help participants apply the insights gleaned to their own lives and communities. This practice was particularly important for the *Invisible*

DOI: 10.34314/wingodigital.00008

Project, whose main objective was to have residents in Porter County better understand what homelessness looks like in their community.

The Process

"Seeking Some Level of Normalcy"

> *It's about, I think, a lot about pride. Nobody wants to be seen as someone who can't make it on their own. We're all human beings, and we all have the same strengths and weaknesses within ourselves, so you just have to be willing to look at yourself and acknowledge that, and say, "I can't do this alone."*[6] (See Appendix D for a full transcript.)

The *Invisible Project* was highly collaborative from the beginning, but any project of this nature needs some management, a role that *Welcome Project* co-director Liz Wuerffel played. She oversaw the various stages of the project and kept communication open among the various partners. She also oversaw the budget, which was raised in several ways. Wuerffel applied for internal funding through the Cultural Arts Committee and received $1,500. The Porter County Community Foundation provided a $1,000 grant, and Shook found a donor through Housing Opportunities who provided an additional $2,000. Given the willingness of partners—including the exhibition team from the Porter County Museum—to give their time in kind, we were able to keep the overall budget to $4,500.

We began our work in the summer of 2015. The nonprofit agencies lined up ten clients willing to be interviewed and coordinated rides for them. (All but one interview took place on Valparaiso University's campus. One took place at the client's apartment.) Interviewees decided beforehand whether to contribute their stories through video or audio, and everyone signed a release form providing their consent and acknowledging they knew how their stories would be shared.[7]

Like most *Welcome Project* interviews, these lasted about 90 minutes, and began with what we consider "low risk" questions, those that people feel confident they can immediately answer. (Their answers also typically provide

DOI: 10.34314/wingodigital.00008

Figure 7.1: Cyanotype prints by Robert Lee impacted the overall design of the mobile exhibit.

background and context that allow the interviewer to get to know the interviewee.) In other words, we seek first to lay a foundation of trust. Interestingly, one of the *Invisible Project's* first lessons occurred when Schuette discovered that for one client our initial questions were anything but easy or low risk, as her experience of home from day one had been fraught. As the client forged ahead, Schuette quickly realized that for some people the experience of homelessness begins long before the physical structure is ever lost.

By the end of the summer, each interview had been edited into several short stories, many of which could stand alone, but several of which worked better in conjunction with each other as chapters in a playlist. All of the stories were immediately made available on the *Welcome Project's* website, and some stories later became a part of the mobile exhibit. Stories have additionally been used in facilitated conversations, sometimes in conjunction with the exhibition, as when Valparaiso students (trained in the Center for Civic Reflection's

DOI: 10.34314/wingodigital.00008

Figure 7.2: Several student posters such as this one by Sarhang Sherwany were used as visual material.

facilitation practice) led a conversation at the Porter County Museum, and sometimes by community members, who discover the stories on our website, as when a Director of Student Ministries at a local church emailed to let us know she was sharing a story with her high-school students.

In the fall, Yeohyun Ahn used the topic of homelessness as the theme for her graphic design course, inviting agency partners to provide her class with regional and local context. Throughout the semester, Tomasek and Wuerffel photographed clients or former clients, some of whom were in shelters and some of whom now had stable housing. The graphic design students were then able to use these photographs, the transcripts from the edited audio and video stories, as well as their own creative content to develop their designs.

At this point, the Porter County Museum stepped in to design and build the mobile exhibit. The Porter County Museum's mission is to connect the rich past to the evolving present to educate, enrich, and inspire Porter County

DOI: 10.34314/wingodigital.00008

communities. Understood as a small but vibrant local history museum, in recent years the museum had begun including more cultural offerings, inviting local artists into their exhibition spaces and encouraging use of the museum building as a site for community meetings and conversations. While the museum may have dealt mostly in history, its staff had experience in distilling and translating information (past and present) for Porter County audiences.

Porter County is generally an affluent community, with a mix of rural farming communities and small suburban towns located on the shore of Lake Michigan. As of July 2018, Porter County had a population of over 168,000.[8] Approximately 30,000 live in the county seat, Valparaiso, a college town containing Valparaiso University, a small historically Lutheran liberal arts college. The 2016 median property value is $168,300 in Porter County, compared to Indiana's median property value of $134,800. Porter County's median income sits at $64,874, compared to the statewide median income of $52,314.[9] This relative affluence presents problems for low-income individuals and families, who struggle to find affordable housing within the county. At the time of the project, 160 individuals were estimated homeless in Porter County on any given day: one in three were children; 72 percent of homeless adults were women.[10]

According to our community partner Mignon Kennedy, these statistics don't mirror national statistics, in which "men have higher rates of homelessness than women." Kennedy suspects Porter County might document higher rates for women because "on average the U.S. homeless population is 40 percent African American," a population underrepresented in Porter County, and because homeless men receive fewer services in Porter County and may not be as easily factored into Point-in-Time counts. Kennedy adds that women experiencing homelessness "are more vulnerable and typically suffer more abuse than homeless men. Women are likely to become homeless due to domestic violence or eviction. The fastest growing homeless sub-population is families headed by a single female."[11]

In some cases, women experiencing homelessness are less likely to be part of the unsheltered homeless population seen in larger cities. Anecdotally speaking, due to childcare responsibilities and fear of physical and sexual

DOI: 10.34314/wingodigital.00008

Figure 7.3: The exhibit needed to be lightweight but heavy duty, three-dimensional but easy to transport.

violence, women are more likely to find accommodations—couch-surfing with friends and family, living out of hotels and cars, etc. This is certainly true of women experiencing homelessness in Porter County, who articulated a feeling of invisibility during the interviews conducted.

Using this knowledge, the exhibition team needed to find a way to combine photos, stories, facts, and designed assets into a physically mobile exhibit intended to reach a varied audience. It was an ambitious undertaking for a small museum; the staff had never designed an exhibition that needed to be compact, flexible, and resilient in order to fit the many display spaces it would inhabit, and to withstand many moves in the coming year. The design that emerged was a durable marriage of form and content.

The exhibition itself was made up of nine lightweight, wood-framed structures reminiscent of houses. The structures were stackable—fitting into themselves for easy transport. The text panels were removable but made of a heavy-duty plastic to survive the many installations and de-installations. This compact and adaptable structure featured a clean design with easily readable and varied types of information.

The overall design of the exhibition was inspired by student Rob Lee's cyanotypes (see Figure 7.1). The color and texture of cyanotype provided a cohesive look to the exhibit and also spoke to its themes: cyanotype prints remain invisible until they undergo a final rinse in water; we hoped our

DOI: 10.34314/wingodigital.00008

exhibit would similarly reveal the realities of homelessness through the lived experience of our storytellers.

Additionally, because the exhibition staff knew that the exhibit would encounter audiences more diverse than those that typically visited the museum, varied media were employed. As counterpoints to the statistics, photos were incorporated into the exhibit to provide a humanizing face to the numbers. Infographics were developed to provide at-a-glance facts for individuals who might only be passing by. The design also helped viewers visualize available resources for homeless individuals alongside what was still needed in Porter County. Pull quotes from the longer interviews foregrounded the voices of those who had experienced homelessness, while longer paragraph text provided interpretation of history, context, causes, and proposed solutions. Finally, and most important, an audio/visual station provided viewers with the chance to engage with the oral histories themselves. Opportunities for joint listening encouraged conversation about the story heard.

Ultimately, the *Invisible Project* mobile exhibit made use of regional history, statistics, and resources; audio and video stories; select student designs; and photographic portraits in order to convey the project's message to a public audience. This physical structure served as a vehicle to take oral histories out of institutional or academic walls to meet people in their day-to-day lives, educating viewers about the realities of homelessness through the words of those who have lived through that experience.

As a hybrid project, with both physical and digital elements, the *Invisible Project* brought the *Welcome Project* "offline" in a way that helped collaborators better realize the objectives of the initiative. Digital stories excel at placing the warmth of the human face and voice front and center, no matter the location of the listener. Through tone and expression, storytellers become tangible and concrete in ways that a transcript or written text can't convey.

At the same time, digital stories in an online space require devices with internet access, and targeting stories to a regional population can be challenging. The physical exhibit in this case provided direct access to those stories in a very specific way by engaging local audiences in the daily spaces they move through.

DOI: 10.34314/wingodigital.00008

Figure 7.4: Opening panel of the mobile exhibit. Color, type, and design draw heavily from student Robert Lee's cyanotype images.

Figure 7.5: Sites were located across the county, including at public libraries, health clinics, churches, civic buildings, and businesses. This site is the Porter County Library.

DOI: 10.34314/wingodigital.00008

Figure 7.6: Panel from the *Invisible Project* mobile exhibit combines portraits with regional context and the project's guiding concepts.

Figure 7.7: Visitor at the Porter County Museum listens to audio stories. Both audio and video stories are integrated into the mobile exhibit by way of mp3 players and a tablet.

DOI: 10.34314/wingodigital.00008

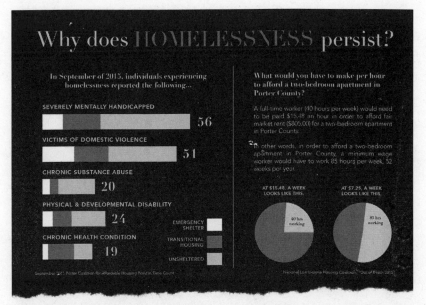

Figure 7.8: Data visualization / infographics deliver statistics and regional information in a visually compelling way.

The physical exhibit additionally contextualized the individual, personal stories in a way that allowed us to draw the public's attention to larger concerns our community needs to address *with each other* in real time, such as lack of affordable housing. Encountering stories online is more likely to be a solitary experience.

Nevertheless, the digital continued to play a role before, during, and after the exhibit. We actively used and continue to use social media as a way to draw the attention of the public to the *Invisible Project*. Not everyone can get to the physical exhibit, especially other communities or nonprofits outside the region who might also benefit from the stories of Porter County residents. By keeping an online, digital presence, we are able to extend the audience for the *Invisible Project* and allow it to have a life far beyond our needs.

DOI: 10.34314/wingodigital.00008

The Impact

Stepping Stones

> *I think people need to step outside of the box and look around for a minute, and see that there are people out there that are really struggling, and that are not taking adantage of the system, and that really, really do need help.*[12] (See Appendix E for a full transcript.)

Between March 2016 and August 2017, the *Invisible Project* exhibit toured eighteen sites—local museums, churches, libraries, the YMCA, a health clinic, a community foundation, and a wealth management company—some of which paired the exhibit with a fundraising project or recruitment for volunteers. It finally came to rest at Housing Opportunities (HO), where it continues to inform and educate. HO still receives requests to have the exhibit brought to the lobbies of churches and libraries, and HO staff regularly use pieces of the exhibit to educate at public-facing events such as the Valparaiso Farmer's Market.

Clients have spoken of both the difficulty and ultimate value of participating:

Gina, who was photographed for the project with her mother, said, "It's important to share your story, even if you're embarrassed about being homeless. It was pride-shattering, not going to lie. I didn't feel human. This sheds light on that it could be anyone—it could be you, it could be your neighbor. Bringing light to that and knowing it is regular people, it could help give a sense of community and relieve those stressors."[13]

Mitch, who was interviewed along with his wife, found value in the process for himself: "I've never sat and talked like that before. It put things in perspective, giving yourself a view of your own life, where you came from and where you're going. The conversation put a lot of things together." But when he reflected on the public aspect of the project, he felt more ambivalent. Having his story heard by so many people made him feel "a bit conflicted because I'm so private, but some people need to hear about homelessness because it is a problem. Folks don't know how people get into that situation. If someone now better understands, then sharing my story was time well spent."[14]

DOI: 10.34314/wingodigital.00008

Figure 7.9: "When you have a child, that child comes first. Sometimes he eats, you don't eat. That's just the way it is."—Truly Unconditional Love

Figure 7.10: "Poor people are looked down upon so badly . . . Well, guess what? There's a lot of people living paycheck to paycheck . . . I'm doing everything I can. I'm not such a bad person. I just have some bad situations."—Made Us Feel Low

DOI: 10.34314/wingodigital.00008

Figure 7.11: "I was 19 years old when I became homeless . . . it could be you, it could be your neighbor." Personal interview.

Figure 7.12: "When they told me I got the apartment I was so ecstatic. I could take a shower when I wanted to. I didn't have no furniture, I had no TV. I had nothing. But I don't care. I had my freedom."—Makes You Strong

DOI: 10.34314/wingodigital.00008

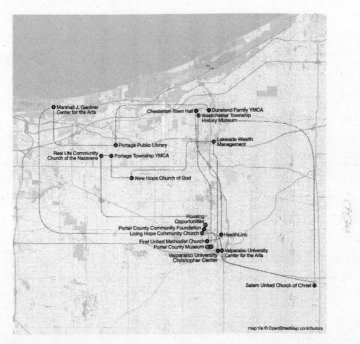

Figure 7.13: The *Invisible Project* exhibit toured eighteen sites in or near northern Porter County, Indiana.

Feedback from community partners indicate that clients like Gina and Mitch can have confidence in their participation.

Mignon Kennedy said, "I believe the most important success was the message the exhibit conveyed: that homelessness exists in our community and that often times people had little or no control over the events that led to their homeless situation. The stories helped the audience to understand the pain, frustration, and feelings of hopelessness experienced."[15]

Caroline Shook agreed that the *Invisible Project* put a real face on homelessness in Porter County. When a new Housing Opportunities board member experienced the exhibit at its opening, she says that he committed himself to HO in a way "no one ever has" because he saw and deeply understood that these folks "are our neighbors, they're in the grocery line with us, they go to school with our kids."[16]

DOI: 10.34314/wingodigital.00008

Not all members of the community were able to hear this message. In October 2016, Valparaiso's City Council turned down a rezoning request that would have allowed Housing Opportunities and Porter-Starke Services to create Aurora View, an ambitious affordable housing complex that would have provided professionally managed, supportive services to its residents. Neighbors in the area, however, resisted, citing safety concerns and declining property values.[17] Shook said a local foundation with investments in the area let city council members know that, if the rezoning request went through, donations the city relied upon would "dry up."[18]

Even so, Shook noted that the *Invisible Project* did influence the mayor of Valparaiso. He had supported Aurora View and was disappointed by the council's decision. Later, he helped ensure that another affordable housing project, first known as Park Place and later renamed Caroline's Place in honor of Shook's efforts, went through quite easily. Housing Opportunities also used the *Invisible Project* to educate neighboring LaPorte County commissioners about the ways in which they could partner with HO to provide affordable housing in their county. The partnership allowed HO both to help current renters buy the homes they rented and to sell vacant houses in need of upkeep to those who had the skills to remodel a home but who didn't have the money or credit to buy a house otherwise. In both cases, HO helped residents create more stability in neighborhoods that many would label "bad."[19]

For the Porter County Museum, the *Invisible Project* was a meaningful success. Not only did it challenge the museum in terms of design, it pushed the museum beyond its four walls. This is, of course, great for museum visibility, but it's more significant than this. The museum staff had been looking for new and innovative ways—from historic photo calls, to oral history interviews, to community conversations—to invite audiences to contribute to the recorded history of their community.

The *Invisible Project* provided them with a way to respond to Nina Simon's call in *The Art of Relevance*: "But what about projects in which the audience co-creates the content? What about projects created in partnership with communities of interest, rooted explicitly in their voices, stories, and experiences?"[20] Instead of an institutional model, in which the museum

DOI: 10.34314/wingodigital.00008

decided what stories were worth sharing and in what ways, partnership with community groups allowed new voices to emerge within the museum space and to speak to a relevant, living issue within the community. "Relevance," Simon writes, "is an exercise in empathy—in understanding what matters to your intended audience, not what matters to you."[21] By listening, being responsive, and saying "yes," the museum was able to reach new audiences, tell new stories, and respond to a need within the community as never before.

The impact on the *Welcome Project* was also notable. In addition to the ways in which we were individually transformed by the stories we heard and edited, we grew our capacity as a project. Previously, collaborations had not required an extended commitment between partners. The *Invisible Project* taught us how to forge relationships between individuals, agencies, and organizations—inside and outside our own institution—and gave us a deadline in which to create a "finished" product. We discovered that working with artists and students on that public product introduced the need to negotiate standards for content and quality and raised the question of creative control and ownership, frank conversations that should have happened on the front end.

Welcome Project participants also found ourselves needing to produce new kinds of stories. Oftentimes, understanding a person's experience of homelessness requires the context of a lifetime. Our standard practice of highlighting a three-to five-minute experience from an hour-long interview works best with discrete moments. Telling the story of homelessness often demanded new approaches (multipart stories, more than one storyteller). Additionally, there were facts and statistics that visitors to the exhibit needed to better grasp the social and political dimensions of homelessness. The *Invisible Project* is not a dramatization of individual choices; it is a story of how individual circumstances within a larger context of regional and national policies and practices leads to outcomes with immense consequences for individuals and communities.

All of these lessons have continued to inform and shape our practice. They have, in fact, prepared us for an even more ambitious initiative, *Flight Paths*, that will document the changing racial and economic demographics of Gary and Northwest Indiana, beginning with the rise of Black political power

DOI: 10.34314/wingodigital.00008

and opportunity in the 1960s, the "flight" of white residents and businesses to the suburbs, and the automation of the steel mills and consequent underemployment of mill workers. *Flight Paths* team members span disciplinary fields, institutions, community partners, and funders. As a seven-year initiative, it will draw upon everything we've learned from the *Invisible Project*.

The *Invisible Project* provides an example of how digital community engagement can succeed. We benefited from eager collaborators at the university and in our community partners. Most challenges arose in the normal course of organizing a project of this size; they were logistical questions that could be addressed given the willingness of everyone to play their part. We recognize that conditions might not always be so conducive: grants might not be given, agencies might not have strong leadership, circumstances might make it impossible for a collaborator to fulfill their role, personalities might clash. But as Elizabeth Allen wrote in response to our request for her assessment: "The talent and expertise of the *Welcome Project*, Valparaiso University graphic art students and Porter County Museum all wrapped around the clients' stories to create a beautiful, clear message to our community: *We're here, we exist, even in pretty Porter County. We're not that different from you, just one or two different turns in the road. With your help and support we can get back on our feet.*"[22] We remain immensely grateful for the clients and collaborators who made this initiative possible.

Notes

1. "Roof Over My Head," *Welcome Project*. July 30, 2015, video, 5:55, https://welcomeproject.valpo.edu/2015/07/30/roof-over-your-head/.
2. Caroline Shook interview by Allison Schuette, telephone interview, March 16, 2018.
3. The Center for Civic Reflection was founded by Elizabeth Lynn, Ph.D. at Valparaiso University in 1998 with support from Lilly Endowment Inc.
4. Shook, interview.
5. Anna Deavere Smith, *Fires in the Mirror: Crown Heights, Brooklyn, and Other Identities* (Anchor, 1993), xxxix.
6. "Seeking Some Level of Normalcy," *Welcome Project*. September 4, 2015, audio, 2:50, https://welcomeproject.valpo.edu/2015/09/04/bad-things-good-people/.

DOI: 10.34314/wingodigital.00008

7. The Welcome Project has received university IRB approval and we renew that approval annually. Team members complete the NIH Protecting Human Research Participants training, and interviewers learn how to review the Welcome Project's release form with interviewees before they sign it. We acknowledge the vulnerability of those we interview and value their right to provide informed consent. Additionally, interviewees may choose to review and approve edited stories before the stories are made public.

8. "Porter County, Indiana," American Fact Finder, U.S. Census Bureau, last modified July 1, 2017. https://factfinder.census.gov/faces/nav/jsf/pages/community _facts.xhtml.

9. "Porter County, Indiana," data.census.gov, U.S. Census Bureau, last modified 2018. https://data.census.gov/cedsci/profile?q=Porter%20County,%20Indiana&g= 0500000US18127

10. "Point in Time Count," Porter County Coalition for Affordable Housing, September 2015.

11. Mignon Kennedy, email to Megan Telligman, October 9, 2018.

12. "Stepping Stones," *Welcome Project*. September 30, 2015, video, 3:38. https://wel comeproject.valpo.edu/2015/09/30/stepping-stones/.

13. Gina, interview by Liz Wuerffel, telephone interview, September 29, 2017.

14. Mitch, interview by Allison Schuette, telephone interview, October 2, 2017.

15. Mignon Kennedy, email to Liz Wuerffel, September 26, 2017.

16. Shook, interview.

17. John Scheibel, "Update: Valparaiso City Council Rejects Rezoning, Donation of Land for Housing Project," *Northwest Indiana Times*, October 25, 2016, accessed October 30, 2018. http://www.nwitimes.com/news/local/govt-and-politics/update -valparaiso-city-council-rejects-rezoning-donation-of-land-for/article_365512b8 -4e24-531f-89ed-471abe43d1a8.html.

18. Shook, interview.

19. Ibid.

20. Nina Simon, *The Art of Relevance* (Santa Cruz: Museum 2.0, 2016), chap. "Co-creating relevance," http://www.artofrelevance.org/2018/04/18/co-creating -relevance/.

21. Nina Simon, *The Art of Relevance* (Santa Cruz: Museum 2.0, 2016), chap. "People Who Don't Normally Show Up," http://www.artofrelevance.org/2017/12/27/peo ple-dont-normally-show/.

22. Elizabeth Allen, email to Liz Wuerffel, September 17, 2017.

DOI: 10.34314/wingodigital.00008

Works Cited

"Seeking Some Level of Normalcy." *Welcome Project*. September 4, 2015. Audio, 8:05. https://welcomeproject.valpo.edu/2015/09/04/bad-things-good-people/.

DataUSA. "Porter County, IN, and Indiana." Accessed January 16, 2019. https://datausa.io/profile/geo/porter-county-in/?compare=indiana#intro.

Gina. Interview by Liz Wuerffel. Telephone interview. September 29, 2017.

Mitch. Interview by Allison Schuette. Telephone interview. October 2, 2017.

Porter County Coalition for Affordable Housing. "Point in Time Count." September 2015.

"Roof Over My Head." *Welcome Project*. July 30, 2015. Video, 5:55. https://welcomeproject.valpo.edu/2015/07/30/roof-over-your-head/.

Scheibel, John. "Update: Valparaiso City Council Rejects Rezoning, Donation of Land for Housing Project." *Northwest Indiana Times*, (Valparaiso, IN), October 25, 2016. Accessed October 30, 2018. https://www.nwitimes.com/news/local/govt-and-politics/update-valparaiso-city-council-rejects-rezoning-donation-of-land-for/article_365512b8-4e24-531f-89ed-471abe43d1a8.html.

"Seeking Some Level of Normalcy." *Welcome Project*. September 4, 2015. Audio, 2:50. https://welcomeproject.valpo.edu/2015/09/04/bad-things-good-people/.

Shook, Caroline. Interview by Allison Schuette. Telephone interview. March 16, 2018.

Simon, Nina. *The Art of Relevance*. Museum 2.0, 2016.

Smith, Anna Deavere. *Fires in the Mirror: Crown Heights, Brooklyn, and Other Identities*. Anchor, 1993.

"Stepping Stones." *Welcome Project*. September 30, 2015. Video, 3:38. https://welcomeproject.valpo.edu/2015/09/30/stepping-stones/.

U.S. Census Bureau. "Porter County, Indiana." data.census.gov. Last modified 2018. https://data.census.gov/cedsci/profile?q=Porter%20County,%20Indiana&g=0500000US18127.

DOI: 10.34314/wingodigital.00008

Appendix A: Transcript of "Roof Over Your Head"

I got to experience homelessness, I got to experience living on others'—I got to experience all that, so it gave me more respect for people who are out there homeless, that they're not in this alone. But I used to be that kind of person—I would judge people because I thought, you know, I wasn't letting things stop me, and I was doing it. What's wrong with them? And then I became that person, and it wasn't until then I understood not to do that—not to judge, not to assume they don't want anything out of life.

My parents are, you know, late eighties/early nineties, and they still live in Gary, in the house that I grew up in, and if you asked me years, and years, and years ago, I'd go, "Well, it's the greatest place, you know, the west side of Gary and—very residential. It's big yards, and kids can play."

My husband was nineteen, and I was sixteen, and so we went to his sister's, and that's where we lived until I had our child, and then, once I had the baby, we had our own apartment. I decided to move from Indiana, and to try to better myself so I could be better for my kids.

I went to school at Ivy Tech, and that's in Minneapolis, Minnesota. I went for a medical assistant, and I did graduate, and began work, and that was the beginning of, you know, me paying my own way. It felt so good, you know? It was so nice to see your name on a paycheck, you know? And know that you created this, and that you can choose how to spend it, you know? In the process of that, I did remarry, you know, to a great guy. He had some of the same goals that I did, and family, being family-oriented. And he helped raise my kids, you know? Gosh, he was just so great, you know, but he passed away. Two years after his death, which was in 2007, I became disabled. My diagnosis was post-traumatic stress disorder—yeah—and depression. And those were very dark times for me. I didn't feel I deserved to be happy because he wasn't there with me to share the happiness that we shared together. And so, everything we worked for, I gave all away. I find myself in a circle—it's like a fish bowl. I want to venture out, because that's the drive I have inside, but that person, I'm like, "Where are you? Push through!" A lot of people don't come back, and I was one of them, that I just didn't have my drive anymore.

Within the last couple of months, my family called and talked about Mom and Dad, how they're declining. That's what brought me back here to Indiana. I may not be able to have gainful employment, but all my skills that I have learned in the medical field, and just everything that I've picked up, I feel so good that I can say I'm using them to help my parents, you know?

DOI: 10.34314/wingodigital.00008

Being a couch-surfer may not be bad for a lot of people, but I've always had the drive to not depend on others, so for me to couch-surf back and forth—it was still, like, a disappointment to myself, you know? Because every parent always wants to keep a roof over their head where their child can come, you know? You may not be able to put the spread out like you used to, but you just want to know you always got a place where your kids can come and have coffee with you, and talk about what's going on in their life.

But I was fortunate to find a program—Neighboring Place. It's a great program for women. They provide quite a bit besides shelter, you know, and I'm just real fortunate to be there. You know, being the bag lady, I finally got a place to put my bags down, and then lay down in my own bed.

Appendix B: Center for Civic Reflection—Three Kinds of Questions

Excerpted from *Civic Reflection Discussions: A Handbook for Facilitators*

by Dr. Elizabeth Lynn

In coming up with a list of questions, it might be useful to consider three *kinds* of questions:

1. Questions of *clarification*—What does it say? What is going on here?
2. Questions of *interpretation*—What does it mean? What do you think of what is going on here?
3. Questions of *implication*—So what? How does what you think of what is going on here impact your work?

You may want to start with **questions of clarification**: *What does it say?* In the case of a story, it might help to find a point in the plot that seems to have a deeper meaning or makes a significant impact on one of the characters. For a poem, it might be a specific image or metaphor that jumps out at you. For an essay, it might be some statement that genuinely catches or puzzles you. In each case, you can ask, what is going on here? Can one literally make sense of what is being said or done here?

Good questions of clarification are open to an answer from anyone who pays attention to the reading. In other words, they do not require any special expertise or experience in order to be answered.

Just as there are good questions, there are also opening questions that are best avoided.

DOI: 10.34314/wingodigital.00008

Avoid questions that:

- Invite opinion without interpretation of the text (Do you like this story?)
- Assert debatable propositions (Why is the concept of social capital so useful?)
- Put people on the defensive (What percentage of your income do you give to charity?).

After you have helped participants clarify what the text says, you will soon be ready to move on to a **question of interpretation**: *What does it mean?*

For instance, in Bertolt Brecht's poem "A Bed for the Night," several participants in the room seem to think that the man on the corner is asking passersby to take homeless folks into their houses for the night. Now the question is, what do you make of the cornerman's request? And why does the poem move from a description of this man's action to the announcement that "it will not change the world"?

These questions of interpretation encourage participants to evaluate the reading, to praise or blame characters, and to talk about values—but to do so using the shared terms provided by the reading everyone has in front of them. At this point, the discussion consists in an exchange of personal opinions, but these opinions are filtered through the shared object of the text, which keeps the discussion from turning personal in a way that might shut some participants out.

As participants get more involved in answering questions of interpretation, there will most likely be a natural push from the reading to the activity they share. That is, participants will move from talking about Brooks' Ladies Betterment League to their service experience in City Year, or from Bambara's Miss Moore to their own kind of teaching, or from Neruda's lamb to the gift they try to pass on.

This motion—from the reading back to civic life—characterizes the best civic reflection discussions, especially when participants have come to see their work anew by looking carefully at the reading before them and thinking patiently about their opinions and beliefs.

In closing, then, you will almost certainly want to move toward **questions of implication**: *So what?*

What do we take away from this reading or discussion as we leave, what do we think about our own activity, our own work, in light of what we have heard or said? These questions simply try to help connect the reading to the experiences of people in the group. Often participants make these connections themselves, but you should still have these kinds of questions ready.

DOI: 10.34314/wingodigital.00008

Here are a few examples of effective "connecting" questions:

- Is Tocqueville describing the kinds of associations in which you participate?
- Do you recognize these characters/dilemmas? Have you experienced them in your own life?
- Is this the kind of leadership your organization has been called upon to provide?
- Are these the kinds of choices we are confronted with in our community?
- Why do these ideas matter? What are some implications of what we have said today for your work, organization, community?

Appendix C: The Practice

Typically, we frame our work on the *Welcome Project* as a practice in community engagement, but a research methodology that takes listening as its primary tool has evolved out of our work and undergirds it. This highly qualitative method involves three practices—interviewing, editing, and facilitating—each of which employ different kinds of listening.

Interviewing, with its focus on asking people what they've experienced and what they think about those experiences, *listens to learn and to establish trust.* Though some may think of interviews as one-sided, where the interviewer merely prompts the responses of the interviewee and attempts to remain otherwise absent, in the *Welcome Project* practice, we attempt to disrupt this power relationship through foregrounding of curiosity. Curiosity, of course, cannot completely divest the interview of power relations, but it can bring the interviewer more fully into the experience as a subject. The interviewer may still refrain from contributing too much to the interview, but they understand that curiosity implies not knowing and requires them to expose their ignorance in a respectful way that demonstrates their own vulnerability. In posing questions, in sharing brief anecdotes, the interviewer makes clear to the interviewee how they are genuinely interested in the interviewee's experiences and how the interviewee is an authority in those experiences. This can generate confidence in the interviewees, who sometimes wonder what they have to share or what is of value in what they share. Curiosity, then, is the ground for establishing trust and the means by which the interviewer learns more deeply about the human experience, whether that experience is familiar or foreign.

Editing, with its focus on revisiting the interview to sound out those stories that are important to the interviewee and to the mission of the *Welcome Project,*

DOI: 10.34314/wingodigital.00008

listens to identify and interpret. Each of our methodological practices entails ethical decision-making, perhaps none quite as palpably as editing. A single ninety-minute interview will produce several three-to five-minute stories. That process leaves a lot of material behind. How does an editor remain true to the intention of the interviewee while crafting stories whose insights will invite, inspire, and/ or challenge future listeners to think deeply about living well with and across our differences? Striking that balance is daunting. An editor's first job, therefore, is to listen again. As the interview replays and is transcribed, the editor begins to identify areas of concern for the interviewee. These areas can be signaled by repetition and recurrence as an interviewee seeks the best way to articulate their experience or insight, or they can be signaled by tone, as an interviewee's cadence demonstrates emotional investment. Editors cannot escape some level of interpretation in this process. Interviewers might have run out of time to probe all areas of conversation deeply; interviewees might have struggled to fully explain their experience. The trust established during the interview has to be borne out in the work of the editor selecting which parts of the interview to bring together into a single story.

Facilitating, with its focus on bringing participants into a story for whose telling they were not originally present, *listens to prepare and to guide.* Facilitators, in preparing to lead a discussion, must take on the role they will later ask of participants. As they listen to and review an edited story, they attend to those parts of the story that resonate and provoke. They ask themselves why they've reacted in these ways and work backwards to distinguish their reaction from the storyteller's description. This gap between reaction and description is the entry point into seeking clarification. From here, the facilitator can create questions that will invite participants to more closely understand what the storyteller means. At the same time, the facilitator listens to prepare questions that will also help participants interpret the meanings of a story and identify the implications both the story and conversation have for their lives going forward. This initial preparation lays the groundwork for facilitators as they shift, during the actual conversation, into *listening to guide*, an act that ultimately aims to both connect and challenge participants. As participants first clarify and then interpret a story, facilitators listen to how participants react and respond. They try to draw out the fullest range of responses and encourage participants to acknowledge points of view different from their own. As the conversation builds and evolves, the facilitator listens to discern how to further connect participants to the storyteller and each other and/or how to allow the storyteller to further challenge them. The ultimate aim of listening to guide is to create meaningful engagement for participants with the storyteller and

DOI: 10.34314/wingodigital.00008

with each other, and to help participants apply the insights gleaned to their own lives and communities. It might appear that the facilitator stands apart from this conversation—and in certain respects, like the interviewer, they do refrain from contributing their perspective. Even so, in essence facilitators and participants co-create a kind of listening that extends the trust first established between interviewer and interviewee as they allow difference to stand, hopefully leaving with more clarity about their own perspective.

Appendix D: Transcript of "Bad Things, Good People"—A Three-Part Story

Part One: "Seeking Some Level of Normalcy"

Speaker 1: It's about, I think, a lot about pride. Nobody wants to be seen as someone who can't make it on their own. We're all human beings, and we all have the same strengths and weaknesses within ourselves, so you just have to be willing to look at yourself and acknowledge that, and say, "I can't do this alone."

Speaker 2: We would sometimes sit in a parking lot in our vehicle at night and just talk all night long like, you know, "Where are we going to go? What are we going to do?" And it's like, well, we didn't know that there was anybody out there that was willing to help us.

S1:   I think we were always seeking some, some level of normalcy, you know? Finding opportunities to be—to look like everybody else, you know? You don't want people to see what's going on.

S2:   During the day, we would spend a lot of time at the parks here in Valparaiso and Lake Station—they have a nice Riverview Park—but most of the parks at ten p.m. close up. Yeah, you're constantly moving from place to place. Lot of times on hot days, we would spend our days at the library—

S1:   Air conditioning.

S2:   —you know, where they had air conditioning and a bathroom facility there.

S1:   And we both loved to read.

S2:   Yeah, we both loved to read. Yeah, nighttime was the worst. And, of course, you know, you don't really have that many belongings, but, you know, what you do have, I mean, you know, you've got everything crammed in your vehicle, and, you know, even sleeping a lot of times—we would park out away from kind of the store, because, you know, we didn't want to, you know, interfere—

S1:   Be in the way.

DOI: 10.34314/wingodigital.00008

S2:—we didn't want to be in the way. You know, and then sometimes it's hard to sleep because you know, you're just not sure of your surroundings, and you don't really feel that safe. And during that time, I think that's most of our resources were making sure, you know, we have gas in the vehicle so we can move if we have to, we have food to eat, which was difficult with no cooking facilities. Everything had to be pre-prepared, and, of course, you know, that's more costly, too. Hygiene. For me, that was the worst part. Restroom facilities, and hygiene. Of course, it was summertime when we were homeless, which, I think, we were fortunate because we could go up to the park, and we could go swimming, and we kept lots of empty gallon jugs—

S1:   We would help each other.

S2:   —and we would fill them, fill them with water. And like I said, it was summertime, so it wasn't so bad, you know, having to wash your hair with cold water, but—

S1:   I'd get to dump a bucket of water over her head.

S2:   Right, you know? And, yeah, we would kind of go to the park in a secluded area, and we would, you know, like bathe each other, and watch and make sure nobody was coming, you know, so we could, you know, help each other do that. And, uh…

S1:   Just because you're homeless doesn't mean you have to surrender humanity.

Part Two: *"Tailspin"*

Speaker 1: When we first came back to Indiana, we went to his sister's, and she let us stay with her for a little while.

Speaker 2: And we got a place.

S1:   And we both got a job, and from there, everything seemed like it was going pretty good. And we had been here four years when his sister passed away. And so…

S2:   And that was, like, the final straw for me. I was broke.

S1:   I was working. My hours got cut. Mitch had developed a lot of physical limitations, and his depression was, like I said, still there—underlying, but started coming out a little bit more when he wasn't able to work, and that kind of threw us in the position where we became homeless.

S2:   Bit of a tailspin. It was just, in a very short time, we went from like, being level, and then her income changed just the slightest bit, and that—that was it. It just kicked the underpinnings right out from under us.

DOI: 10.34314/wingodigital.00008

S1:   Right. When you're living, like I said, paycheck to paycheck, you know, by
       the time it would get two or three days before payday, and, you know, I
       wouldn't have a penny in my pocket. And when, you know, my hours started
       getting cut due to the economy—you know, business wasn't as good—I was
       working at a restaurant, you know. It's like, I'm driving eighteen miles one
       way to get to work, and eighteen miles back. Well, that's, you know, taking
       a lot of gas—I need something closer to home. Due to my age, people kind
       of were more looking at me not as an asset, but as a risk. "Wow," you know,
       "She's not gonna be somebody long term. She may develop health issues.
       She may call off work. We don't know what's gonna go on." And I think
       that was where I started having difficulties finding employment. So, when
       we couldn't pay our lot rent, they, you know, basically—you have fifteen
       days to either pay or evacuate. And not having any immediate family or
       anybody that could help us, or provide a place for us to stay—you know, our
       children were in Wisconsin, and neither one of them was really in a position
       to do anything for us. It was kind of a snowball effect. We did live in our
       vehicle for approximately four months before one of my coworkers had told
       me about Housing Opportunities. We checked into that, and took us about
       another month, and they accepted us into their program, and provided us
       with a place to stay.

Part Three: *"We Were Them"*

Speaker 1: What we're doing here is very outside our comfort zone.
Speaker 2: Yes.
S1:   And that's one of the things we are trying to do different. Because people
       need to learn these things. It's not easy for people to open up about this sort
       of thing. Trust—it doesn't come easy to me.
S2:   It is, it's very hard to know who you can talk to, and who you can be honest
       with, because a lot of people in my past—my experiences were, that the
       more people know about you, the more judgmental they become. Asking
       for help wasn't something that I ever really did. That, for both of us, was a
       big step—having to ask for help.
S1:   When we were living out of our vehicle, necessity drove us to have to go
       here and go there, because, you know, you don't have resources, you know.
       We would park in the Walmart parking lot through the night for sleeping,
       because we knew they had restroom facilities we could use. And when you
       live like that, you start meeting other people in a similar circumstance. And
       I was astounded at the number of people with vehicles and such, so I mean,

DOI: 10.34314/wingodigital.00008

typically if you saw them, you wouldn't even know that they're suffering in this way. And they're all around us. We were them, you know, and I never understood any of this. But I got a pretty good grasp of it now.

S2: I don't think I ever even really considered people being homeless. It wasn't anything that I ever thought about, you know. I wasn't a person who was going to be like, "Oh, there's homeless people out there. I should do something to try to help them," because the thought never even crossed my mind. And then, when it happens to someone like us, where then I have to take a step back and say, "Wow, it happened to me. It can happen to anybody." Because I would've never in a million years dreamed that I would end up homeless.

S1: What I've learned is that life is not a straight line. There's curves, turns, and you even go back upon yourself many times. And it's easy to get lost, you know, to take one misstep, to take one wrong turn: left, when you should've went right. And, so, to stereotype all these people, and say they're this, this, or this—I can't tell you how wrong that is. Bad things happen to good people, and it ain't through no fault of their own. It's life. And I'll never hesitate to help somebody up after this.

Appendix E: Transcript of "Stepping Stones"

There's some people out there—they don't want the help. They just, they don't want it. And I've seen people who don't take the help, and then they end up in the same predicament that they were in. They don't have the same opportunities because they didn't take the opportunities that were given to them. But there are people out there that really need help, and there are people out there that don't want to be on the system forever, that don't want welfare, that don't take advantage of it. They're just trying—they're taking stepping stones to get where they need to get, and for that period of time, they have to let their pride go, and get the help that they need.

Housing Opportunities helps me by providing a roof. We go over goals. They help you find steps to finding a job. They give you resources to help you go to school. They introduce you to other nonprofit organizations that help you with other things. Like, they help my son with his speech therapy. They referred me to somebody. They referred me to First Steps. They referred me to Early Head Start—Head Start. The Family Youth Services Bureau—they paid for my car insurance for the first six months when I first got my car. I graduated from them, I guess you can say now, but they were truly amazing. Every single one of them

DOI: 10.34314/wingodigital.00008

that I had were amazing. Geminus Head Start—the nonprofit organization—my son went there for two years, and I loved the teachers that he had. They were amazing. One time, I didn't have enough money to pay for my son's pictures, and they—the teachers—put in the money to buy his pictures. I mean, then you have food stamps and welfare, that helps provide food, medical coverage, and that helps a lot, too.

My case manager, Cindy, is an incredible role model. She comes out to the apartment, she talks to us, she goes over the goals. She's taught me how to be a mom. She's amazing. She is more than just a case manager to me.

Right now, things are pretty good. I do watch children out of my house. Yes, it's not a lot of money, but I'm able to pay my bills. I'm able to buy my son what he needs, I'm able to keep a roof over our head right now. I was looking for another job, and I'm going to start looking for another job again as soon as I have a reliable car. It's still hard—you still struggle, especially when your car is constantly breaking down. You don't have enough money to pay for everything and fix your car, so the bills have to come first, and then the car, but I'm managing. We eat. We have a roof. He has clothes.

I think people need to step outside of the box and look around for a minute, and see that there are people out there that are really struggling, and that are not taking advantage of the system, and that really, really, do need help. Not everybody is the same. I think that it's just the way you look at it. And if you've ever been in that situation. If you've never been in that situation, then it's hard for people to understand what it's like. I think, sometimes you have to step back and take yourself out of your situation, and put yourself in somebody else's shoes.

DOI: 10.34314/wingodigital.00008

8

Hear, Here

Digital History and Community Engagement
Activating Social Change

Ariel Beaujot

In 2015 a member of the Ho-Chunk Nation recorded the following oral history while standing at the foot of a two-story-tall statue portraying a Native American:

> I just turned my back, symbolically, on what the [University of Wisconsin-La Crosse] Native American students used to refer to as "The Colossus of Kitsch" or as Riverside Park calls "The Big Indian."
>
> My name is Kera Cho Mani ga. That means "the person who paints the sky blue." You know me as Dan Green—what Malcolm X might call my slave name. [In] the late nineties, the Chamber of Commerce in La Crosse [Wisconsin] proposed [putting] fifty thousand dollars into a paint job on the Colossus—something that reinforces stereotypes about Native Americans. As a sociology student, I had for years looked into the influence of imagery, statuaries, and I was a part of the national anti-Native American sport mascot movement. I traveled to University of Illinois, University of North Dakota, and Cleveland, Ohio, on a regular basis to demonstrate and to teach about the harms, the largely psychological harms, of this kind of imagery of the Big Indian standing behind me. So that was my interest, that here it is, in my hometown where I'm raising children that look like me—they're brown-skinned, they're dark-haired, we don't get mistaken for anything but Native American, and here's something in our hometown reinforcing harmful thinking about us, so I was compelled to do something.

This oral history is one of the first recordings logged for a critical public history project called *Hear, Here: Voices of Downtown La Crosse.*[1] *Hear, Here* seeks to bring previously overlooked or unheard stories to light as a way of enhancing

DOI: 10.34314/wingodigital.00009

Figure 8.1: Hear, Here sign beside "Hiawatha" statue in Riverside Park. Photo courtesy University Communications, UW–La Crosse.

traditional narratives of the region that highlight Protestantism, prosperity, and whiteness, and ignore indigeneity, race, and cultural difference. Launched in 2015, *Hear, Here* is a place-based oral history project brought to life through *Hear, Here* signs scattered throughout downtown La Crosse, Wisconsin. Each sign is placed where a story happened and the public can access each story by dialing a toll-free number. Once the stories are heard, callers are encouraged to stay on the line to add their own story about that site or any other site in Downtown La Crosse. In this way the stories become user-generated and the project comes to represent both the living and lived history of the community. The only requisite for a *Hear, Here* story is that it be told by the person who experienced it.

Of the sixty-nine stories collected over the four-year-long project, "The Big Indian" is the focus of more recorded narratives and voicemail comments than any other site in the eight-block downtown area. The reason many want to comment on the statue becomes obvious when we consider its place and meaning in the community. The statue is twenty-five feet tall. It is placed in

DOI: 10.34314/wingodigital.00009

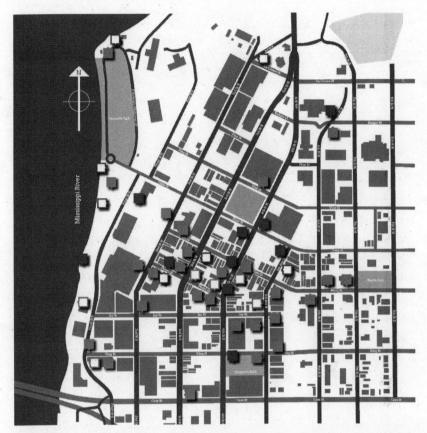

Figure 8.2: Hear, Here downtown La Crosse map of stories. Image courtesy of Marc Manke, Graphic Designer.

a popular downtown park situated at the convergence of three rivers, ground the Ho-Chunk consider sacred. The statue also stands beside three major tourist draws—a steamboat attraction, the visitor's information center, and an international garden.

Officially called "Hiawatha," it has been controversial since its inception in 1958. The city created it as a tourist attraction to entice motorists off a scenic highway to spend money in the downtown area. The representation of "Hiawatha" includes a cartoon-like conglomeration of visual stereotypes regarding Native American people—prominent nose, high cheekbones, strong jawline, pigtails, feathered hair ornament, peace pipe, fringed buckskin

DOI: 10.34314/wingodigital.00009

pants, moccasins, and exposed chest. The name "Hiawatha" comes from a Haudenosaunee chief from a territory around Lake Ontario made famous in the non-Native community by the 1855 Henry Longfellow poem, "Song of Hiawatha." The reasons for the controversy are many: its location, its purpose, its name, its visual representation. The statue does not represent Native Americans within the region, and was based on fictional caricatures.

The mission of *Hear, Here* is to create a culture of conversation around places. The "Hiawatha" statue generated a number of stories through *Hear, Here*, and resulted in a renewed groundswell of activism from various community groups that ultimately worked together to change local policy. While the controversy over the statue spans six decades and came to a head three times, the final push to retire the statue happened concurrently with the stories collected via *Hear, Here*.[2]

Without the tireless work of students and community members both in and out of the classroom to create a successful digital public history project, it would have been difficult for *Hear, Here* to join the conversation and affect change. This chapter will explain: 1) how the project functions; 2) the execution of *Hear, Here* in the university classroom; and 3) the larger social justice work a project like *Hear, Here* contributes to through a case study of the campaign to retire "The Colossus of Kitsch."

A Look Under the Hood of *Hear, Here*

The three main digital aspects of *Hear, Here* are the phone system, the website, and student collaboration via Google Drive.

Interactive Voice Response System

From the user's perspective, *Hear, Here*'s phone system is a toll-free number on street-level signs. The toll-free number includes a story and location number for each sign. When a person calls and enters the numbers, they hear a story of the place on which they stand. The caller can choose to stay on the line and leave a message. Because this is a toll-free number, there is no cost to the user,

DOI: 10.34314/wingodigital.00009

unless they pay for their phone calls by the minute. We have tried to make the work as democratic as possible, using the simplest front-end technology invented in the late nineteenth century and used for generations—a phone number. There is no need for a smart-phone, and there are no QR codes to scan or apps to download. As long as a person has the now ubiquitous cell phone they can access the project in real time on the streets of La Crosse.

On the back end, the phone system is an Interactive Voice Response system (IVR) called EZ Route, hosted by CenturyLink. An IVR system is most commonly found in large companies to direct calls to a specific department or individual. *Hear, Here* is backed by the same technology, but employed in a more user-friendly way. While many IVR systems are used to triage callers and restrict access to the decreasing number of human agents, *Hear, Here* uses the technology to increase human connection. We use a system designed to eliminate humans to amplify and expose users to voices from a wide range of people.

This IVR system works via a phone tree. *Hear, Here*'s phone tree is based on the initial toll-free number, then on a location and story numbers. There are nine numbers on a standard keypad. In order to create the capacity for eighty-one stories, we developed a single-level phone tree that is 9x9. Adding deeper levels to the phone tree allows us to include more than one story at some locations. Here we use the IVR business technology to give access to specific stories on certain days and other stories on other days, just like a business phone system might be set up differently for the weekends and evenings than during business hours.

We use standardized welcoming messages—"Please select your location number" and "Please select the number of the story you would like to hear"— and concluding messages—"Would you like to tell your own story about this location or any other location in the downtown? If so stay on the line and leave us your name, phone number, and story." Otherwise, we include no contextual information for the stories. Rather, each story stands on its own merits, and one must listen to several stories to notice a pattern or narrative. Therefore, the users and not the content creators frame the stories.

DOI: 10.34314/wingodigital.00009

IVR technology provides another benefit: we are able to track the days and times of the calls, the call volume for the months, the area codes for each call, and the length of calls. This allows us to see that certain seasons create change in people's use of the project: call volumes diminish in the colder Wisconsin months of November through February, and they pick up in March and are especially strong from July through October. The average call time is 1 minute and 50 seconds.

We can also track whether or not promotion and events increase the use of the system. For example, our two major launch events that included thematic tours increased the regular call volume by factors of two and four respectively, and also contributed to a more robust call-in month overall.[3] Interestingly, the years in which we scheduled large launches for new stories, call volume increased not only for April, the month of the launch, but also for May and June. There is a clear benefit in reminding the public that this is an ongoing user-generated project.

IVR also allows us to track the area codes of calls. As of March 2019, people in 49 states and Canada have called the system. Between April 2015 and March 2019, we received a total of 9,612 calls to the system; of those, 52 percent are local calls and 48 percent non-local. Tracking the number of non-Wisconsin calls each month indicates that for the first two years, 2015 and 2016, primarily local residents used the system. This pattern shifted in 2017 during an eight-month stretch in which there were more out-of-state calls to the system. This spike was likely due to our membership in "Explore La Crosse," the local visitors' bureau, that promoted *Hear, Here* and distributed flyers about the project.

The EZ Route system is not without its problems, but it is easy to program, it fit our budget, and it provided the lowest barrier to access. One of our biggest issues is that EZ Route only records audio in VOX, a low-quality audio file, and only for 180 seconds at a time. EZ Route is also a lesser-known product of a large company. It took a long time to coordinate access, and it is currently only available in America. When we began the project in 2014, EZ Route was the most affordable IVR system.[4] However, technology is ever-evolving and our latest *Hear, Here* project in London, Ontario, utilizes

DOI: 10.34314/wingodigital.00009

Amazon Web Service's IVR product Connect.[5] This is a less costly option that affords higher quality recordings of any length, and can be used worldwide. It is, however, more complicated to program.[6]

Hear, Here's Homepage

Our website consolidates and backs up all our stories, and provides a central portal for our marketing. It appears on our signs, Facebook page, and pro-motional materials. The website includes an interactive map that shows the location of each story with the audio, links to the transcript, and a photo gallery. It also provides more information about the project, including five external reviews, all media stories, another way to submit a story, informa-tion on how to add your community, and K-12 education programming. Our Google Analytics demonstrate that the website is an important com-ponent, with 59 percent of users accessing the website from outside of the United States.[7]

We employ a media agency to maintain our website and there are ongoing costs for any changes and updates. Best practice is to overhaul the site at least once in the first three years and probably two or three times over ten years.[8] As per our agreement with the media agency, we developed all the wording, content, and images for the website. We also input all the stories, associated photographs, and news media coverage. The agency handles web development and maintenance.

Collaboration in Google Docs

Google Drive holds a *Hear, Here* masterfile: it acts as a working file that allows everyone associated with the project to contribute to the work as well as edit working documents that will eventually appear to the public. Google Drive holds all the work from audio files, web content, and newspaper editorials. Its collaborative platform allows for a democratic process in content creation, especially in the classroom.[9] However, all digital technology has the potential to fail, and is subject to funding and personnel changes. To mitigate issues

DOI: 10.34314/wingodigital.00009

of sustainability and longevity, we have an agreement with Murphy Library Archives at University of Wisconsin-La Crosse (UW-L) to hold hard copies of all materials generated for *Hear, Here*.[10]

Teaching *Hear, Here* in a University Classroom

Teaching *Hear, Here* means teaching the fundamentals of social history, oral history, and public history, and demonstrating how a combination of these elements can lead to activism and social change. We begin with the fundamentals of social history: the idea that anyone and everyone can contribute to the history of their community, city, state, and nation. I then have students read about the methodology and importance of oral history, focusing on the philosophy of Marxist historian Paul Thompson, who encourages the collection of stories from historically underrepresented and marginalized people.[11] Students then read articles about the impact of other radical public history projects that incorporate oral history, such as the *Montreal Life Stories Project* and the *Cleveland Homeless Oral History Project*.[12] These projects demonstrate that once challenging stories are placed in the mainstream, they generate conversations about the state of the community, what it has been, and where it is going.

Beyond the historiography, a crucial element of teaching this class is to do it in a community setting. I lead the *Hear, Here* classes in the boardroom of Downtown Mainstreet, Inc. (DMI), a local business association office and one of our community partners. Having the class at an off-campus and downtown location contributes to students seeing this not just as a school project but as work in a field that would benefit the community. The downtown location of the class also embeds the class into the space we research and serve.

The students in these classes do two types of interviews. For the first interview, students found narrators of excellent downtown-based stories that we heard about in our larger analysis of downtown. This series of interviews includes stories about a fight to move a monument of the Ten Commandments out of a public park, a campaign to save and move an 1850s home turned garage out of a construction zone, and the story of a student who was offered

DOI: 10.34314/wingodigital.00009

work at a strip club. This first set of interviews, along with the required background archival research about each story, teaches students best interview practices and helps them get comfortable with their role as project creators.

For the second set of interviews, students sought stories from historically underrepresented and marginalized groups. In order to build trust with these community members in advance of class, I contacted communities of color in La Crosse, as well as organizations working with people facing homelessness. For example, I attended events put on by the Office of Multicultural Student Services and Campus Climate at UW-L, Human Rights Commission events, and meetings at the city; I also helped organize events in conjunction with all three organizations. I further worked with organizations who provide services for marginalized people to combat poverty. This laid the groundwork for in-class meetings with representatives from service organizations that do work on behalf of the vulnerable. These meetings were supplemented by readings from academic journals and books about topics such as white privilege, Marxist interpretations of gentrification, and the systemic issues surrounding homelessness.[13] Through these in-class meetings, students got to know the individuals within the community who could help them find narrators.

The stories that came out of the second set of interviews are profound. Some of the stories students collected are difficult to hear but they lead to important changes in people's lives, and in the communities of color that many of our narrators work in, with, and for. One story is told by Antoiwana Williams describing her experience of being called the N-word on the day of her graduation. Another story is told by ChongCher Lee about the significance of a photograph of the Ban Vinai Refugee Camp in Thailand where he lived after fleeing Laos. Yet another story is told by Martin Peeples, a formerly homeless man who once slept in the garden behind the Catholic cathedral. Most of the stories collected are like these three; they are stories of struggle, survival, hope, memory, difficult times and lessons learned, community and sharing, and protecting one another.

For some students, their involvement with *Hear, Here* acted as a gateway into activism. One student in particular, Jennifer DeRocher, became interested in anti-racism, attended the White Privilege Conference, and ultimately

DOI: 10.34314/wingodigital.00009

produced a capstone project based on the interview that she conducted about the false arrest of Shaundel Spivey due to his critique of the police. As I have discussed elsewhere, this particular story drew fire from some local business people, politicians, and city officials who wanted the story taken down. Later the signs that lead to the story were stolen, effectively silencing the voice of a Black man in our community.[14] DeRocher's reaction to this was to study sources such as oral histories and the local newspaper for incidents of racism of various types. Her capstone posits that La Crosse had been a "sundown town," or a city that purposely maintained itself as white since the 1890s. James Loewen, the preeminent scholar on sundown towns, later confirmed DeRocher's findings.[15]

Digital Community Engagement as an Element of Local Policy Change

More recently the story told by Dan Green (Kera Cho Mani ga), excerpted at the outset of this chapter, began to take a heightened meaning in the collective imagination of La Crosse, acting as another rallying cry for activists. The remainder of this chapter will be an examination of the influence *Hear, Here* had in the most recent movement to retire the "Hiawatha" statue. As we will see, *Hear, Here* helped to bring some important stories into the mainstream, and thus joined a river of less-public discussions about the statue that resulted in conversations and eventually new understandings and attitudes.

Three stories emerged in the first three years of the *Hear, Here* project that acted as a catalyst for the retirement of the gigantic statue along the Mississippi. The first narrator was Dan Green (Kera Cho Mani ga) in 2015. He explains that many long-term residents of La Crosse believe the statue honored Native Americans. His response is one of both understanding and resistance. The second phase of the project included a 2017 poetry contest, which generated a poem titled "Fun." In this poem, William Stobb explains the "look" of the statue as cartoonish, and its meaning in context of the 1960s. Finally, in the most recent 2018 additions to the project, Lutheran pastor Benjamin Morris moves the meaning of the statue far beyond La Crosse

DOI: 10.34314/wingodigital.00009

itself into the larger colonialist endeavor of the United States. He articulates a personal connection made between the statue and the protests he participated in against the Dakota Access Pipeline at Standing Rock.

By no means is *Hear, Here* the first forum to air La Crosse citizens' opinions about the statue. As a history project, one of the things that we do is overlay stories of past events, thoughts, and ideas, making them constantly and consistently present in the landscape. In no other *Hear, Here* location is this more true than for the "Hiawatha" statue, which has been embroiled in controversy for sixty years. There are three major periods where the arguments surrounding the meaning of the statue became particularly intense: 1) in 1958–1963, when it was first conceived, created, and named; 2) in 2000, when it was in need of a costly repair; 3) and in 2015–2018, when *Hear, Here* and other organizations came together and created pressure to change local policy.

The initial controversy beginning in 1958 centered on naming and placement. The naming debate revolved around whether the statue should be called "Hiawatha," after a well-known Disney cartoon *Little Hiawatha*, or Chief Decorah, after a prominent member of the local Ho-Chunk band.[16] In the end, the City of La Crosse named the statue "Hiawatha" because they believed the connection to Disney would bring more tourists to the area.[17] The second controversy in the initial period was about placement. The proposed, and ultimately chosen, location for the statue is at the convergence of three rivers, an area the Ho-Chunk consider sacred ground.[18] This location was also near where the United States removed the Ho-Chunk people via steamboat under the Indian Removal Act of 1830.[19] The Disneyfied statue representing a person unrelated to the local Native American group helps create a collective amnesia that denies the colonial violence that occurred at the location where the statue now stands.

In 2000 the statue once again became news, this time because it needed repair.[20] At this moment the city put together a committee to decide the fate of the statue—retirement or repair. A number of local debates were held and the local paper covered the story extensively. The family of Anthony Zimmerhakl, the deceased artist who created the statue in 1958, had a large voice in this debate. They believed that taking the statue down would dishonor the artist.

DOI: 10.34314/wingodigital.00009

Ho-Chunk people, on the other hand, argued that keeping the statue up was a dishonor to them and their culture. In the end the committee chose to repair rather than retire the statue.[21]

This brings us to the 2015–2018 debate, the debate in which *Hear, Here* took part. It's worth establishing a timeline of events. In 2015, the *Hear, Here* project launched Dan Green's (Kera Cho Mani ga) narration about what he calls "the Colossus of Kitsch." Then in 2015, students in Timothy Gongaware's capstone class in Department of Sociology and Criminal Justice at UW-L produced a 24-minute video about the statue. In 2016, Gongaware and top administrators at UW-L shared the video broadly with the university and the public.[22] This same year, William Stobb contributed his poem "Fun," which characterized the statue as a cartoon-like portrayal, to *Hear, Here*. In 2017, because of national controversy around Confederate monuments, the Arts Board and the Human Rights Commission at the City teamed up to create a listening session hosted at the Ho-Chunk Nation's Three Rivers House on December 6, 2017.[23] And in 2018, Pastor Morris added the third *Hear, Here* story about the statue by relating its history to the Dakota Access Pipeline protests in which he participated. In January 2018, Tracy Littlejohn (Cooninaziwi) created a Facebook group titled "Hiawatha Statue Removal." Later in March, a petition for retirement and a letter-writing campaign began, and in April an anti-statue citizens' group was formed.

The anti-statue arguments presented in 2015–2018 were sophisticated—possibly because Gongaware's students' 24-minute video focused on an Indigenous representation in La Crosse allowed for a fuller examination of the issue. In the video, we find arguments that stereotypical imagery affects the self-esteem of Native American people, and that stereotyping creates identity crises that contribute to increased suicide rates among Native Americans. The video also states that Native American peoples do not form a single group, but many groups, and therefore it is offensive to assume that "Hiawatha" represents the Ho-Chunk. Along the same lines it is asserted that images of Native Americans are always placed in the past, which is detrimental for people's understanding of Native peoples in today's society. The video culminates by arguing that keeping Native American peoples as a single

DOI: 10.34314/wingodigital.00009

group and representing them in the past are forms of white supremacy that perpetuate the imbalance of the power between Native Americans and white Americans.

In addition to the video, there was a marked shift in representation of this side in the mainstream media as well. In a *La Crosse Tribune* article, Shaundel Spivey, head of the Human Rights Commission, explains the issue thus:

> Why does just the thought of [the statue] being taken down, remodeled and reframed hurt so many people's feelings? Who it doesn't even represent? In the context of the history of race in the U.S., it does make sense. At some point we have to break that cycle and this could be the start. It's not just a point of "yup, it's important for the reconciliation and healing of the Ho-Chunk." It's also important for reconciliation and healing for white folks. White people in La Crosse should own up to the historical racist actions of the white people in both La Crosse and the nation as a whole.[24]

Herein we see a major shift from the earlier two anti-statue groundswells: the Ho-Chunk and their supporters are now the ones defining the narrative, their voices are amplified, and they often choose to not directly address the narrative formed by the family and statue supporters.

The pro-statue arguments in this phase relied on the argument from 2000, focused on its traditional place in the city, honoring the Ho-Chunk people, and nostalgic memories about the deceased creator Anthony Zimmerhakl.[25] Two new arguments in this camp emerged: claims that the Zimmerhakls have Native American ancestry, and that Zimmerhakl taught his students reverence for Native American peoples.[26]

Because of this renewed discussion around the statue, Mayor Tim Kabat called together a group on February 14, 2018. The group included council members, members of the Ho-Chunk Nation, and members of the Zimmerhakl family. The purpose of the group was to discuss the possibility of taking down the statue, ideally with the consent of the Zimmerhakl family. The mayor learned from the 2000 debates that media coverage could inflame the issue, creating retrenchment on both sides. Creating an unofficial group that bridged the different perspectives in the debate successfully kept the conversation out of the media and away from City Council Chambers where it

DOI: 10.34314/wingodigital.00009

was less certain how the chips would fall. The mayor hoped to resolve the issue peacefully and quietly.

Around the time the group began meeting, I prepared a letter to the editor with a colleague, Kate Parker, in response to a column that we thought overrepresented those who wanted to keep the statue.[27] I checked with Tracy Littlejohn (Cooninaziwi) who told me to keep the issue out of the paper and instead persuaded us to start a letter-writing campaign that might increase the support to retire the statue. So, along with Parker and in consultation with members of the Ho-Chunk Nation, we drafted an email to colleagues and other interested parties. Someone forwarded the email to student Aaron Batoya. Along with a larger group of students, he began to gather signatures at the clock tower on campus, at farmers markets, and as part of a door-to-door campaign. Batoya and his colleagues also requested letters from faculty and community members interested in writing against the statue. In this way, Batoya collected 1,328 signatures and eleven letters. Individuals sent various other letters and emails directly to the mayor based on the original email that Parker and I wrote and a subsequent letter-writing request made via the Facebook group "Hiawatha Statue Removal."

In the meantime, city council member Jacqueline Marcou, one of the people who was at the meeting with the mayor, organized a group of concerned citizens: two council members, three faculty members (myself, Parker, and Dan Green), *Hear, Here* narrator Benjamin Morris, and Aaron Batoya. We met to discuss the next steps in helping to continue the momentum for the statue's retirement. More letters were added and we circulated the petition to new groups.

On July 24, 2018, the group convened by the mayor five months earlier met once more. On this same day, the petition and letters gathered by the UW-L students were delivered to the mayor's office. At this meeting, the Zimmerhakl family expressed that they would like the statue preserved, and if that meant moving the statue onto private land they would be amenable. Both sides viewed the compromise to move the statue, which will cost an estimated $50,000, as a good solution to their opposed goals.[28]

DOI: 10.34314/wingodigital.00009

This third movement to retire the statue was different from the earlier two in a number of ways. First, the Ho-Chunk and their supporters brought the issue to the fore *themselves* using the platform of *Hear, Here* and the student video, which allowed them to create and control the narrative. Open debates about the statue were held on Ho-Chunk property and sanctioned by two government committees: the Arts Board and the Human Rights Commission. Two powerful city boards were supporting the anti-statue debate, helping to maintain and support the Ho-Chunk narratives. This left the Zimmerhakl family and their supporters scrambling to form a new narrative that did not relate to the arguments articulated and controlled by those against the statue. That the mayor was a progressive also gave the debate an opening to affecting policy change. The mayor astutely created a group with key players—family members of the artist, city council members for and against the statue, and Ho-Chunk people—that could craft a policy behind closed doors that La Crosse residents would respect no matter what side of the debate they were on. Advocates for statue retirement, through a petition and letter-writing campaign, provided additional pressure. In the end it became obvious to the Zimmerhakl family that they were not going to win the long game: "Council members are going to change. Mayors are going to change. Ideas are going to change. We might win this time around but next time around, we may lose."[29]

While this is a win in some ways—a stereotypical statue is being taken down after sixty years of debate—it is but a small victory that does little to affect the larger goal of respect and understanding of the history of Native peoples. While the pain of the statue is removed, the tragedy of imperialism and white-is-right history remains. This is true not only of the "Big Indian" statue but also of all the anti-Black Confederate statues removed throughout the Southern United States. Controversy over monument removal is not relegated to the South or the former Confederacy; there is much work to be done in northern states as well. Until the powerful white population can understand and appreciate the position of the groups they have oppressed, express their sympathy and regret, and consider reparations, this story will not be over. Statues may come down but it's the hearts and minds of those that would have them remain that are the real battlegrounds for change.

DOI: 10.34314/wingodigital.00009

Sixty years of controversy around the statue generated many different arguments and moments of influence. *Hear, Here* intersected with these histories and actions, serving as a way for Dan Green's (Kera Cho Mani ga's) story to be told and retold. The project made his story consistently visible rather than relegated to historical editorials, university classrooms, or ephemeral Columbus Day protests. Creating yet another—and in some ways more permanent—source of visibility for Green's (Kera Cho Mani ga's) voice was one link in a sequence that included the filming of a documentary, community discussions, social media groups, advocacy by private citizens, municipal-sanctioned discussion groups, and petitions, letter-writing campaigns, op-eds, articles, and letters to the editor. *Hear, Here* was a link in the chain that would ultimately lead to a decision to move the statue.

I would like to thank first and foremost archivists Laura Godden at Special Collections Murphy Library and Scott Brouwer at the La Crosse Public Library Archives for their help identifying and scanning important sources that form the basis of this article. To Rebecca Wingo and the editors of DiCE for asking me to participate and patiently reviewing my work numerous times. Thank you to Katrina Bjornstad, my Research Assistant at Western University, for work on the footnotes and fact checking. To my readers Jennifer DeRocher, Michelle Hamilton, Patricia Skidmore, and Kate Parker. To Dan Green, Tracy Little John and Tim Blackmore who are always available for consultation. And to all the students and narrators who have participated in Hear, Here. *This project would not be what it is without you.*

Notes

1. Ariel Beaujot, *Hear, Here: Voices of Downtown La Crosse*, http://www.hearherelacrosse .org/. All *Hear, Here* materials are also housed at *Hear, Here*: Voices of La Crosse Manuscript Collection, LAX Mss 2015/01. University of Wisconsin-La Crosse Murphy Library Special Collections and Area Research Center, La Crosse, Wisconsin.
2. The use of the term "retired" rather than "removed" was suggested as part of the campaign by Tracy Little John, a member of the Ho-Chunk Nation and also the creator of the Facebook page. The language of removal harkens back to the removal of Native groups from the areas east of the Mississippi and this is why the group opposing the statue chose to use different terminology.
3. First launch was on April 12, 2015 and resulted in 250 calls that day and 776 calls for the month. The second launch on April 28, 2018 resulted in 380 calls,

adding to the 581 calls for that month. In comparison April 2016 had 84 calls and April 2017 had 96 calls.

4. Initial start up cost for EZ route was just under $2,000 for the first year (or $167 a month) and just over $1,000 for subsequent years (or $84 a month). Custom-building an IVR system is about twelve times the cost.

5. For more information about how to build a *Hear, Here* project using AWS Connect see: Fabrizio Napolitano and Mark Tovey, "Hear, Here at City of London: Build a DIY Audio-Tour with Amazon Connect," *AWS Contact Center,* April 9, 2019.

6. Initial start-up cost for AWS Connect: $190.02 (or $15/month) and $90.09 (or $8/ month) for every year thereafter.

7. La Crosse *Hear, Here* Google Analytics data since the website launch on March 4, 2015 shows 10,039 total users. Unfortunately, we do not have any data from approximately January 12, 2018 – January 9, 2019. We also noticed an issue starting June 2017, as there are only small spikes of data reported starting then until this issue was fixed on Jan. 9, 2019.

8. Initial costs will vary but quotes will likely range between $10,000 and $25,000 with a yearly maintenance cost of about $2,500.

9. In Google Drive, we keep records of the full and edited audio, transcripts, anno-tated bibliographies, interview questions, IRB and consent forms, photographs for each story, walking tours, presentations, analytics of the phone system, charts and tables for all stories, grants written, university class material like syllabi and readings, poster and pamphlet designs, "how to" documents for future contribu-tors, maps and mapping information, web design information, and all writing done about the project including OpEds, journal articles, manuscripts, and book chapters.

10. Special Collections Murphy Library holds all the audio on files, transcripts, ques-tions, consent forms, annotated bibliographies, all the class work, and all the extra materials generated in Google Drive, along with print-outs of all the web changes, and many (but not all) emails that have been exchanged about *Hear, Here.*

11. Paul Thompson, *The Voices of the Past,* 3d ed. (Oxford: Oxford University Press, 2000).

12. Daniel Kerr, "We Know What the Problem Is: Using Oral History to Develop a Collective Analysis of Homelessness from the Bottom Up," *Oral History Review* 30, no. 1 (2003): 27-45; Steven High, *Oral History at the Crossroads: Sharing Life Stories of Survival and Displacement* (Vancouver: University of British Columbia Press, 2014).

13. Robin DiAngelo, "White Fragility," *International Journal of Critical Pedagogy* 3, no. 3 (2012): 54-70; George Lipsitz, "The Racialization of Space, the Spacialization of Race: Theorizing The Hidden Architecture of Landscape," *Landscape Journal,* 6, no. 1 (2007): 10-23; Robert Weyeneth, "The Architecture of Racial Segregation: Challenges of Preserving the Problematic Past," *The Public Historian* 27, no. 4 (2005): 11-44; J. Kuo Wei Tchen and L. Ševčenko, "The 'Dialogic Museum' Revisited: A Collaborative Reflection" in: *Letting Go? Sharing Historical Authority in*

DOI: 10.34314/wingodigital.00009

a User Generated World, ed. Bill Adair et al. (The Pew Center for Arts & Humanities, 2011): 80–97; Dan Collins, "Community Mapping: From Representation to Action" in *Proceedings of the 19th International Symposium on Electronic Art,* ed. K. Cleland, L. Fisher, and R. Harley (Sydney: International Symposium on Electronic Art, 2013).

14. Ariel Beaujot, "Sun Up in a Sundown Town: Public History, Private Memory, and Racism in a Small City," *The Public Historian* 40, no. 2 (2018): 43-68.

15. Nathan Hansen, "Sociologist discusses La Crosse's history as a 'sundown town,'" *La Crosse Tribune,* October 28, 2016, accessed May 30, 2016; Jourdan Vian, "La Crosse mayors, community pledge to work toward equality," *La Crosse Tribune,* December 9, 2016, accessed May 30, 2017. See also: James Loewen, *Sundown Towns: A Hidden Dimension of American Racism,* (New York: Simon & Schuster, 2006).

16. "Hiawatha No Native: Koch Objects to Idea for Riverside Statue," *La Crosse Tribune,* June 29, 1958, in vertical file: La Crosse: Art-Statues/Sculptures- Hiawatha/"Big Indian," University of Wisconsin-La Crosse Murphy Library Special Collections and Area Research Center, La Crosse, Wisconsin; "For Indian Statue: Society to Oppose Name of 'Hiawatha,'" *La Crosse Tribune,* April 3, 1961, in vertical file: La Crosse: Art- Statues/Sculptures- Hiawatha/"Big Indian," University of Wisconsin-La Crosse Murphy Library Special Collections and Area Research Center, La Crosse, Wisconsin; "Hiawatha vs. Decorah: Aldermen Hear Debate On Name For Statue," *La Crosse Tribune,* September 12, 1961, in vertical file: La Crosse: Art- Statues/Sculptures- Hiawatha/"Big Indian," University of Wisconsin-La Crosse Murphy Library Special Collections and Area Research Center, La Crosse, Wisconsin.

17. Press Release from City County Tourist Publicity Committee, April 20, 1962, La Crosse Series 13- Box 16- Folder 5, La Crosse Public Library Archives, La Crosse, Wisconsin.

18. Kidder, "Object to Hiawatha Statue: Indians on Warpath Against Chamber Unit," *La Crosse Tribune,* March 29, 1961.

19. For information about Ho-Chunk removal see: *La Crosse County Historical Sketches Series 1* (La Crosse: Liesenfeld Press, 1931), pg 31, La Crosse County Historical Society, La Crosse, Wisconsin; George Nichols, *Recollections of a Pioneer Steamboat Pilot Contributing to the Early History of the Mississippi* (La Crosse: Tucker and Company Printers, 1883), 17-18.

20. David Holstrum, "Hiawatha Big Indian Construction," May 11, 2000, Series 013, Box 16, File 5_2000-5-11, La Crosse Public Library Archives, La Crosse, Wisconsin; Joan Kent, "Donation increases funds for Hiawatha statue restoration,"July 20, 2001, *La Crosse Tribune* vertical file: La Crosse: Art- Statues/ Sculptures- Hiawatha/"Big Indian," University of Wisconsin-La Crosse Murphy Library Special Collections and Area Research Center, La Crosse, Wisconsin.

DOI: 10.34314/wingodigital.00009

21. Joan Kent, "Indian statue repairs on hold," *La Crosse Tribune*, June 16, 2000, in vertical file: La Crosse: Art- Statues/Sculptures- Hiawatha/"Big Indian," University of Wisconsin-La Crosse Murphy Library Special Collections and Area Research Center, La Crosse, Wisconsin; Betsy Bloom, "Family Wants Statue to Stay," July 3, 2000, *La Crosse Tribune*, in Hiawatha Statue Folder, University of Wisconsin-La Crosse Murphy Library Special Collections and Area Research Center, La Crosse, Wisconsin; Joan Kent, "Park Board to Discuss Fate of Hiawatha Statue," July 19, 2000, *La Crosse Tribune*, Hiawatha Statue Folder, Special Collections Murphy Library; Joan Kent "Committee Disagrees on Fate of "Hiawatha"" November 16, 2000, *La Crosse Tribune,* In Hiawatha Statue Folder, University of Wisconsin-La Crosse Murphy Library Special Collections and Area Research Center, La Crosse, Wisconsin.

22. Nathan Hansen, "UW-L Students Tackle 'Big Indian': Native American imagery in La Crosse topic of class video 'Patterns,'" *La Crosse Tribune*, February 1, 2016, in vertical file: La Crosse: Art- Statues/Sculptures- Hiawatha/"Big Indian," University of Wisconsin-La Crosse Murphy Library Special Collections and Area Research Center, La Crosse, Wisconsin.

23. Jourdan Vian, "Controversy Over Hiawatha Statue," *La Crosse Tribune*, December 7, 2017, in vertical file: La Crosse: Art- Statues/Sculptures- Hiawatha/"Big Indian," University of Wisconsin-La Crosse Murphy Library Special Collections and Area Research Center, La Crosse, Wisconsin.

24. Jourdan Vian, "Controversy Over Hiawatha Statue," *La Crosse Tribune*, December 7, 2017.

25. Arla M. Clemons, "Arla M. Clemons, Indian Statue Highlights Native Heritage" *La Crosse Tribune*, February 28, 2016, in vertical file: La Crosse: Art- Statues/Sculptures- Hiawatha/"Big Indian," University of Wisconsin-La Crosse Murphy Library Special Collections and Area Research Center, La Crosse, Wisconsin; Steve Kiedrowski, "Steve Kiedrowski: Hiawatha Statue is a Tribute," *La Crosse Tribune*, February 21, 2016, in vertical file: La Crosse: Art- Statues/Sculptures- Hiawatha/"Big Indian," University of Wisconsin-La Crosse Murphy Library Special Collections and Area Research Center, La Crosse, Wisconsin; Lilly Nelson, "Lilly Nelson, "Hiawatha" Represents Our Diversity," *La Crosse Tribune*, February 19, 2018, in vertical file: La Crosse: Art- Statues/Sculptures- Hiawatha/"Big Indian," University of Wisconsin-La Crosse Murphy Library Special Collections and Area Research Center, La Crosse, Wisconsin.

26. Jourdan Vian, "Hiawatha Statue Debate Heats Up," *La Crosse Tribune*, December 9, 2017, in vertical file: La Crosse: Art- Statues/Sculptures- Hiawatha/"Big Indian," University of Wisconsin-La Crosse Murphy Library Special Collections and Area Research Center, La Crosse, Wisconsin; Jourdan Vian, "Controversy Over Hiawatha Statue," *La Crosse Tribune*, December 7, 2017; Steve Kiedrowski, "Steve Kiedrowski: Statue Is a Tribute to our Heritage," *La Crosse Tribune*, December 17,

DOI: 10.34314/wingodigital.00009

2017, in vertical file: La Crosse: Art- Statues/Sculptures- Hiawatha/"Big Indian,"
University of Wisconsin-La Crosse Murphy Library Special Collections and Area
Research Center, La Crosse, Wisconsin.

27. Peggy Derrick, "Things That Matter: Hiawatha Nostalgia," *La Crosse Tribune*,
March 4, 2018, in vertical file: La Crosse: Art- Statues/Sculptures- Hiawatha/"Big
Indian," University of Wisconsin-La Crosse Murphy Library Special Collections
and Area Research Center, La Crosse, Wisconsin.

28. Scott Behrens, "Hiawatha Statue in Riverside Park may be removed soon," *News
8000 WKBT-TV*, July 24, 2018; Jordan Vian, "'Hiawatha' could find a new home
outside of Riverside Park," *La Crosse Tribune*, July 29, 2018.

29. Scott Behrens, "Hiawatha Statue in Riverside Park may be removed soon," *News
8000 WKBT-TV*, July 24, 2018.

Works Cited

Beaujot, Ariel. *Hear, Here: Voices of Downtown La Crosse*, http://www.hearhere
lacrosse.org/.

Beaujot, Ariel. "Sun Up in a Sundown Town: Public History, Private Memory,
and Racism in a Small City." *The Public Historian* 40, no. 2 (2018): 43–68.

Behrens, Scott. "Hiawatha Statue in Riverside Park may be removed soon." *News
8000 WKBT-TV*, July 24, 2018.

Bloom, Betsy. "Family Wants Statue to Stay." *La Crosse Tribune*, July 3, 2000. In
Hiawatha Statue Folder, University of Wisconsin-La Crosse Murphy Library
Special Collections and Area Research Center, La Crosse, Wisconsin.

Clemons, Arla M. "Arla M. Clemons, Indian Statue Highlights Native Heritage."
La Crosse Tribune, February 28, 2016. In vertical file: La Crosse: Art-Stat-
ues/Sculptures-Hiawatha/"Big Indian," University of Wisconsin-La Crosse
Murphy Library Special Collections and Area Research Center, La Crosse,
Wisconsin.

Collins, Dan. "Community Mapping: From Representation to Action." In *Pro-
ceedings of the 19th International Symposium on Electronic Art*, ed. K. Cleland,
L. Fisher, and R. Harley. Sydney: International Symposium on Electronic
Art, 2013.

Derrick, Peggy. "Things That Matter: Hiawatha Nostalgia." *La Crosse Tribune*,
March 4, 2018. In vertical file: La Crosse: Art-Statues/Sculptures-Hi-
awatha/"Big Indian," University of Wisconsin-La Crosse Murphy Library
Special Collections and Area Research Center, La Crosse, Wisconsin.

DiAngelo, Robin. "White Fragility." *International Journal of Critical Pedagogy* 3, no.
3 (2012): 54–70.

DOI: 10.34314/wingodigital.00009

"For Indian Statue: Society to Oppose Name of 'Hiawatha.'" *La Crosse Tribune*, April 3, 1961. In vertical file: La Crosse: Art-Statues/Sculptures-Hiawatha/"Big Indian," University of Wisconsin-La Crosse Murphy Library Special Collections and Area Research Center, La Crosse, Wisconsin.

Hansen, Nathan. "Sociologist discusses La Crosse's history as a 'sundown town.'" *La Crosse Tribune*, October 28, 2016. Accessed May 30, 2016.

Hansen, Nathan. "UW-L Students Tackle 'Big Indian': Native American imagery in La Crosse topic of class video 'Patterns.'" *La Crosse Tribune*, February 1, 2016. In vertical file: La Crosse: Art-Statues/Sculptures-Hiawatha/"Big Indian," University of Wisconsin-La Crosse Murphy Library Special Collections and Area Research Center, La Crosse, Wisconsin.

Hear, Here: Voices of La Crosse Manuscript Collection, LAX Mss 2015/01. University of Wisconsin-La Crosse Murphy Library Special Collections and Area Research Center, La Crosse, Wisconsin.

Holstrum, David. "Hiawatha Big Indian Construction." May 11, 2000, Series 013, Box 16, File 5_2000-5-11, La Crosse Public Library Archives, La Crosse, Wisconsin.

"Hiawatha No Native: Koch Objects to Idea for Riverside Statue." *La Crosse Tribune*, June 29, 1958. In vertical file: La Crosse: Art-Statues/Sculptures-Hiawatha/"Big Indian," University of Wisconsin-La Crosse Murphy Library Special Collections and Area Research Center, La Crosse, Wisconsin.

"Hiawatha vs. Decorah: Aldermen Hear Debate On Name For Statue." *La Crosse Tribune*, September 12, 1961. In vertical file: La Crosse: Art-Statues/Sculptures-Hiawatha/"Big Indian," University of Wisconsin-La Crosse Murphy Library Special Collections and Area Research Center, La Crosse, Wisconsin.

High, Steven. *Oral History at the Crossroads: Sharing Life Stories of Survival and Displacement*. Vancouver: University of British Columbia Press, 2014.

Kent, Joan. "Donation increases funds for Hiawatha statue restoration." *La Crosse Tribune*, July 20, 2001. In vertical file: La Crosse: Art-Statues/Sculptures-Hiawatha/"Big Indian," University of Wisconsin-La Crosse Murphy Library Special Collections and Area Research Center, La Crosse, Wisconsin.

Kent, Joan. "Indian Statue Repairs on Hold." *La Crosse Tribune*, June 16, 2000. In vertical file: La Crosse: Art-Statues/Sculptures-Hiawatha/"Big Indian," University of Wisconsin-La Crosse Murphy Library Special Collections and Area Research Center, La Crosse, Wisconsin.

Kent, Joan. "Park Board to Discuss Fate of Hiawatha Statue." *La Crosse Tribune*, July 19, 2000. In Hiawatha Statue Folder, University of Wisconsin-La Crosse

DOI: 10.34314/wingodigital.00009

Murphy Library Special Collections and Area Research Center, La Crosse, Wisconsin.

Kent, Joan. "Committee Disagrees on Fate of 'Hiawatha.'" November 16, 2000, *La Crosse Tribune.* In Hiawatha Statue Folder, University of Wisconsin-La Crosse Murphy Library Special Collections and Area Research Center, La Crosse, Wisconsin.

Kerr, Daniel. "We Know What the Problem Is: Using Oral History to Develop a Collective Analysis of Homelessness from the Bottom Up." *Oral History Review* 30, no. 1 (2003): 27–45.

Kidder, "Object to Hiawatha Statue: Indians on Warpath Against Chamber Unit." *La Crosse Tribune*, March 29, 1961.

Kiedrowski, Steve. "Steve Kiedrowski: Hiawatha Statue is a Tribute." *La Crosse Tribune*, February 21, 2016. In vertical file: La Crosse: Art-Statues/Sculptures-Hiawatha/"Big Indian," University of Wisconsin-La Crosse Murphy Library Special Collections and Area Research Center, La Crosse, Wisconsin.

Kiedrowski, Steve. "Steve Kiedrowski: Statue is a Tribute to our Heritage." *La Crosse Tribune*, December 17, 2017. In vertical file: La Crosse: Art-Statues/Sculptures-Hiawatha/"Big Indian," University of Wisconsin-La Crosse Murphy Library Special Collections and Area Research Center, La Crosse, Wisconsin.

Kuo Wei Tchen, J. and Liz Ševčenko. "The 'Dialogic Museum' Revisited: A Collaborative Reflection." In: *Letting Go? Sharing Historical Authority in a User Generated World,* ed. Bill Adair, et al., 80–97. The Pew Center for Arts & Humanities, 2011.

La Crosse County Historical Society. *La Crosse County Historical Sketches Series 1.* La Crosse: Liesenfeld Press, 1931.

Lipsitz, George. "The Racialization of Space, the Spacialization of Race: Theorizing The Hidden Architecture of Landscape." *Landscape Journal* 6, no. 1 (2007): 10–23.

Loewen, James. *Sundown Towns: A Hidden Dimension of American Racism.* New York: Simon & Schuster, 2006.

Napolitano, Fabrizio and Mark Tovey. "Hear, Here at City of London: Build a DIY Audio-Tour with Amazon Connect." *AWS Contact Center*, April 9, 2019.

Nelson, Lilly. "Lilly Nelson, 'Hiawatha' Represents Our Diversity." *La Crosse Tribune*, February 19, 2018. In vertical file: La Crosse: Art-Statues/Sculptures-Hiawatha/"Big Indian," University of Wisconsin-La Crosse Murphy Library Special Collections and Area Research Center, La Crosse, Wisconsin.

DOI: 10.34314/wingodigital.00009

Nichols, George. *Recollections of a Pioneer Steamboat Pilot Contributing to the Early History of the Mississippi.* La Crosse: Tucker and Company Printers, 1883.

Press Release from City County Tourist Publicity Committee. April 20, 1962. La Crosse Series 13-Box 16-Folder 5, La Crosse Public Library Archives, La Crosse, Wisconsin.

Thompson, Paul. *The Voices of the Past,* 3d ed. Oxford: Oxford University Press, 2000.

Vian, Jourdan. "Controversy Over Hiawatha Statue." *La Crosse Tribune,* December 7, 2017. In vertical file: La Crosse: Art-Statues/Sculptures-Hiawatha/"Big Indian," University of Wisconsin-La Crosse Murphy Library Special Collections and Area Research Center, La Crosse, Wisconsin.

Vian, Jourdan. "La Crosse mayors, community pledge to work toward equality," *La Crosse Tribune,* December 9, 2016. Accessed May 30, 2017.

Vian, Jourdan. "Hiawatha Statue Debate Heats Up." *La Crosse Tribune,* December 9, 2017. In vertical file: La Crosse: Art-Statues/Sculptures-Hiawatha/"Big Indian," University of Wisconsin-La Crosse Murphy Library Special Collections and Area Research Center, La Crosse, Wisconsin.

Vian, Jourdan. "'Hiawatha' could find a new home outside of Riverside Park." *La Crosse Tribune,* July 29, 2018.

Weyeneth, Robert. "The Architecture of Racial Segregation: Challenges of Preserving the Problematic Past." *The Public Historian* 27, no. 4 (2005): 11–44.

DOI: 10.34314/wingodigital.00009

You Can't Make *Ketchup* Without Smashing a Few Tomatoes

Reflections on a University-Community Partnership

Aubrey Thompson and Ildi Carlisle-Cummins

Though most ketchup-eating Americans don't know it, one machine—the mechanical tomato harvester—allows California's Central Valley to play a critical role in ensuring that we never run out of that classic condiment. The invention of the mechanical tomato harvester took a feat of engineering that had tremendous impact on the tomato industry. But a backlash to the machine's invention among activists also sparked the early California food movement. When it was released in 1964, the machine put tens of thousands of farmworkers and 95 percent of tomato farmers quickly out of work. This led to national debates about the role of land-grant universities in developing industry-altering technologies that benefit only a select few.

In 2015, the two of us—Aubrey Thompson and Ildi Carlisle-Cummins—joined together to produce a podcast, *Cal Ag Roots*. The first episode is about the invention of the mechanical tomato harvester and its complicated story of technological triumph and social failure. In some ways, the story begged us to tell it. We're both products of UC Davis, the public university where the harvester was invented, we were both taught about the value and inevitability of technological developments, and we were both striving to make agriculture better for everyone. As it turned out, the institutions where we were working while producing this story have their roots in the conflict over the tomato harvester.

In other ways, the story was much bigger than us. The mechanical tomato harvester carries an almost mythological weight for many in our situation; young academics and advocates in California hear echoes of the

DOI: 10.34314/wingodigital.00010

harvester story, but rarely the original voices of those involved. As a team, we thought it was important to bring those voices back to the fore. We wanted to allow those involved with the invention of the harvester and its fallout to interact with young academics and activists to inform their professional paths in food and agriculture.

We told this story through our first podcast episode, "There's Nothing more Californian than Ketchup." Through this, we found ourselves forced to navigate the politics of our positionality, roles, and identities to tell this story in the right way. Ildi Carlisle Cummins is an activist who was educated at UC Davis. Aubrey Thompson, also a UC Davis alumna, continues to work as a staff member at the university. This article introduces you to the process we went through to tell a politically charged story from our positions inside and outside of the university. It also reflects on how we navigated (and continue to navigate) our individual roles in institutions trying to do activist-and research-oriented work.

Since it has been four years since this collaboration, we decided the best way to revisit the project was to record a conversation between the two of us. We've been able to reflect on the process, and wanted to share those reflections directly using our favorite medium: audio!

NOTE: the audio transcripts below have been edited for cohesion.

Transcript

> Aubrey Thompson (AT): Do you have your radio voice on?
> Ildi Carlisle-Cummins (ICC): Here we are in the middle of Aubrey's workday, remembering work done three years ago. But yeah, we're gonna try and, like, think about how and why we made this story about the tomato harvester and what it was like to work together, like from very different roles. As friends [giggle], but coming at it from very different roles.
> AT: Well, should we break it down a little bit? [Yes] Well, from my perspective, I work at a public university that has decreasing public funds as the years go on and yet is consistently responsible to the public that it serves and needs to better learn how to do that.

DOI: 10.34314/wingodigital.00010

Figure 9.1: Ildi Carlisle-Cummins (L) and Aubrey Thompson (R) first told the story of the mechanical tomato harvester aboard an Amtrak train as it crossed through California's agricultural fields.

AT: [. . .] A public university with public funds is one thing, but a public university that actually responds to the needs of its public, is another challenge altogether. And I see it as my work, in my current role and my past role, to . . . improve that.

By clicking on each of the audio clips as you read, you'll be able to hear directly from us on some of the major themes we discussed and lessons we learned:

*   We're not journalists, but instead work for institutions that cultivate their own voices.
*   Telling this story together helped propel each of us toward the kind of academics and activists we want to be; it clarified our paths and helped make our work more meaningful.
*   We're both committed to helping build strong connections between the university and community-based organizations. The work we did together is one of the ways that happens, but we explore the ideas of

DOI: 10.34314/wingodigital.00010

"community engaged research" and "research engaged practice" to help others explore how their work might better engage outside of their standard working silos.

If you're setting out on a project like this—one that might push you from your comfort zone and make you grapple with your role in storytelling—we'd like to offer some basic rules that we learned in the process of working together on this story. These rules form the backbone of this essay and are found at the beginning of each section.

Before you go much further, we recommend you listen to the full episode "There's Nothing more Californian than Ketchup." While we've organized this article to stand alone, without the podcast, you'll likely glean much more after a listen.

Rule # 1:

Trust the stories of your interviewees to guide you, but talk to plenty of people to find balance. Seek an understanding of all the perspectives at your institution or in your community–and make sure your audience knows who you, the story producer, represent (or at least work for).

To tell the story of the mechanical tomato harvester, we called upon people who were closely involved in its creation and the backlash against it. While the engineers who invented it are no longer alive, academics at UC Davis and California historians know the story well and provide first-hand accounts of the harvester's release. We spoke with activists who first protested against the harvester, farmers who were impacted, academics who testified in court, and the lawyers who litigated the harvester lawsuit.

Through the story production process, we learned more about our own institutions, and how we were actually part of the story we sought to tell.

Transcript

ICC: Do you want to say who you are?

AT: I'm Aubrey Thompson. I'm currently the Community Engagement Manager for the Environmental Health Sciences Center here at

DOI: 10.34314/wingodigital.00010

> UCD. I was previously at the Agricultural Sustainability Institute which is the role I was in when we did this project . . .
>
> [. . .] That org has been around for 10 years. . . . But the name to really remember is UC SAREP [UC Sustainable Agriculture Research and Education Program] and that program was started as a legislative mandate following the tomato harvester lawsuits that took place.
>
> ICC: Ok, well I am sitting here with Aubrey. I'm Ildi Carlisle-Cummins, I direct the *Cal Ag Roots* project. [. . .] And the org that I work for, CIRS [California Institute for Rural Studies], has its roots in this particular conflict over the development of the tomato harvester.
>
> AT: The podcast "There's Nothing More Californian Than Ketchup" is a story of an instance when the public university did not serve the public evenly. It served some needs and did not serve others.
>
> ICC: I would say it's also an origin story about some key organizations that have been at the forefront of California food movement work. . . . for the past fifty years.

At the heart of the tomato harvester story is a tension over who has access to the university, and how the university accepts and addresses criticism of its work. As a UC Davis employee heading into her tenth year of service to the University as either a student or staff member, Aubrey grappled with telling this story as a university insider alongside a story critical of the university. For Aubrey, her path within the university is focused on making it a more accessible and public-serving institution. Her work in community engagement and science communication is all about making connections between researchers and the public need, and making complex science understandable and useful for those without advanced scientific training.

But the issue of directly criticizing the work of the university presents a different challenge. Is an internal staff member free to criticize? Or should she, as a representative of her institution, defend its mission and work? For Aubrey, she found her role more as an arbiter, working to understand and empower ideas and intentions both inside and outside the university. Often, it's the groups outside of the university that need a louder microphone to be heard in place of power like universities.

DOI: 10.34314/wingodigital.00010

Transcript

> AT: I learned through this process that it's ok, as a staff member of the U,
>   to be critical of the U, but that it has to be . . . it's almost like it has
>   to be done as an external voice . . . trying to bring an external voice
>   internal, you know? In some ways I'm an open door or something to
>   allow it a space inside of the walls of the university.
>
> ICC: So you needed a community partner, or somebody on the outside, to
>   knock on that door or stroll through that open doorway in order to
>   raise those questions and tell that story? Is that fair to say?
>
> AT: Yeah, I think so. That's not to say that I work at a place that says
>   you're not allowed to be critical . . . but I think that for the story,
>   this kind of story is about the community perspective and that it does
>   require that partnership with an outside org to bring that into the
>   fold.

Rule #2:

The role you inhabit at your institution is not a barrier or a shield. Use your role to push for improvement and growth at your institution.

Of course, collaborations inside and outside of the university are not just about critique. Carolina Balazs and Rachel Morello-Frosch, among many others, argue that community-based participatory research—that is, research that incorporates non-university partners in the research design and implementation—can increase the relevance, rigor, and reach of science.[1] Building partnerships with people directly impacted by research, or designing research to respond to the needs of those people, strengthens the work.

For Ildi, the reciprocal is also true: communities benefit from engaging with public institutions like the university. She terms this "research-engaged practice," which builds on a long tradition of thought related to community-engaged scholarship. Building those connections and the capacity for each of these groups to engage with each other are key goals for both of us in our own roles.

DOI: 10.34314/wingodigital.00010

Transcript

> AT: I wonder if we could each talk about those two terms—community-engaged scholarship and research-engaged practice. How do you see it and what do you see as *Cal Ag Roots*' role in it?
>
> ICC: You want me to go first? [. . .] I think there's an increasing number of scholars now that put themselves in the community-engaged scholarship camp, so really wanting to be vitally engaged over the long term with communities to produce data that is relevant to them and that creates change.
>
> AT: I think there's a spectrum of community-engaged scholarship and that the . . . there is a guiding light of research being guided by communities: that communities are able to come to the university and ask for something and that the university researchers are able to deliver something to them that is in an equitable partnership, that at the outset they know who owns the data and where things are going and what they'll be used for. But at the same time communities know the research process, they know how to identify what good research is and what high-quality research is. And they can see it, and they question it, and they can engage with it.
>
> ICC: I firmly put *Cal Ag Roots* in a "research-engaged practice" vein. I think that's a big part of our goal. To encourage people to be informed about where we've been and to be prepared to reach out to a whole set of paid public thinkers who are theorizing and collecting data and informing our understanding of the world and who are ready and wanting to work with community members.
>
> [. . .] I think it's really important that this project illuminates who's doing thinking particularly around food and farming in our public research institutions and that we make those people available to folks outside of the university. If that could be one of the things that *Cal Ag Roots* accomplishes, that would be really cool.

Rule #3:

If you work for a university or advocacy organization, your story is not a piece of journalism. Use that fact to improve your story—seek feedback on your script, work with your interviewees to make sure you get the story right. Use every step of the storytelling process to understand your own role at your institution.

DOI: 10.34314/wingodigital.00010

Throughout the storytelling process, we kept running into the same tension: how can we tell this story objectively when we work for institutions that have and want their own voices? This storytelling project originated from Ildi's work as an advocate, and she approached the story with an explicit goal of informing future advocacy efforts in the so-called California food movement. So together, we had to wrestle with how to do that while respecting the sensitivity around this story within the university.

We consistently remind ourselves that we are storytellers, not journalists. While we did strive for balance, we did not consider ourselves neutral reporters. We wanted to maintain independence as storytellers but not so much that we restricted people from providing direct feedback on how we told the story, particularly from UC SAREP, the organization the story was partially about. In the end, we felt like our approach provided good scaffolding for the story.

Transcript

> AT: I became intimately aware of that history through my time there and talking with people who had worked there in its inception over the years, and was able to speak as a representative of that organization, right? Like, I didn't separate myself in our podcast as not a representative of that org—which brought its own challenges when we had to write scripts that met the needs of SAREP as a stakeholder.
>
> ICC: Were you running scripts by people in the org?
>
> AT: We ran one script by . . . I think the reaction was positive . . . But the reaction was in part that SAREP always feels slightly under threat of losing its funding. And like so many institutes at universities that's maybe not the straight-and-narrow, or mainstream, I guess, so some of the reaction from people was "you need to boost the language about the positive things that SAREP has done in the story." And we did that.
>
> [. . .] I think it impacted how we ended the story, too. We were a little bit less negative at the end, and a little more inquisitive. Which I think was actually better. [. . .] We ended the podcast with these questions of how do we develop these partnerships and how do we get the university to be better responsive to community needs? And so I think their feedback was good—if at times we felt like it . . . we questioned the integrity of the story-telling.

DOI: 10.34314/wingodigital.00010

[. . .] But we kind of had to keep remembering, this isn't journalism. We're not journalists. We are two people with perspectives and with roles in this story, in some way, you know?

ICC: We didn't take the teeth out of the story, but it made it a story that could be heard within the wall of the institution. Which was pretty powerful . . . I mean, I think that if there's a place that needs to hear it. [. . .] The fact that it had a track inside the university was really important to the life of the story.

The story's potential reach inside of the university was important. But for Ildi—who was beginning to articulate the *Cal Ag Roots* Project's role in the current California food movement—how the story played outside of the university mattered just as much.

Transcript

ICC: Well, there was another layer to my identity at the time, which is that I was fresh out of grad school at UC Davis, which is the place—the location of the story. [. . .] That student version of Ildi was really curious about all sides of the story and really blown away by the wonder of the invention and wanted people to recognize what a breakthrough that invention was. And at the same time sort of have a critical lens about who the public university is producing technology for. So at a personal level, I was interested in the complications and the nuances of that story, which is one reason why I think we were a good match at that moment.

[. . .] But the *Cal Ag Roots* project in general, is designed to put some historical roots on the food movement. So there are goals related to that project that are definitely unique to an organization outside of the university that would have movement-building, strategy-building goals. And this podcast was the first that we produced. So those goals about movement-building were just being articulated.

[. . .] So in an interesting way it's sort of like this story that emerges from scholarly, student interest—and from the very particular place where I was and where I met you—and then begins to converge with these other goals of an activist org that's trying to educate and mobilize people for effective change.

[. . .] I've never said that out loud before! [Laughter]

DOI: 10.34314/wingodigital.00010

So together we had feet firmly planted both inside and outside of a powerful institution, this land-grant university that we were both connected to. And we wondered as we reflected back on the production of this story if there was something special about that moment—when we were both more recently students of the university, when we were forming our identities, when we worked for organizations that were so closely tied to the story we told—that let our collaboration flourish.

Transcript

ICC: So do you think that was a unique moment?

AT: You mean because you were in this initial thought process of what the strategy of *Cal Ag Roots* was going to be? No . . . I don't think that it was particular to that, and I think that in some ways it maybe would be even stronger now because I think we both have a stronger sense of our own . . . the process of this podcast was a lot about navigating what roles we were allowed to play and expected to play in this story-telling process. And I think we both have a stronger sense now of what that role is and what the rules are . . . and what rules we can bend, what boundaries we can push. I think we sifted through it together pretty intensely at that time. And I think if we did it again we would have stronger . . . we would feel more self-confident in it.

ICC: So what rules would you be willing to break with me? [Laughter]

Last Thoughts

It wasn't easy to produce this story for all of the reasons that we have explored in this essay. And yet, when we reflect back on the story and the conversations it has sparked about the land-grant university's mission, the inherent trade-offs at play in technological development, and the relationships between universities and their publics, we know that we would do it all over again. It can pay to deviate from the standard path of academic achievement that is lined with peer-reviewed journal articles. Creative partnerships that extend beyond publishing research can open rewarding doors and sometimes benefit community partners much more than any research paper.

DOI: 10.34314/wingodigital.00010

Just recently, Ildi was asked to perform "There's Nothing More Californian Than Ketchup" at a meeting for UC Cooperative Extension Advisors and Specialists. The story's balanced university-community perspective combined with the engaging delivery of audio and visual materials created ideal conditions for a rich conversation about the current possibilities for shifting university attention to the social impacts of agricultural research. We expect this story will have long-lasting impacts—and we hope that sharing reflections on our process encourages other researchers to produce audio pieces that spark productive dialogues in other places.

Notes

1. Carolina L. Balazs and Rachel Morello-Frosch, "The Three R's: How Community Based Participatory Research Strengthens the Rigor, Relevance and Reach of Science," *Environ Justice* 6, no. 1 (February 2013).

Works Cited

Balazs, Carolina L. and Rachel Morello-Frosch. "The Three R's: How Community Based Participatory Research Strengthens the Rigor, Relevance and Reach of Science." *Environ Justice* vol. 6, no. 1 (February 2013): 10.1089/env.2012.0017.

DOI: 10.34314/wingodigital.00010

DiCE Biographies

Editors

Rebecca S. Wingo is the Director of Public History and an Assistant Professor of History at the University of Cincinnati. She is a scholar of the Indigenous and American West and co-author of *Homesteading the Plains* (University of Nebraska Press, 2017). She is completing her third book on adult education and housing on the Crow Reservation.

Jason Heppler is the Digital Engagement Librarian and Assistant Professor of History at the University of Nebraska at Omaha. He is completing his first book on the environmental history of Silicon Valley with the University of Oklahoma Press.

Paul Schadewald is the Senior Project Director for Community-Based Learning and Scholarship in the Civic Engagement Center of the Kofi Annan Institute for Global Citizenship at Macalester College. He is the Vice Chair of the National Advisory Board of Imagining America, a consortium that advances public scholarship and engagement.

Contributors

Marvin R. Anderson is the co-founder of Rondo Avenue, Inc. (RAI), an organization representing the Rondo neighborhood in his hometown of St. Paul, Minnesota. In 1980, the Minnesota Supreme Court appointed him State Law Librarian, a position he held until retiring in 2002. He is still an active member of the Rondo community.

Ariel Beaujot is Professor of Public History at the University of Wisconsin-La Crosse. She is currently working on her second book, *Uncomfortable Truths: Public History and Race in 21st Century North America.*

Julia Brock is a public historian and Assistant Professor of History at the University of Alabama. She is co-editor, with Daniel J. Vivian, of *Leisure, Plantations, and the Making of a New South: The Sporting Plantations of the South Carolina Lowcountry and Red Hills Region, 1900–1940.*

Ildi Carlisle-Cummins is the Director of the *Cal Ag Roots Project* at the California Institute for Rural Studies (CIRS). She holds an M.S. in Community Development from U.C. Davis. She leads projects that bring people together to shift California agriculture toward sustainability and justice.

Patrick Collier is professor and chairperson of English at Ball State University. His publications include *Modern Print Artifacts: Literary Value and Textual Materiality in British Print Culture* (Edinburgh, 2016) and *Modernism on Fleet Street* (Ashgate, 2006). He is director of the *Everyday Life in Middletown* online database.

James Connolly is George and Frances Ball Distinguished Professor of History at Ball State University, where he directs the Center for Middletown Studies. His scholarship, including publications and digital projects, examines U.S. urban, political, and cultural history. He co-directs the *Everyday Life in Middletown* project.

Karlyn Forner served as project manager for the *SNCC Digital Gateway Project* and is a continuing collaborator in the ongoing partnership between the SNCC Legacy Project and Duke University. She is a historian and the author of the book, *Why the Vote Wasn't Enough for Selma* (Duke University Press, 2017).

Melissa Hubbard is a doctoral fellow in the Graduate School of Education at the University at Buffalo researching academic libraries and the public good. She has more than ten years of experience as an academic librarian, previously serving as the Head of Special Collections & Archives at Case Western Reserve University.

Elayne Washington Hunter holds a BS in Psychology from Morris Brown College and an MS in Human Resource Management from the University of Utah. After a multi-varied and award-winning career in nonprofit and municipal leadership, she recently retired as manager of Human Services for Dekalb County, Georgia. She is a board member of United Way of Greater Atlanta Dekalb and the proud parent of two sons and five grandchildren.

Robin Morris is Associate Professor of History at Agnes Scott College in Atlanta, Georgia.

Shaneé Yvette Murrain is the Community Manager at the Digital Public Library of America. Shaneé holds a B.A. in Religion and Philosophy from Bethune-Cookman University, the Master of Divinity from Drew Theological School, and Master of Library Science from North Carolina Central University.

Allison Schuette documents lives through a variety of mediums and genres. Written work has appeared in *Michigan Quarterly Review*, *Gulf Coast Review*, and *Mid-American Review*. An Associate Professor at Valparaiso University, she co-directs the *Welcome Project*, an online, digital story collection that fosters conversations about community life and civic engagement.

Amy C. Sullivan (Ph.D University of Illinois at Chicago) teaches history at Macalester College in St. Paul, MN. Public history projects include the Bakken Museum's *Inventing for Health/Minnesota Made* and various online exhibits with the National Library of Medicine. Her book, *When "Rock Bottom" Is Death: Reckoning with Opioids in the Rehab State* is forthcoming (Fall 2021) with the University of Minnesota Press.

Megan Telligman currently serves as a program manager at Indiana Humanities. Previously she was a coordinator at the Porter County Museum in Valparaiso, IN, where she contributed to the *Invisible Project*. She received her B.S. in Biology from Valparaiso University and M.A. in English Literature from the University of Montana.

Aubrey Thompson manages the community engagement efforts at the UC Davis Environmental Health Sciences Center, where she works with community-based organizations and researchers to ensure research meets the needs of Californians affected by environmental contaminants. She has a master's degree in community development from UC Davis.

Liz Wuerffel (MFA Columbia College Chicago) is an artist and filmmaker who teaches digital media art at Valparaiso University where she also co-directs the *Welcome Project*. Wuerffel directed a short documentary about Syrian refugees, *Kawergosk: Home Made of Cloth*, and the short animation *The Four Hijabs*.

Index

Carlisle-Cummins, Ildi, 21, 215–25, 217*f*

Caroline's Place (housing project), 176

Carroll, Eric, 80

Carter, Melvin, Jr., 90*f*

Carter, Melvin III, 91

Case Western Reserve University, 51

Castile, Philando, 89

Caswell, Michelle, 59

CDP. *see* Cleveland Division of Police

Center for Civic Reflection, 161, 165–66

Center for Documentary Studies (CDS). *see* Duke University

Center for Middletown Studies, 142

CenturyLink, 195

Chafe, William, 33*f*, 36*f*, 39, 46*f*

Chief Decorah, 201

children

and *A. M. E. Digital Archive* project, 95, 107

death of black, 49

education of black, 72

homeless, 159, 166, 170*f*, 173–74*f*

Christensen, Todd, 43*f*

Cifor, Marika, 59

Civic Engagement Center, 80

Civil Rights Movement, 32, 38

clarification, questions of, 182–83*a*

Cleveland Division of Police (CDP), 50, 54

Cleveland Homeless Oral History Project, 198

Cobb, Charlie, 31, 32, 33*f*, 37, 43*f*, 45, 46*f*

Coleman, Chris, 73, 91

Collier, Patrick, 12, 19–20, 142, 147

colonialism, 64

"Colossus of Kitsch, The" (Indian statue), 191, 194, 202

see also Hiawatha (statue)

community-academic partnerships

advice about working with academics, 3–4

community engaged scholarship, 12, 14, 80, 220–21

effect upon tenure and promotion, 16

formation, 2–3

imbalances of power in, 16, 59–60

impact upon science, 220

research-engaged practice, 220–21

see also specific partnerships

condom distribution, 119

Confederate monuments, 202, 205

Connolly, James, 12, 19–20

consent forms

for A. M. E. Digital Archive, 97

ethics of, 60

for *Invisible Project,* 163

and *PAPVC* project, 60–61

Cooninaziwi (Littlejohn, Tracy). *see* Littlejohn, Tracy

copyrights

in Antioch A. M. E. project, 97

in *PAPVC* project, 60

for SNCC partners, 36, 42–43

Corella and Bertram F. Bonner Foundation, 13

counter-stories, 53–55

Cox, Courtland, 31, 33*f*, 38*f*, 40, 44, 45, 46*f*

Creative Commons licenses

for Antioch A. M. E., 97

for SNCC partners, 42

crisis diary, 153

Crosby, Emilye, 33*f*, 40, 41, 46*f*